Criminology in Perspective

Israel Drapkin

Criminology in Perspective

Essays in Honor of Israel Drapkin

Edited by
Simha F. Landau
Leslie Sebba
The Hebrew University of Jerusalem

Lexington Books
D.C. Heath and Company
Lexington, Massachusetts
Toronto

31697

Library of Congress Cataloging in Publication Data

Main entry under title:

Criminology in perspective.

CONTENTS: Cohn, H. Foreword.—Landau, S.F. and Sebba, L. Introduction.—Historical and theoretical perspectives: Sellin, T. Beccaria's
substitute for the death penalty. Pinatel, J. Twenty-five years of criminology. Wolfgang, M.E. Real and perceived changes in crime. [etc.]
  1. Crime and criminals—Addresses, essays, lectures. 2. Drapkin Senderey, Israel, 1905-   I. Drapkin Senderey, Israel, 1905-   II. Landau, Simha F. III. Sebba, Leslie.
HV6028.C77   364   76-50437
ISBN 0-669-01281-5

Published simultaneously in Canada.

Printed in the United States of America.

International Standard Book Number: 0-669-01281-5

Library of Congress Catalog Card Number: 76-50437

Contents

Foreword

On the occasion of his recent retirement from active teaching, Professor Israel Drapkin, founder of the Israel Society of Criminology, was honored by a special convocation of the society attended by the President of the State of Israel and criminologists from all walks of life. Tribute was there paid by scholars, disciples, academicians, and practitioners to the personality of Israel Drapkin, as well as to his manifold achievements as teacher, writer, researcher, and administrator, and more particularly, to the decisive role he played in introducing criminology into Israel and gaining recognition for it as a full-fledged discipline. After two decades, his own Institute of Criminology at the Hebrew University of Jerusalem no longer works in (however splendid) isolation, but enjoys the cooperation and adherence of three additional thriving centers of academic criminology at the Universities of Tel-Aviv, Bar-Ilan, and Haifa, respectively—and Professor Drapkin, the founding father of criminology in Israel, can now look down upon a whole generation of lawyers, magistrates, and police, probation, and prison officers practicing criminology in action.

But praises sung *viva voce*, however pleasant and impressive they sound, lack permanence; they may linger for a while in the memory, but then they fade away into oblivion. Even if the honoree himself (hopefully) keeps the memory of such celebrations as long as he lives, he will cherish that memory as something wholly personal to himself rather than as an event in the life of his science or profession. It was, I think, in order to invest tributes paid to a great scholar on the occasion of his jubilee with permanent durability and at the same time to elevate those tributes from a purely personal to a scholarly level that German professors invented, at the beginning of the last century, the *Festschrift*, which by now has become standard usage all over the academic world. You honor the scholar not only (and not mainly) by singing his praise but also by gathering together the best and select fruit of the labors of his more intimate colleagues and disciples. On the one hand, you can offer him no gift more attractive or congenial than a collection of essays in his own field of interest; and on the other hand, the more important the contributions collected in his honor, the greater and longer-lasting will be the fame of the name so honored. It was therefore highly fitting that two of Professor Drapkin's eminent disciples, Drs. Landau and Sebba, take the initiative of adding to the *Festschriftenliteratur* yet another volume—not only to gladden the heart of their master and teacher but to erect in his honor an everlasting monument of what is best and most enlightened in the discipline of his vocation.

The editors have collected essays covering a vast range of subjects—there is hardly any aspect of modern criminology on which there is not a notable contribution in this volume. To pay tribute to Israel Drapkin, all the greatest figures in criminological theory and practice have gathered together here from many countries—testifying by their collaboration not only to the international repute and standing of Drapkin himself, but also to the place which, thanks to his untiring efforts, this small and poor country has earned for itself on the world map of criminology. It is indeed the encouragement and guidance that we have been fortunate enough to receive from great minds throughout the free world that has enabled us, adversities notwithstanding, to pursue our own ways of humanitarian progress; and if we too are as yet far away from the ultimate goal, we derive some consolation and much confidence from the fact that we cannot find ourselves in better company than that so eminently represented in this volume. May Drapkin and all of us joining together to honor him live to see the days, in a more peaceful world, in which the ideas and ideals of today find their practical realization.

Jerusalem, 1977

Haim Cohn, Justice
The Supreme Court of Israel

Introduction

As two of Professor Israel Drapkin's former students, we take great pleasure in presenting a collection of papers contributed in his honor by a number of distinguished friends and colleagues. The retirement of Israel Drapkin from his official duties at the Hebrew University and the celebration of his seventieth birthday provided us with the formal opportunity for this endeavor. In the following lines, in addition to some comments on the papers contributed, we wish to mention some of the highlights of Professor Drapkin's career. We should emphasize that the biographical material presented here is not intended to be comprehensive; for this would be inappropriate for a person still at the peak of his abilities.

While Drapkin's almost unbounded energies were in the last twenty years directed mainly at the development of criminology in Israel, his impact was no less significant both in Chile and on the international scene. From 1936 to 1959 he directed criminological research on behalf of the Chilean government; for the last ten of those years he held the position of Professor in Social Pathology and Criminology at the University of Chile. A fitting tribute to his role in the development of criminology in Chile was paid to him recently when the University of Chile dedicated its new Institute of Criminology in his name. On the international level, Drapkin was for more than twenty years a member of the board of directors of the International Society of Criminology, during the last five of which (1966-1971) he served as Vice-President of the Society. Since 1950 Drapkin has undertaken a number of missions on behalf of the United Nations in various parts of the world. It was in his capacity as UN expert on Criminological Studies and Services that Drapkin was initially invited to Israel in 1957. However, what was planned as just a brief advisory mission resulted in his becoming the founding father of Israeli criminology: for following this visit, the law faculty at the Hebrew University of Jerusalem decided to establish an Institute of Criminology, and invited Drapkin to be its first director.

As the Director of the Institute of Criminology in Jerusalem, Professor Drapkin drew up a multidisciplinary program which subsequently served as a model for similar programs both in Israel and in other countries. For this purpose he engaged a wide range of experts, at the same time encouraging a number of younger scholars to serve as a nucleus for the future development of the Institute. Drapkin's conception of an Institute of Criminology was not limited to an academic role in the narrow sense, but also encompassed providing a service to the community at large. Therefore, in addition to the regular teaching and research activities of the Institute, annual symposia were organized dealing with subjects of public interest and general social relevance. During this period Drapkin also organized in Jerusalem two events on the international level: the XIIth International Course on Criminology in 1962; and the First International Symposium on Victimology in 1973. As indicated earlier, the activities mentioned here constitute only a small fraction of the manifold achievements of Israel Drapkin. Moreover, his retirement as Director of the Institute of Criminology has enabled him to devote more time to his writing while continuing to be most active on the international as well as local levels.

Perhaps because of Drapkin's strong historical orientation he has always shown a remarkable gift for analyzing contemporary criminological issues in their proper perspective, showing a foresight toward future developments which frequently imbued him with a skepticism regarding fashionable trends in criminology. This skepticism has generally proved, in retrospect, to have been justified. This somewhat philosophical approach of Israel Drapkin led us to adopt the theme of this volume as reflected in its title; and accordingly, the individual contributors were invited to adopt a similar approach in dealing with their topics. The four sections into which the book has been divided reflect, moreover, the main areas in which Professor Drapkin has shown active interest.

The first section of this volume, "Historical and Theoretical Perspectives," opens with Thorsten Sellin's essay entitled "Beccaria's Substitute for the Death Penalty." In an original analysis of some implications of one of the famous reforms advocated by Beccaria, the author points out that a proposal renowned for its progressive and enlightened nature (the abolishing of capital punishment) frequently proved in its actual implementation to be a more protracted and horrifying method of arriving at the same outcome—death. Apart from their own intrinsic interest, such exercises in historical research may enable us to add a larger perspective in considering contemporary movements in penal reform.

An historical perspective related explicitly to the contemporary era is provided by the second chapter of this section in which Jean Pinatel reviews European developments in criminology over the past quarter of a century. The account of how the clinically-oriented European criminologists defended their approach during this period is particularly appropriate here, not only in view of Professor Drapkin's own inclinations in this respect, but also as a counterweight to the prevailing skepticism regarding this approach in much contemporary criminological literature.

While the first two chapters of this section deal with two of the most important issues in criminology (i.e., the death penalty and the clinical approach to criminology, respectively), these are topics which always have to be considered in their historical context. Stephen Schafer, on the other hand, endeavored to cope with a topic of which both the relevance and the framework of analysis are eternal. The problem of free will versus determinism has occupied the human mind from time immemorial. Schafer's chapter deals with this repeatedly raised but never settled topic, focusing on the specific area of criminal behavior. Schafer's polyglot training stood him in good stead for this purpose, and his untimely death in July 1976 has been a sad blow not only to his friends and admirers, including many of the contributors to this volume, but also to criminology as a whole.

Schafer (like Drapkin) considered much of the empirical research with which the criminological literature is replete as somewhat mechanistic and restrictive, tending to confuse or even evade issues rather than face them. Such research, however, when properly conducted and applied, can actually clarify the issues to an extent to which mere theorizing, however erudite, can never succeed in doing. Perhaps the most well-known advocate of this approach is Marvin Wolfgang, and an illustration is provided in his contribution to this volume entitled "Real and Perceived Changes in Crime." This chapter shows how perspicacious analysis of criminal statistics, when combined with the results of Wolfgang's own studies (pioneered jointly with Thorsten Sellin) on the public's perception of the seriousness of crime, places in true perspective the dimensions of the crime problem. This approach enables Wolfgang not only to explain recent trends in crime in America but also to project probable future developments.

The second section of this volume deals with some of the topical contemporary issues in criminology. The first chapter in this section by Simon Dinitz, "Economic Crime," provides a comprehensive survey of the literature on this subject (which increasingly occupies the headlines of the mass media), as well as an account of some attempts made by academics to research this problem. It appears that such attempts have had very little success. In Dinitz's view, moreover, little progress can be expected in this respect owing to the lack of social consensus on the definitions or even the very criminality of the behaviors falling under this heading.

Similar problems of definition and scope arise in connection with political crime and terrorism, a topic dealt with by Nicholas Kittrie. The attitude adopted by a particular regime or individual to the specific issues encountered in this area will depend upon their political sympathies. In the words of Kittrie: "What is terrorism to some is heroism to others." Further, a balance has to be reached between the desire to expand international control of terrorism and the recognition of the rights of individuals to take action against oppressive regimes.

The issue tackled by Rita Simon in the third chapter of this section is the role of the female in contemporary crime. The writer, well-known for her analysis of this problem in the context of the United States, adds a cross-cultural dimension based upon an investigation she conducted in Israel. Whereas in the United States a connection was found between the rise of the movement for women's liberation and an increase in the rates of female property offenses, this pattern was not applicable to the Israeli scene. In Israel, there was little indication of change in either the status of women or in their criminality.

A section devoted to contemporary issues in criminology in a volume dedicated to Israel Drapkin would not be complete without a chapter on victimology. Such a chapter has been contributed by Walter Reckless. The writer provides a survey of the "state of the art" of victimology, bringing together some of the more relevant recent statistical findings and discussing current trends in the area of victim compensation.

As hinted earlier in this introduction, Professor Drapkin's training (he holds an M.D.) and approach to criminology has been first and foremost clinical. The third section of this volume has therefore been devoted exclusively to this approach. The section opens with a comprehensive review of psychological theories of delinquency by Franco Ferracuti and Graeme Newman. The authors analyze the main contemporary psychological theories, focusing on their relevance to the explanation and prevention of criminal behavior. In their discussion, the crime problem is dealt with not merely on the level of the individual, but also from a wider social perspective. In this context they do not refrain from voicing somewhat unorthodox views on the relationship between intelligence and criminal behavior and the preventative measures indicated thereby.

The second chapter in this section, by contrast, deals with a specific and somewhat neglected area in psychological research with delinquents, namely, their temporal experience. This chapter, written by one of the editors of this volume, illustrates the relevance of situational factors (such as institutionalization) on so-called personality traits frequently attributed to offenders.

The last two chapters in this section, both dealing with the treatment of offenders, reflect the extensive experience of their authors. In the first of these two chapters, Sigmund Manne discusses the treatment of the dangerous offender in the special setting of the famous Patuxent Institution. He analyzes the stages through which the offender passes in the course of group therapy within this setting, pointing out the pitfalls which the therapist must take care to avoid. Noël Mailloux, writing on the reeducation and rehabilitation of the criminal, focuses on the treatment of the juvenile offender. Implicit in this essay is a compassionate appeal for a more understanding approach to the offender both within treatment institutions and on the part of the society to which he returns. From both these chapters the concept emerges that post-release support and treatment are an integral part of the rehabilitation process.

The last section of this volume deals with aspects of the criminal justice system. The section opens with Bernard Cohen's chapter "Police Theory: New Perspectives," which provides a welcome contribution in an area in which there has been a paucity of innovative sociological theorizing. Focusing on police violence, the author challenges the widespread view that this phenomenon derives from a built-in conflict between formal legal norms and the pressures inevitably exerted by police bureaucracy. It is his view that the existence of police bureaucracy rather than conflicting with the legal order may actually be instrumental in promoting it. The real conflict lies in the author's words, ". . . between bureaucratic means and the legal order, on the one hand, and the realistic means provided by the police subculture on the other." It is this concept of police subculture, elaborated by the author, which he proposes as the clue to explaining the phenomenon of police violence.

The last three chapters of this section deal with juridically-oriented subjects.

David Reifen reflects upon the developments in legislation regarding juvenile offenders in Israel. The writer, as the founding father of Israel's juvenile court system, is eminently qualified to write about this topic. His emphasis on the necessity of adopting a treatment approach within the juvenile court, while yet strictly preserving the legal safeguards, is particularly relevant in the light of contemporary controversies in this field.

The next chapter, written by Eryl Hall Williams, deals with a specific but vitally important stage in the judicial process, namely sentencing. Following upon some issues raised in an essay by Drapkin on the same subject, Hall Williams discusses three main topics: the training of judges; the presentence report; and the structure of sentences; and raises some fundamental issues in connection with them. Among the important questions raised in this chapter are the proper length of sentences of imprisonment and the role of parole in this context. However, perhaps the most provocative issue dealt with is how far a sentencing judge should be required to possess criminological expertise—or whether "a little knowledge is a dangerous thing."

The final chapter, contributed by one of the editors, takes us beyond the regular machinery of the criminal justice system to the rather special institution of clemency. An historical analysis reveals that the clemency powers have not only been assailed on ideological grounds, but have also been rendered somewhat superfluous as a result of the development of alternative institutions. Thus the ultimate issue with which the chapter attempts to grapple is whether this institution is not merely ancient but also archaic, destined for extinction within the foreseeable future.

The historical-futurological perspective employed in this last chapter reflects the main theme of this festschrift. Yet while both this general theme and the specific areas into which the papers in this volume fall were selected with reference to Israel Drapkin's special interests, the outcome represents a rather comprehensive coverage of many of the focal topics of contemporary criminology, dealt with by leading scholars belonging to different schools of thought. It is surely appropriate that what was intended primarily as a tribute to Israel Drapkin should constitute a modest but in our view significant contribution to the criminological literature.

Simha F. Landau
Leslie Sebba
The Hebrew University of Jerusalem, 1977

Acknowledgments

The editors wish to express their gratitude to Professor Eliahu Harnon, Director of the Institute of Criminology at the Hebrew University, for placing the services of the Institute at their disposal for the purposes of the preparation of this volume; to Professor Marvin Wolfgang, Director of the Center for Studies in Criminology and Criminal Law at the University of Pennsylvania, for similar services provided at that Center during the period one of the editors was in residence there; to Maya Landau who assisted with the editing; and to Hemda Kirschenbaum, the dedicated Secretary of the Institute of Criminology in Jerusalem, for her assistance with this project.

Most of the credit, however, for this volume must undoubtedly go to the distinguished contributors who were kind enough to participate in this venture. These colleagues agreed to submit original chapters on topics which were both within their special expertise, while at the same time falling within the general framework of the volume. Moreover they endeavored to comply with our special request to deal with their subject matter in the perspective of the passage of time.

**Part I
Historical and Theoretical
Perspectives**

1

Beccaria's Substitute for the Death Penalty

Thorsten Sellin

Medieval ways of dealing with criminals still flourished in the eighteenth century. Their aim was to instill the fear of punishment in the minds of potential offenders, and the means employed testify to the disdain of the ruling class for the life and rights of the lowly. Those found guilty of serious crimes suffered the penalty of death, publicly executed, in more or less tormenting forms, depending upon the gravity of the offense. The headsman's axe was the quickest way of terminating life, but it was usually reserved for nobles. Commoners were hanged by slow strangulation, broken on the wheel, burned alive, and, if possible, their bodies gibbeted by the highways or their severed heads exhibited in cages or on spikes affixed above the city gates. If their lives were spared as a result of their rulers' needs for a cheap and expendable workforce, they were sent to galleys, arsenals, fortresses, or mines, where they would labor in chains as slaves of the state. Lesser offenders were mutilated, branded, whipped, pilloried, sent to ignominious labor in chains on public works, or confined to notoriously noxious jails. Courts used torture to extract confessions and possessed wide arbitrary power in the choice of punishments.

Opposition to this penal system and the aristocratic or despotic political regimes that engendered and maintained it grew during the eighteenth century, fostered by philosophers and their disciples, producing an intellectual climate that would ultimately, by revolution or otherwise, replace autocratic with democratic governments and result in the abolition of judicial torture, the reduction of the use of capital punishments, the nearly total abandonment of corporal punishments, and the introduction of new forms of the deprivation of liberty as the dominant means of punishing serious offenders. In the achievement of these aims, the Milanese Marquis Cesare Beccaria (1738-1794) would play an important role. His instrument was a tract, *Dei delitti e delle pene* (Of Crimes and Punishments), which he published in 1764, when he was twenty-six years of age.[1] In this work, which reflected the great influence on his thinking of the French philosophers, especially Rousseau, Montesquieu, Helvetius, and the Encyclopedists, as well as the English philosopher John Locke and others, he theorized on the aim of punishment, argued against the use of judicial torture, and pleaded for the abolition of the death penalty. I propose to examine briefly this plea, which made Beccaria famous as the father of the abolition movement. Further, I will examine the substitute punishment he proposed and the effect of his ideas on legislation, especially in the empire to which Milan belonged, but first a few words should be said about his general ideas about the aim and nature of punishment.

3

The aim of punishment is not to torment and afflict a sentient person. . . . [It is] none other than to prevent the criminal from doing more damage to his co-citizens and to deter others from doing likewise. Those punishments, then, and the method of inflicting them should be preferred, which while proportioned to the crime will make the most effective and enduring impression on human minds and be least tormenting to the body of the criminal. . . . For a punishment to achieve effectiveness, it is enough that its painfulness just exceed the benefits derived from the crime. Anything more is superfluous and tyrannical. Men regulate their conduct by the repeated effects of the evils they know and not by those of which they are ignorant. If there were two nations, in one of which the most severe penalty in the scale of punishments, proportionate to the scale of crimes, were slavery for life, while in the other it were [breaking on] the wheel, I say that the former will fear its most severe punishment as much as will the latter [fear the wheel].[2]

The aim of penal law, then, should be to prevent crime by making punishments deterrent and not unnecessarily afflictive. Beccaria could find no evidence that the death penalty had deterrent force; the experience of centuries yielded none. Therefore, he could find no justification for the execution of offenders, except possibly when the death of a powerful leader, already in custody, would thwart an attempt by his followers to overthrow the government. Generally, executions failed to deter potential criminals because they left only a fleeting impression on the minds of the spectators. For most spectators, "the death penalty becomes a spectacle and for some an object of compassion mixed with abhorrence. Both of these sentiments dominate the minds of the spectators more than the salutary terror which the law wants to inspire." Hence, a punishment more deterrent than death was needed, and Beccaria believed he had found it in penal slavery, which by its *duration* would be a constant reminder of the consequences of crime.

In the case of an execution, a crime can furnish only one example to the nation, but in the case of lifelong penal slavery a single crime can provide numerous and lasting warnings. Were one to say that slavery for life is as sinful as death and therefore equally cruel, I would reply that, adding all the unhappy moments of slavery together, the former would be even worse, but these moments are spread over a lifetime, while the death penalty expends its total influence in a single moment. . . . Therefore the intensity of the punishment of penal slavery, as substitute for the death penalty, possesses that which suffices to deter any determined soul. I say that it has more. Many look on death with a firm and calm regard—some from fanaticism, some from vanity which always accompanies men beyond the tomb, some in a last desperate attempt either to live no longer or to escape misery—but neither fanaticism nor vanity dwells among fetters and chains, under the rod, under the yoke or in an iron cage, when the evildoer begins his sufferings instead of terminating them.[3]

Beccaria's arguments and conclusion raise some interesting questions. His claim that lifelong penal slavery would have greater deterrent force than capital punishment obviously could not be demonstrated, because no data existed at the time to validate it. Nevertheless, that argument would impress his readers and influence the actions of legislators. Furthermore, penal slavery, which present-day readers of his tract might assume to be a Beccarian invention, could not have been thus conceived by him because it had ancient origins, was well-established in the Roman empire, was a common punishment in his time in the form of forced labor in galleys, arsenals, fortresses, and mines, and was undoubtedly known to him, at least as it was administered in Italian bagnes. In European penal laws it ranked immediately below the death penalty in the scale of punishments and was quite commonly imposed directly instead of capital punishment, or by a commutation of that penalty. Beccaria's "substitute" was no substitute at all, but rather an already existing punishment that simply would be promoted to the first rank through the abolition of the formerly top-ranked penalty of death. But how could lifelong penal slavery be made more "painful" and "cruel" and thus worse than death? "Fetters and chains," whippings, forced labor "under the yoke," and confinement in an "iron cage" already were familiar devices in use everywhere and did not seem to deter people from committing crime. More drastic means would be called for to achieve the deterrence envisioned by Beccaria as the chief purpose of penal slavery and of punishment generally.

Within six years of its first publication, translations of Beccaria's tract had been published in France, Germany, England, and Sweden.[4] Since French was universally used in polite discourse by the upper classes, the many French editions of the work could not fail to attract the attention of leaders of public opinion and government everywhere. There is no place here for a discussion of all the revolutionary ideas that made the tract one of the most important and seminal publications in the history of criminal law reform. Only one of Beccaria's ideas concerns us here, namely his suggestion that penal slavery be made the most severe punishment of all. Of further concern is the effect this suggestion had on legislation.

A Penalty "Worse than Death"

The prime example of the legislative effect of Beccaria's suggestion occurs in Austria. Beccaria had no more conscientious a disciple than Joseph II, who was a true product of the Enlightenment. Coregent with his mother Maria Theresa since the death of his father in 1765, he may well have considered Maria Theresa's penal code, *Constitutio Criminalis Theresiana*, outmoded, since it retained traditional customs that he would soon change. He may have been responsible in part for the abolition of judicial torture and reduction in the use of capital punishment decreed by his mother in 1776. When he succeeded her in 1780, he hastened to order a revision of her code. Years passed before this work was completed, but early in 1787 it was ready. It abolished the death penalty, except under martial law. However, since the emperor had put a stop to executions in 1781, Beccaria's "substitute" had already been in use for several years.

The alternatives were forced labor of excruciating kinds or frightful imprisonment, for life or long terms. The once popular forced labor on fortifications, a common form of penal slavery in the landlocked nations that could not resort to galley slavery, was abandoned in 1783, when the War Department stopped building fortresses.[5] Barge-towing up the Danube in Hungary was then introduced, partly because prisons were overcrowded and maximum security institutions too few.[6] When John Howard visited the house of correction in Vienna in 1786, he noted that

The criminals sent off to Hungary are brought first to this prison. They are clothed in a uniform and chained by companies, five and five together, with *irons* around their necks and *on* their feet; besides a chain about ten inches long *between* the feet of each of them, and another chain about six feet long for fastening each of them to the person next to him. I was told that the hard work in which they are employed of drawing boats up the Danube wears them out so fast that few of them live in this state above *four* years.[7]

He did not mention how these prisoners were transported to the work site, but we may assume that they were sent on foot, since this was common practice in all countries at the time.

The hard life of the penal slave was described by the military general of the south Hungarian border command post in the following terms: "Criminals, already emaciated, wasting away from hunger, harnessed in rows to the vessels, often to the waist or even to the neck in water, wading through morasses and constantly forced to labor,"[8] driven by the whips of their military guards, actually were subjected to a prolonged death penalty. Of 1173 men subjected to this form of penal slavery between 1784 and 1789, death claimed 721, or about 61 percent.[9] "The unsound climate, the hard labor in foot and neck irons, the single meal evenings (by grace, a drink of vinegar water twice daily) led to certain death in about two years. Most prisoners died from exhaustion and bad fever," writes Hartl.[10] When the new penal code was promulgated in 1787, an imperial decree ordered that all persons sentenced to "hard imprisonment" be sent to towing "whether or not their health permits it."[11] The procedural code of 1788 (par. 180) provided that males convicted of murder, robbery, or arson (or other crimes) and sentenced to hard imprisonment and public labor for long terms (8-15 years) be similarly sent to towing. If the conduct of anyone serving a prison sentence proved him to be incorrigible, he could also be sent to towing, no matter what his crime was (par. 191).[12]

All the "worst" criminals were not sent to Hungary. Some were sentenced to "irons," which ranked as an even harsher punishment. "The punishment of irons (*Anschmiedung*) consisted of chaining the criminal in the prison so closely that there was room for only the absolutely necessary movements of the body, and in annual canings publicly administered."[13] The sentence imposed in 1787 on a Viennese man found guilty of robbery and murder was characteristic:

He shall on three successive days be exposed on the scaffold with a tablet hung on his chest and inscribed with the words robbery and murder, be given on the lower back fifty strokes with a cane the first and the last day, such beating to be repeated annually as a warning to the public, depending on his physical condition, and kept in severe prison for thirty years leaving him room for only necessary bodily movements.[14]

An even more severe degree of such confinement was used, in which a prisoner wore an iron band, riveted to the wall, around his waist and was loaded with chains. When John Howard saw the Great Prison on his visit to Vienna, he found,

very few of the dungeons empty; some had three prisoners in each dungeon; and three horrid cells I saw crowded with twelve women. All the men live in total darkness. They are chained to the walls of their cells, though so strong and so defended by double doors, as to render such a security needless. No priest or clergyman has been near them for eight or nine months. . . . [The new prison to which the prisoners were soon to be transferred had] twenty dungeons at the depth of twenty-two steps below the surface of the ground, boarded with thick planks, in which are strong iron rings for the purpose of chaining the prisoners.[15]

The fortresses of Spielberg in Brünn, the then capital of the provinces of Moravia-Silesia, the Schlossberg in Graz, Styria, and the Kufstein in the Tyrol were also used as state prisons.

The worst criminals, who according to pars. 186ff. of the procedural code were to be delivered to Schlossberg were housed in casemates or in the ten solitary cells. Of the two casemates, one had neither light nor fresh air, and in 1784, after an inspection visit by Emperor Joseph II, they were divided into twenty-one cells, walled with planks (so called blockhouses) for holding the worst criminals sentenced to irons for life. A report by the government of Inner Austria, dated September 20, 1790, stated about the prisoners in the block-houses that "the irons, weighing nearly fifty pounds hinder them in working and sleeping. The confined air, the bread and water diet and the hard bed [they slept on bare planks] changed these wretches into semi-corpses and living skeletons. Consumption, dropsy and scurvy took their lives in a short time. Even the healthiest and strongest man could not last under this extreme kind of punishment more than four years."[16]

This was surely a penalty worse than death.

Joseph II died in 1790 and was succeeded by his brother Leopold, who had for 14 years ruled the Grand Duchy of Tuscany, where, inspired by Beccaria, he had commuted death sentences until he abolished capital punishment altogether in 1786. Leopold II was more of a humanitarian than his brother. When he assumed the throne he promptly abolished the towing penalty and the punishment of irons, as well as branding, which had consisted of burning a symbol resembling a gallows into the cheeks of the criminal. He also tried to ease imprisonment by ordering that prisoners be given straw mattresses and blankets.[17] However, his fear of repercussions from the revolution in France led him to restore the death penalty for "all who dared to inflame the people and lead them to oppose the orders of the government by public violence."[18] After his death in 1792, his brother Francis II made not only high treason but also several other crimes capital offenses; and in his penal code, which took effect in 1804, we still find that under the most severe of three grades of imprisonment, the prisoner was to receive only "that amount of light and room necessary for his health." A prisoner was to:

wear heavy irons on hands and feet constantly and an iron band around his waist, by which, when not at work, he could be attached with a chain. Every other day, he would receive a warm meal but no meat and on other days only bread and water. He would sleep on bare planks, and no one could meet or speak with him.[19]

Many decades would pass before such inhumane punishments would disappear.

Beccaria's brand of penal slavery, like executions, left no room for the reformation of the offender, which had for a long time been thought by many to be one of the aims of punishment. Indeed, nowhere in Beccaria's tract is this aim mentioned. His great achievement was the program he proposed for the reform of the administration of justice and his redefinition of crimes to meet the requirements of a democratic society, which should be protected against the abuse of power by making every punishment "above all things public, speedy, necessary, the least possible in the given circumstances, proportioned to its crime, [and] dictated by the laws."[20] As for the punishments to be used, his advocacy of penal slavery encouraged the invention of horrid forms of imprisonment believed to be more deterrent than death.

Notes

1. Cesare Beccaria, *Dei delitti e delle pene*. Printed in Livorno by the press of Marco Coltellini (no date).

2. My translation is from Cesare Cantú, *Beccaria e il diritto penale* (Florence: Barbera, 1862), pp. 381-462. A recent translation of the Becarria tract into English by Henry Paolucci was published in 1963 in Indianapolis, Indiana, by Bobbs-Merrill Co.

3. Ibid.

4. The richest bibliography of Beccaria's writings, commentaries, and translations is that of Giacinto Manuppella, *Cesare Beccaria: Panorama bibliografico* (Coimbra, 1963), from Boletim da Faculdade de Direito da Universidade de Coimbra, Vol. 39.

5. Friedrich Hartl, *Das Wiener Kriminalgericht. Straftechtspflege vom Zeitalter der Aufklärung bis zur österreichischen Revolution* (Wien: Bohlau, 1973), p. 408.

6. Ibid., p. 128.

7. John Howard, *An Account of the Principal Lazarettos in Europe* (Warrington, 1789), p. 72.

8. Eberhard Schmidt, *Einführung in die Geschichte der deutschen Strafrechtspflege*, 2d ed., (Göttingen: Vandenhoeck & Ruprecht, 1951), pp. 183-184.

9. Ibid., p. 246.

10. Hartl, *Das Wiener Kriminalgericht*, p. 425. He added that "it must be remembered that in contemporary prisons (*Zuchthäuser*) few prisoners survived sentences of two or three years."

11. Schmidt, *Einführung in die Geschichte*, p. 246.

12. Hartl, *Das Wiener Kriminalgericht*, pp. 23-24.

13. L.V. Bar, *Geschichte des deutschen Strafrechts und der Strafrechtstheorien* (Berlin: Weldmann, 1882), pp. 159-160.

14. Hartl, *Das Wiener Kriminalgericht*, p. 408, n. 7.

15. Howard, *Principal Lazarettos*, p. 66.

16. H. Kaut, "Leibes- und Freiheitsstrafen," in *Strafrechtssammlung der Nö. Landesmuseum im Schloss Greillenstein* (Wien: Museum, no date), p. 52.

17. Hartl, *Das Wiener Kriminalgericht*, p. 25.

18. Cited by Cantú, *Beccaria e il diritto penale*, p. 253.

19. Schmidt, *Einführung in die Geschichte*, pp. 247-248, quoting paragraph 14 of the code.

20. Cantú, *Beccaria e il diritto penale*, from the concluding paragraph of the tract.

2 Twenty-Five Years of Criminology: A European View

Jean Pinatel

The very sincere homage I wish to pay to Professor Israel Drapkin for the scientific activity he has unceasingly deployed in the field of criminology provides me with the opportunity to evaluate a quarter of a century of criminology covering the period from 1950 until the end of 1974. I shall endeavor to give an account of this period as I have lived it. That is to say, my perspective will essentially be subjective. My point of view will not be that of an objective historian, complete and impartial, but rather that of a deeply involved witness and participant.

The Rise of Clinical Criminology

The year 1950 was that of the Second International Congress of Criminology, which was held in Paris from the 10th to the 19th of September, presided over by H. Donnedieu de Vabres, Professor of the Faculty of Law in Paris, and assisted by the Reverend Father Piprot d'Alleaume. The aim of the organizers of this meeting was to give criminology the status of an autonomous, unified, and interdisciplinary science. This involved replacing the distinct biological, psychiatric, psychological, psychoanalytical, and sociological approaches with a universalistic and synthesized approach. To achieve this objective, two methods were proposed: first, a recapitulatory method requiring the organization of elements diffused by their specialist approaches in the matter of the genesis of crime, that is, by reference to the formation of the personality of the criminal; and second, a method centered on predelinquent situations and the processes which are connected with them, which are destined to bring to light the dynamics of the criminal act and the concept of *l'état dangereux*.

The views of Etienne De Greeff strongly influenced the organizers of the congress. Moreover, this meeting proved to be a triumph for the great Belgian criminologist. Previous to the congress, it had seemed sufficient to enumerate the criminogenic factors individually, but from then on it became a matter of grasping the interaction of criminogenic factors and linking them to the essence of the subject. It was in this manner that clinical criminology became the focus of interest.

The years that followed were devoted primarily to airing and placing in perspective the achievements of the Paris congress. Clinical criminology became

11

organized on both the practical and the theoretical levels. The 1951 United Nations and Cycle of Brussels study of the adult offender and the International Society of Criminology's 1952 and 1953 International Courses in Paris were devoted, respectively, to the medico-psychological and social examination of the criminal and the *état dangereux*. Both of these contributed appreciably to the development of the clinical method. In 1958 M. Benigno di Tullio organized, in Rome, the first large-scale international meeting devoted exclusively to clinical criminology.

The Third and Fourth International Congresses in London (1955) and the Hague (1960) were largely dominated by the clinical approach in tackling the problems of recidivism and the mentally abnormal delinquent. Finally, in France, Article 81 of the new code of criminal procedure promulgated in 1958 provided for the examination of the individual as an integral part of the judicial process.

During the period which began with the Paris congress and ended with that of the Hague, the positions taken in the name of criminology were supported by the doctrine of social defense, while uncompromising opposition was displayed by the defenders of the classical penal doctrines.

The Middle Period: Confusion

Following the Hague congress, criminology appeared to be developing along the lines of the clinical principles laid down during the preceding period. In France, the National Congresses of 1960, 1961, and 1962 had as themes the study of the individual and *l'état dangereux*. Very rapidly, however, differences became apparent among the upholders of clinical criminology. It is true that the method followed by De Greeff was developed with greater depth by the systemization of the concept of the criminal personality; the report presented in 1963 in Bellagio by the late Ch. Andersen was very significant in this regard. Yet, here and there, and in Lyon in particular, the basis of the clinical approach came into question. Clinical criminology suffered from a reaction to the developing crisis in psychiatry, which was manifest in criticism of the traditional nosography. The clearest result of this crisis was the development of arguments, independent of the wishes of the innovators themselves, against those who endeavored, in a manner consistent with the circumstances of the day, to put the classical doctrines back into the place of honor.

Another current was developing elsewhere on the international level which also had the effect of undermining prevailing criminological thought. In 1963 the Council of Europe instituted a Scientific Committee for Criminology and took the initiative in encouraging criminological research. In this committee a majority emerged in favor of the idea that priority should be given to applied or evaluative research. The consequences of this choice were twofold. On the one hand, concern for the causes and dynamics of crime was abandoned in favor of the treatment of delinquents. And on the other hand, results obtained by the new approach constituted a source of discouragement to practitioners.

Putting the accent on the treatment of delinquents was in no way designed to displease clinicians. Treatment can in effect permit discoveries about the personality of the delinquent, which can in turn illuminate the genetic and dynamic mechanisms. Moreover, clinical criminology was becoming aware that it could not limit itself to diagnosis and prognosis, but rather that it should engage in treatment. If clinical criminology were to go beyond the stage of knowledge for its own sake, it would need to try to influence the personality of the delinquent by means of a psychomoral cure. Clinical criminology oriented itself of its own account toward the treatment of delinquents. The French Congresses of Strasbourg (1963) and Toulouse (1965), and above all the International Congress in Montreal (1965), were dedicated to this theme.

Commitment to this way of treatment required the execution of experiments, with adequate provision for both personnel and institutions or services. In reality, very little effective implementation of this occurred. Yet, on the other hand, there was astounding success in evaluative research. However, evaluative research could not be applied to clinically oriented treatments, since these did not exist. It had to concentrate on punishments and traditional measures, modified by treatments according to the needs of the case. Despite the clinical adornment, therefore, it remained essentially dominated by either a *repressive* or a *philanthropic orientation*. The linguistic confusion brought about the surprising result that research specialists believed they were evaluating clinical methods, when in fact they were testing methods that were clinical only in name.

The results obtained, thanks to sophisticated statistical techniques, made it appear that homogeneous delinquent groups were involved and that failures and successes were constant whatever the methods employed, whether it was a matter, for example, of prison or probation.

These results had a debilitating effect among the practitioners. "What is the good," they said, "of striving to perfect or at least improve our methods, when in any case the results will be unaffected?" By the same token, those responsible for criminal policy, given to deep discouragement, took the view that it would be pointless to endow clinical criminology with the necessary tools. This was the situation in criminology when the events of May 1968 in France occurred. The impact of the political ideologies held by the proponents of the student uprising was felt universally; and criminology, too, was not left untouched.

Challenge of Critical Criminology

Following the events of 1968, a new movement emerged among practitioners, especially among those specializing in the treatment of minors. This movement challenged the very purpose of the treatment of delinquents, namely, their rehabilitation in society. It was thought that to reintegrate delinquents into an unjust society, the disappearance of which was highly desirable, was valueless.

The argument was taken up again and developed on the theoretical level by the interactionists and their followers. Based on scientific observation of the existence of dark figures, the process of discretionary decision-making on the part of police and the judiciary, the dangers of labeling in terms of the delinquent stereotype, and the stigmatization of the criminal on the part of society, the arguments of the interactionists opened the way to an extreme position that saw no longer in crime a single personal response to a situation but rather a general response to a sociojudicial process that operates constantly to the prejudice of the deprived classes.

This new criminology presented itself essentially as a *critical* criminology. In many respects it was to criminology what antipsychiatry was to psychiatry. It directed its attacks against traditional criminology, reproaching it for compromising with the political establishment in the matter of the treatment of delinquents. As a result, it called for study of the dominant ideologies and political processes through which penal laws evolve and are maintained.

This perspective has put clinical criminology under great strain. Putting stress on the criminal personality tends, it is claimed, to make one believe that the crime is an individual phenomenon, to be judged by psychoeducational methods, when actually it is a social and, even more so, political phenomenon.

While academic sociology has been engaged in these conflicts, criminality has exploded around the world: criminality deriving from poverty in the underdeveloped countries, political criminality in countries at war, and American-type criminality, i.e., white collar crime, organized crime, gangsterism, violence of the young, and drug abuse. In most countries, these three types of criminality were evident and interacted with one another.

In the face of this challenge, a new tendency developed—an organizational approach to criminology. It adopted the point of view of the engineer in social sciences and was applied to the police, judiciary, and penitentiary systems. It emphasized the importance of studying the administration of justice itself. This organizational approach found itself confronted, however, with clinical criminology at the International Congress of Belgrade in 1973. And clinical criminology, which had patiently developed its research on the criminal personality while the other movements had occupied the front of the stage, brilliantly resisted the attacks of the organizationalists.

Therefore, the conclusion that can be drawn from this quarter of a century of criminology is that even if this period was particularly brilliant on the intellectual plane and stimulating on the political level, it has turned out to be rather disappointing from the point of view of the challenge of criminality.

There are, however, several scholars who have not ceased to draw attention to the foreseeable developments of criminality and who have always insisted that the only viable method to relief is the clinical method. To study the individual delinquent, evaluate his dangerousness and capacity for social adaptation, and formulate in terms of these elements a favorable program for social readaptation, such is the mode of action they have unceasingly recommended.

For this clinical approach to give satisfactory results, however, proper conditions are needed. In fact a criminological system can function only if magistrates, police, prison officials, educators, doctors, psychiatrists, psychologists, chaplains, and other well-meaning citizens are educated in criminology. It is to Professor Drapkin's credit to have contributed so greatly to the organization and development of this indispensable area of education.

3 The Problem of Free Will in Criminology

Stephen Schafer

Hardly any intellectual or practical discipline is in a more confused state at present than criminology, and fundamental questions about the nature of crime and punishment remain to confound and should often embarrass the thinker. Crime has been intensively studied for more than a century, but it is doubtful whether we are now much nearer to an understanding of man's criminal conduct. As it appears, a considerable amount of theoretical work remains to be done, one such area being the problem of freedom of will, an issue on which an ideological stand must be taken. However complicated this might be for various scientific and ethical reasons, it is necessary as a foundation on which empirical research can be more intelligently built, and without it the contemporary turmoil of the crime problem may result in more scope for criminological mischief.

The issue of free will is seldom featured in conventional textbooks on criminology or among the titles in professional journals, nor does this profoundly critical problem receive attention in the presentation of research reports. Yet, a *tour d'horizon* of the immense volume of empirical investigations seems to indicate a covert suggestion that a deterministic inclination or even strategy exists among the quantifying researchers of our time. This is not to say that they would overtly state, or even consciously assume, that we have no free choice, that our conduct is determined only by external forces which annihilate the human will, or that we are helpless toys in the hands of superhuman, social, or other outside powers which can play with us at will. It may be that while they lean toward determinism, they do not even contemplate the problem; rather, they are just trying to follow the nineteenth century scientific thinking in terms of causality, being so obsessed with numerical techniques and tables that they lose sight of the basic qualitative issues. For many years quantitative research has been a flourishing industry, where both the funding agencies and the investigators, with some exceptions, place heavy emphasis upon the correct construction and use of statistical and methodological rules and cloud any preference to the promise of theoretical propositions and their justification with laboring on

It is the author's great personal and professional privilege to offer this paper in honor of Israel Drapkin, man, thinker, and friend. It would be difficult to tell the most important issue among the many historical, victimological, biological, and other criminological problems that Israel Drapkin has explored and promoted to the lasting enrichment of criminology. The basic theme of this chapter, the freedom of man, has also been inspired by Professor Drapkin who so often has taken a firm stand for a scholar's freedom and integrity—and free choice of action.

founding problems. This is one of the major reasons why a distinction between accidental and causal regularities has been much too often missed or misinterpreted, and only through skepticism and its attendant sense of the complication of what one sees can one sustain anything like equanimity and avoid cynicism and despair.

There has been, beyond a doubt, a great deal of observation and record keeping of man's behavior. And although my attempt is not meant to deflect attention from the many solid virtues of a deterministic kind of quantifying, I still believe there is a danger in accepting these observations and records without making efforts to resolve the relevant theoretical issues. It hardly needs saying that the roots of crime are buried much deeper and their ramifications are vastly more complicated than is suggested by the way they are usually treated by our quantifying researchers, whose deterministic approach avoids any explanation or justification as to why this stand on the problem of free will has been taken. This might be one of the explanations of why so many of these projects, and even their subject matter, are remarkably superficial, a deficiency which leads them to the principal conclusion of banality. There are too many unresolved theoretical problems for a critic not to be cautious about lightly accepting those numbers and figures; and one of the major unresolved theoretical issues is man's free will.

The problem of man's free will is one of the most difficult problems of the area of knowledge that is supposed to deal with ultimate realities, yet it is one of the most popular and most significant problems in spite of its almost insoluble nature and the inordinate Sisyphean intellectual labor that is unavoidable even for taking a side in its centuries' old dispute. Three hundred years ago Gottfried Wilhelm Leibniz simply called it "the great question,"[1] and Nicolas Malebranche has viewed it as a "mystery."[2] Two centuries ago Immanuel Kant, historically the first who exposed this problem to a confrontation between science and ethics, bitterly complained that a thousand years' work had been expended in vain on its solution,[3] and Jonathan Edwards has seen it as the "grand question" that can be approached only with "candor and calm attention."[4] In the twentieth century, Nicolai Hartmann found free will to be the real *exemplum crucis* of ethics, the perfect solution of which could not even be hoped for at the present time;[5] and Heinrich Gomperz has called attention to the fact that both the conservative and the liberal thinkers have in a manner inconsistent with their ideologies tended to reverse the stands traditionally taken by them on the problem.[6] Indeed, as M.R. Ayers expressed it, "The free will problem is certainly the heaviest millstone around the neck of anyone who inquires into the nature of potentiality."[7]

It should not be surprising, therefore, that nothing is further from these thoughts than a lightly offered solution to this troublesome and perplexing "grand mystery." However, while this writing has none of the comprehensiveness or coherence suggested by its title, it is its intent to point to this free will problem as a pivotal question of criminology so sadly neglected by many of those who venture to treat the struggling issue of crime. The problem of the freedom of will—often called *freedom of action*[8] or *freedom of the self*—actually mirrors the seemingly endless debate on the issue of causality, i.e., in terms of determinism versus indeterminism, ultimately leading to the question of man's freedom of choice in acting or not acting and his consequent responsibility for this conduct. Determinism suggests that man's will—if there is such a thing as a "will"—does not motivate action; conduct therefore results from extraneous sources. Indeterminism, however, suggests that the human will is not motivated by physical and environmental factors; thus man can do anything he wants to do, for if "will" did not exist, causal reality would be an illusion. It is clear from the legion of arguments that an unconditional acceptance of the law of causality (determinism) would be as grandiose a hypothesis as would be the endorsement of unlimited free will (indeterminism) as a metaphysical concept only. From the point of view of criminal law and criminology, this means that should the determinists be correct, criminals, as we understand them now, would not exist, since all impulses from which actions stem are irresistible. Consequently only the determining extraneous physical and environmental factors ought to be blamed for crime—punishing, correcting, or reforming man would be an illogical and meaningless effort. On the other hand, should the indeterminists be right in their view of "willing" to commit crimes, punishment ought to be equal for all criminals, or perhaps the value of the criminally attacked target could justify distinctions, since man willed the action and could have acted otherwise by choice. Thus the criminal would be fully and exclusively responsible for his choice of violating the law, regardless of the conduct of his victim and irrespective of his social and physical environment. This would point up, if it were correct, the illogical and meaningless nature of all empirical research projects.

The assumption of all penal systems seems at a glance to be indeterministic. The philosophy of officially punishing the criminal lawbreaker indicates the lawmaker's premise that the criminal has a freedom of choice, and this choice was crime. Criminal law assumes that man has a freedom of action, and as Morris Ginsberg contended, he is able to form a "more or less impartial judgment of the alternative actions" and can act "in accordance with that judgment."[9] Ted Honderich poses the thesis that to say that something can happen in a given situation is to say that something else is not "caused" to happen.[10] It would be pointless, so the argument runs, to offer the option of reward or punishment if the freedom of choice were not a fact; after all, the liability for crime is based on this choice of committing the criminal violation of the law. Criminal law, as it appears, operates not only on the presumption that we humans have the free will to decide our action, but, at the same time, with the implication that we are intelligent and reasoning creatures who can recognize values (whatever the term *value* may cover) and who can distinguish between right and wrong (whatever these terms may mean). In other words, as criminal law seems to assume, only those can and should be punished who *willed* to commit a crime or neglected *to will* otherwise. In the first case, persons should be *directly responsible* for what they willed to do; in the latter, they should be *held responsible* for their being careless or negligent in their willing to avoid crime.

At the same time, criminological research, mainly the quantifying kind in the last three decades, seems to assume the power of external forces which do not allow man to freely exercise his will and make the actions of the criminal agent causally explicable. As somehow seen in the so-called prediction studies, "it can be known *a priori* that every event has a cause."[11] And accordingly, in opposition to the practice of the administration of criminal law, empirical investigators may be seen as reaching for the proposition that nobody is ever really, or at least not fully, responsible for his actions. In their search for a cure for crime they believe that crimes, at least most of them, are unfree and involuntary actions; and although they are obviously not reflexes, they are done against the will of their performers, and with certain regularities extraneous influences actually determine or guide their lawbreakings.[12] What they really say is that if something does not happen in a given situation then something else was caused to happen; they give the impression of looking for guilty factors other than the criminal himself. But, even their deterministically flavored research would prove to be purposeless and unnecessary should the totalitarian-inclined and strictly deterministic behavior modifiers be correct. Whatever the deterministic external factors revealed by researchers, in the Fourier-type phalansteries of those subscribing to behavior modification such technical brainwashing—or more correctly, will-washing—would take place under the pretext of punishment or treatment as would make any research result irrelevant and would overpower all kinds of external forces by completely determining the choice of man. The determinist behavior modifiers seem to be more deterministic than the determinist researchers.

However, unless we are ready to deny that freedom is one of the higher attributes of man, and so discard the philosophical and theological aspects of the behavior modifiers' ideas, which prefer evil to good, the chances of reaching *the* solution of the problem of the free will are necessarily slim. Are we wholly a part of the natural world and our actions the necessary outcomes of causal processes? Or are our actions free and can we thus be made responsible for them? Further, can we suggest that only one of these questions has an answer and thus deny the validity of any answer to the other? Just as materialistic monism concludes in strict determinism, so spiritual monism leads to an absolute indeterminism. They are so formidably in opposition to each other that neither of them would tolerate the other. Many philosophical ideologies tend to divide the human universe into two parts: the world of empirical realities (*mundus sensibilis*) on the one hand, and the world of values and ideas (*mundus intelligibilis*) on the other. Apparently, however, these ideological views do not offer room for strict indeterminism in the former world and strict determinism in the latter world. Any monistic view would expose the two independent worlds to an unavoidable and confusing clash, and man would be tormented by not recognizing which of them is his real world and which is to guide his conduct. Thus, since man could hardly exist in two independent worlds at the same time, only with a dualistic view can human society function, where a man's position and role in functioning demands the merger of the two worlds. Victor Cathrein contends that freedom of the human will does not make the acceptance of the laws of causality impossible;[13] and Constantin Gutberlet claims that the will is so strongly subjugated to the causal laws that if this were the only question in the debate between determinism and indeterminism, then even his own indeterministic stand could be qualified as a deterministic view.[14] Gyula Moor also supports the dualistic outlook by suggesting that in the willed choice the idea of value is playing an important role since man has the capability of choosing and his choices may develop causal effects.[15]

This is why, as it appears, only a moderate determinism *or* a moderate indeterminism (the former with a limited range of causality, the latter with an arrested freedom of will) offer at least some answer to the problem of "free will." From a pragmatic point of view, and in order to approach the crime issue somewhat more safely, usable answers have to contain a mixture of both the indeterministic and deterministic elements. Thus they actually differ primarily in terms of how much each contributes to such a compromise. Such a golden mean, such an estimate of the volume of freedom of will (in other words, is the deterministic or the indeterministic view more dominant in judging crime) may also have been necessary because there is no philosophical guarantee either that the adherents of the indeterministic view possess any real freedom of will in reaching their conclusions or that the supporters of the deterministic thesis express their judgment only as mouthpieces of external forces. *Compatilism* (that is, that the two independent worlds, freedom and physical determinism, can coexist) is often proposed, but *incompatilism* (that they cannot coexist) is even more often contended. Yet, in a dualistic view, only *libertarianism* (and not *necessitarianism*) seems to offer a viable foundation for judging a person's action or conduct because it leans toward freedom and yet saves deterministic causality. This is without the claim of absolute freedom of will, which might lead to the *liberum arbitrium indifferentiae* where the will could fall into a guideless position resulting in chaos, and without a statement of the absolute rule of the *causa finalis*, the ultimate cause, which is not really known and where in any case the more deterministic strength of possibly competing causes can be measured only *ex post facto*, since obviously the stronger one is that which finally wins and determines the action.[16]

For an unsophisticated person, determinism (and maybe even incompatilism) is of course easier to assert than freedom of will. He may say that something cannot come out of nothing, so everything therefore must have a cause. But Plamenatz contends "whereas it is not at all clear that he requires an event always to have the same cause, he does seem to require the former to be produced by the latter in some sense which makes the causal law something more than a necessity of succession or concomitance."[17] This, however, makes possible such questions as how can the cause cause its effect if it ceases to exist at the moment when the effect comes into existence. Determinism, by the nature of its apparent logic, can be easier to comprehend than indeterminism where the will is less tangible and provable. Yet, even the devoted determinists often seem to feel a sort of fallacy in their view, and they often look for a place for freedom of choice. Moreover, sometimes they even try to arrive at their deterministic position by using free will as the starting point of the argument. For example, Heinrich Rickert, clearly a determinist, places free will in a "prophysical" world that is supposed to be a metaphysical sphere that functions before we become acquainted with the realities, thus he adjusted Aristotelian ideas in favor of the will's freedom.[18] David Wiggins, a "reasonable libertarian," criticizes determinism by suggesting that "if determinism is true and every action of every agent depends in its particular circumstances upon some specific physical condition being satisfied, then actions cannot be torn free from the nexus of physical effects and fully determining causes."[19] The agent thus could not have done otherwise, and, continues Wiggins, "if that is the character of the causal nexus we live within, then it makes no particular difference to this point whether or not actions are identical with movements of matter."[20]

While, however, it is the belief of the libertarians that determinism cannot operate in the real world without accepting the validity of indeterminism, and "it is characteristic of the libertarian to insist that for at least some of the things which the man with freedom does, or plans, or decides to do, he must have a genuine alternative open to him,"[21] *strict* indeterminism does not exist. As Anthony Kenny pointed out, "the fact that we can do what we want does not mean that we can want what we want."[22] A fully indetermined choice ought to be totally beyond the reach of all influences, but—as was admitted even by the staunch indeterminist Jonathan Edwards—because it could be influenced, it could be determined and therefore would not be free choice. This might be true even in case of mental disease—as contrasted with physical illness by Antony Flew—since mental derangement is culturally relative.[23] Jonathan Edwards' free choice refers, as an example, to asses who can choose between alternative bales of hay. But, in this example, there is an important difference between asses and men: when asses make their choice, the issue of moral responsibility, or moral blameworthiness or praiseworthiness, does not appear in the question. This is because asses are not moral agents, and only moral agents can be properly subject to moral judgment. What then is meant by a *moral agent* in common speech and in the evaluation of the criminal law system? According to Edwards, a moral agent is a being who satisfies two conditions. First, he has a moral faculty, that is, he is capable of distinguishing between right and wrong. And second, he has the capacity to reason. The latter might be the more important of the two conditions since this makes the agent subject to influences on his actions by "moral inducements or motives"—whether these inducements take the form of commands, exhortations, or persuasive arguments.[24] Since the central thrust of this chapter is primarily to call attention to the problem of free will in criminology and to translate these theses and thoughts into understandable criminological issues, "it follows from these premises that our actions are never free or voluntary," [yet] "the theses of determinism . . . are incompatible with the existence of this responsibility."[25] Thomas Hobbes, who is known as a determinist, at least a scientific determinist, in his description of "liberty" nevertheless maintains that a man can act freely even though he acted necessarily and could not have acted otherwise.[26]

However, *in thesi*, one may claim that even *moderate* indeterminism does not exist; and moreover, because of the force of socialization processes, it could be claimed that the will has no freedom whatsoever. The socializing measures develop man's biases and prejudices, likes and dislikes, beliefs and disbeliefs, and affirmations and negations regarding the basic and guiding questions of the world in which he is expected to live, choose, decide, and function. The ideas of this world and the prescriptions of the ruling sociopolitical power are infused into man long before his faculties of knowing, reasoning, evaluating, and choosing have had a chance to develop to maturity. "Prescribed socialization makes the individual what he is."[28] He knows, reasons, assesses, and makes his choices; but, normally, what he would will to know, how he would will to reason, and what choices he would will to make are acts of a will that is imbued and arrested by ideas socialized into it and that is limited by the sociopolitical power that in fact dictates the range of his choices. Thus he is not deciding and doing according to a will that could have been otherwise genuinely free from these influences; moreover, he is expected to will as other persons (who are more powerful than he is) will him to will. He will not be deprived of his choices, and almost always he "can do otherwise." But, how many and which of these choices will be at his disposal, what he can do otherwise, and what he can want to want are all influenced, limited, and arrested already, long before he can begin to will, by the socialization processes, which in turn are assumed to operate according to the influencing, limiting, and arresting prescriptive will of the ruling power. The question, therefore, is not whether physically he can *do* otherwise; rather, it is a question of whether he can *will* to do otherwise. Since, if the role of the socialization processes is posited correctly, he can not will doing otherwise. Consequently, it might be safe to say that man does have a freedom of will, yet it is a will that has been influenced, limited, and arrested even before it could evolve to a stage where man could will to will freely.

A qualitative concentration on this point may guide the quantifying researchers to a better understanding of what they are doing, and it may assist the administrators of criminal law in better understanding what they are judging.

Clearly, the less effective is the socialization process, the broader is the freedom of man's will; and the more successful is the socializing operation, the narrower is the freedom of will and the range of choices from which actions can result. In the former, there is more space to will an action that is qualified as crime; in the latter, more, or only such, actions can be willed that do not pull man over to the territory of criminality. The state of crime in different cultures may support this proposition. In the former alternative, man may will to belong to a world other than the one he inhabits under the rule of its sociopolitical power. In that case, because of his broader freedom of will, he sees no reason to restrain that will or not to will what he can will,[29] and his undesirably extensive, or even unlimited, freedom of will may create a potentiality for crime or even a revolt against those dominating sociopolitical powers who will his freedom influenced, limited, and arrested, and who will the world according to their reasons, assessments, and choices.

If this is so, is it correct to blame and punish the criminal? Is he really *responsible* for his crime (and not those who failed to influence, limit, and arrest his will)? Or are we *making* him *responsible* (instead of blaming and punishing the socializing agents)? Do we have, for example, juvenile delinquents or criminal parents? As it appears, man does have *a* freedom of will, but one's indeterminism (at least its range) is determined by other indeterminists.

Notes

1. Gottfried Wilhelm Leibniz, *Nova methodus docendae discendaeque jurisprudentiae* (1686).

2. Nicolas Malebranche, *De la Recherche de la vérité, ou l'on traite de la nature de l'esprit de l'homme et de l'usage qu'il en doit faire pour éviter l'erreur dans les sciences* (1675).

3. Immanuel Kant, *Kritik der praktischen Vernunft* (1788).

4. Jonathan Edwards, *Freedom of the Will* (W. de Gruyter, 1754).

5. Nicolai Hartmann, *Ethik*, 2d ed. (Berlin, W. de Gruyter, 1935), pp. 572-579.

6. Heinrich Gomperz, *Das Problem der Willensfreicheit* (Jena, E. Diederichs, 1907), pp. 3-11.

7. M.R. Ayers, *The Refutation of Determinism: An Essay in Philosophical Logic* (London, Methuen, 1968), p. 1.

8. Ted Honderich (ed.), *Essays on freedom of action* (London, Routledge & Kegan Paul, 1973), p. vii.

9. Morris Ginsberg, *On Justice in Society* (Harmondsworth, Penguin, 1965), p. 168.

10. Ted Honderich, "One determinism," in Honderich, *Essays*, p. 202.

11. Ayers, *The Refutation of Determinism*, p. 3.

12. J.P. Plamenatz, *Consent, Freedom and Political Obligation*, 2d ed. (London, Oxford University Press, 1968), p. 116.

13. Victor Cathrein, *Das Strafrecht der Zukunft* (Stimmen aus Maria-Lach, 1896), Vol. 50, pp. 366-367.

14. Constantin Gutberlet, *Die Willensfreiheit und ihre Gegner*, 2d ed. (Fulda, Fuldaer Actiendruckerei, 1907), p. 23.

15. Gyula Moor, *A szabad akarat problémá ja* (Budapest, 1943), p. 8.

16. See Wilhelm Windelband, *Uber Willensfreiheit*, 2d ed. (Tübingen, J.C.S. Mohr, 1905), p. 38.

17. Plamentaz, *Consent, Freedom, and Political Obligation*, pp. 108-109.

18. Heinrich Rickert, *System der Philosophie*, Vol. I., *"Allgemeine Grundlegung der Philosophie"* (Tübingen, 1921), p. 201.

19. David Wiggins, "Towards a reasonable libertarianism," in Honderich, *Essays*, pp. 41-42.

20. Ibid., p. 59.

21. Ibid., p. 34.

22. Anthony Kenny, "Freedom, Spontaneity and Indifference," in Honderich, *Essays*, p. 91.

23. Antony Flew, *Crime or Disease?* (London, Macmillan, 1973), p. 67.

24. Arnold S. Kaufman and William K. Frankena (eds.), Introduction to Jonathan Edwards, *Freedom of the Will* (Indianapolis, Bobbs-Merrill, 1969), pp. xvii-xviii.

25. Honderich, "One determinism," pp. 205 and 208.

26. Thomas Hobbes, *Elements of Philosophy* (1841).

27. Ayers, *The Refutation of Determinism*, pp. 4-5.

28. Stephen Schafer, *The Political Criminal: The Problem of Morality and Crime* (New York and London, The Free Press, 1974), p. 109.

29. Ibid., pp. 139-140.

4

Real and Perceived Changes in Crime

Marvin E. Wolfgang

Expansion of Deviance, Contraction of Crime[1]

The definition of crime is culturally subjective. So is society's response to persons who commit crimes. *Crime* is an act that is believed to be socially harmful by a group that has the power to enforce its beliefs and that provides negative sanctions to be applied to persons who commit those acts.[2] Although crime, like pornography, may be in the eye of the beholder, subjective perceptions about crime come closer to universality and retain more temporal stability than do definitions of obscenity and pornography.

At least this generalization applies to serious crime and the meaning of seriousness. Acts that are defined in American culture as victimless crimes and do not involve physical injury, theft, or damage to property have a greater range of perceived seriousness; whereas acts that involve injury, theft, or damage have a narrow range of seriousness and considerable stability over time and in their rank order of gravity.[3] It is commonplace to refer to the cultural relativity of crime and to mention that the crime of yesteryear is noncriminal today. What is less trite and certainly not trivial is Emile Durkheim's notion that crime is normal, not pathological. In his *Rules of Sociological Method*, Durkheim said that even in a society of saints there would still be crime, by which he meant that if all acts we know as crime were eliminated, small differences in behavior that now appear to have no moral significance would take on a new and important meaning. Slight breaches of manners and good taste could become serious crimes. In his terms, crime involves acts that offend strong collective moral sentiments. If these sentiments weaken, then what were formerly considered more serious offenses would be considered less serious; when the sentiments grow stronger, less serious offenses are promoted to the more serious category. The degrees of enforcement and severity of sanctions are correlated with the intensity and degree of commitment to the collective moral sentiments.

I shall return to these propositions later in this essay. However, for the moment my concern is with emphasizing the extent to which behaviors that are defined as deviant but not criminal have been and will continue to expand, while simultaneously our definitions of delinquency and crime will contract.

If the crimes we now know as serious—murder, rape, robbery—were to disappear and the society of saints were constructed, "the very cause which would thus dry up the sources of criminality would immediately open up new ones."[4] Without empirical evidence but with convincing reasoning, Durkheim argues that

27

these strong states of the collective consciousness cannot be thus reinforced without reinforcing at the same time the more feeble states, whose violation previously gave birth to mere infraction of convention—since the weaker ones are only the prolongation, the attenuated form, of the stronger. Thus robbery and simple bad taste injure the same single altruistic sentiment. . . . But, if this sentiment grows stronger, to the point of silencing in all consciousness(es) the inclination which disposes men to steal, he will become more sensitive to the offenses which, until then, touched him lightly.[5]

In his extraordinarily provocative lecture entitled "The Elasticity of Evil" Albert Cohen, in quoting this same passage, suggests that there would be a short step to argue from Durkheim's position that the amount of crime in any given society would tend to approximate a constant: "That is, if the collective sentiments were to grow weaker rather than stronger, more serious offences would then be considered less serious, the barriers to the commission of those offences should be reduced, and their frequency should cease to be regarded as criminal altogether."[6] Neither Durkheim nor Cohen push the argument this far, and for the latter "[it] is not the constancy of evil, which is debatable, but its elasticity, which I take to be a fact. . . ."[7]

While deviance may have both an inevitability and elasticity, my major point is that we are currently experiencing in American culture, and perhaps in Western society in general, an expansion of acceptability of deviance and a corresponding contraction of what we define as crime. The total quantity of criminal and noncriminal deviance may indeed be constant, both in our value definitions and in the statistical frequency with which acts are committed. But the line of demarcation between criminal and noncriminal deviance, the threshold of tolerance, the statutory definition of crime is being positioned at a different point in the total line segment we call deviance.

The notion of rapid social change implies not only institutional variations stemming from technology but changes as well in the mores, in what conduct is considered acceptable or objectionable. Historically, changes in sex mores have probably been the most dramatic, and the deviant of a generation ago may be a conformist today. Behavior that was radical and expressed mostly by the literati in Greenwich Village during the 1920s is now so diffused and expressed by such large groups that it is no longer the form of behavior but the size of the groups participating which draws our attention. There has been a value stretch to what is acceptable, or at least tolerated, behavior. The statistical and dominant prescriptive norms are increasingly different in a pluralism that permits more subcultural enclaves. Perhaps for quite a while in our culture, homosexuality, use of marijuana and psychedelic drugs, sex experimentation, and so forth will still be considered deviant from dominant behavior prescriptions, but not criminal.

Expansion of membership by persons holding these deviant values and manifesting deviant behavior can be expected. The group will stretch the dominant culture's range of tolerance, so that what was formerly viewed as *contraculture*, to use Yinger's term, will become tolerated subculture. What may have begun in protest to the establishment or authority changes from an antithesis to an alternative. The retreat to drugs and other nonviolent forms and symbols of deviance and defense against being sucked into the mold of middle-class conformity takes on a prescriptive posture of its own. Youth will be seduced no longer by the titillation of rebellion but by the prospect of membership in an acceptable alternative.

While the dominant value system of society is expanded to accommodate formerly defined contraculture behavior into the sphere of what is tolerated by the system, there will be a concomitant contraction of acts now defined as delinquent or criminal. In the United States, juvenile-status acts that are now included under juvenile court laws as delinquency will be subsumed under some other rubric, such as misbehavior or family problems. Running away from home or being declared incorrigible or truant should no longer be labeled delinquency, as was requested by a resolution of the United Nations.[8] But more than this change, it is already evident that such acts as homosexuality between consenting adults, public drunkenness, abortion, and certain drug use will be removed from criminal codes. There are undoubtedly other acts in the realm of public and private morality that are still regulated by criminal law but which will be eliminated from that framework in the future. Gilbert Geis expressed this sentiment in strong terms:

I would therefore suggest that the most efficacious method of dealing with deviancy is to ignore, to the furthest point of our tolerance, those items which we find offensive. Such response is predicated upon the assumption that there exists in our society a core of values which exert enough appeal to win over the deviant ultimately, or at least to keep him within the society in terms of other aspects of his behavior, provided that he has not been irresolutely shut off from conformist living.[9]

By a contraction of what is deemed delinquent, the criminal law will be made more enforceable. The more narrow range of behavior considered criminal will mean a stronger link of consistency with history; for the persistently serious offenses like homicide, rape, and thefts, which have almost everywhere and always been viewed as criminal, will constitute the hard core of criminality, and the actors will continue to be viewed as criminals.

Philip Rieff writes persuasively about cultures as moral-demand systems that have a kind of dialectic set of remissions which are counterinterdictory. Cultural revolutions, he claims, occur when the remissive elements become dominant.[10] A *remission* is a relapse from the dominant culture-value, or moral-demand, system. Remissions that become institutionalized modes have indeed taken over, but not through revolution, however long or short the process may take. They are adaptations or mutations which a culture, to remain viable, must tolerate, i.e., accommodate. Remissions may be grafted to the dominant value system and thereby enrich or mute the force of the latter without wiping it away. Homosexuality, pornography, drug usage, abortion, and the like may change from being nasty, evil, or anti-God to being defined as illness and social disorganization, and ultimately, as neutral notions of how some segments of society act and are permitted to act. It is not that the moral-demand system will then have a more weakened posture; at most, we can say it is changing. However, historically and anthropologically, it is very clear that uniform interdicts about ingroup murder, injury of persons, or theft of property are not rudimentary remissions reaching toward positions of dominance.

There is some indication from cross-cultural research of the validity of this point and the stability of subjective perceptions of the relative degrees of seriousness of various kinds of crimes. In 1964 Thorsten Sellin and I published *The Measurement of Delinquency*, which was a study of the psychophysical scaling of the seriousness of crime.[11] We asked approximately 1000 persons to use the number system to provide score values for the relative seriousness of 141 offense descriptions. The principal method we used was called a *magnitude estimation* or *ratio scale*, which requested respondents to assign any number above zero and less than infinity to the stimuli presented and the ratios of numbers assigned to offenses contained enormous stability, which we declared statistically significant among university students, juvenile court judges, and police officers. The hierarchical ordering and the numerical differences among offenses were most stable for the offenses rated most serious, i.e., offenses involving physical injury, theft, or damage to property. The greatest fluctuations and numerical distances among offenses involved what the FBI in the Uniform Crime Reporting System calls *nonindex offenses*, or those not used in the crime index of the United States. The taking of a life, murder, was considered the most serious offense. Additivity of offensivity was reflected in the higher scores given to murder with rape or murder with some other felony. Rape was the second most serious offense, with aggravated assault, robbery, burglary, and varying degrees of monetary loss the other most serious offenses. The greater the amount of money loss, the more serious the stealing offense. These may not be surprises to the public in general, but the relative assigned weights to each of these offenses was the intriguing and novel aspect of the study.

Of considerable interest since the publication of that study has been the equally stable finding in a variety of other cultures. Replications of the psychophysical scaling were performed in such diverse cultures as Taiwan, England, Italy, Germany, the Belgian Congo, Puerto Rico, and Canada.[12] Even among prisoners in New Jersey institutions, the same ratios and rank ordering of offenses of injury, theft, and damage were recorded and corresponded to the ratios and rank ordering in the Congo, Taiwan, Puerto Rico, and elsewhere.[13]

Thus interdicts of acts of high seriousness retain a near universality for cultural ingroup behavior. These findings say nothing about killing, maiming, raping, or robbing outgroup members in times of conflict, war, or revolution.

Graeme Newman, in a recent study covering such different cultures as Iran, Indonesia, Yugoslavia, the United States, Sardinia, and India, found similar responses. As Newman says,

There is a consistency across cultures in their disapprobation of traditional crimes, a consistency of such strength as to warrant the treatment of these acts or prescriptions as universals, or functionally absolute values.[14]

The Center for Studies in Criminology and Criminal Law at the University of Pennsylvania has launched a new and elaborate study to obtain a national representative sample of perceptions of gradation of the seriousness of crime.[15] By a joint effort of the Bureau of the Census and the Law Enforcement Assistance Administration, the study involves interviewing persons in approximately 30,000 households across the United States. They will be asked to assign numerical values to the seriousness of approximately 200 different offenses. This is the first study of this magnitude to obtain a national recording of what the Supreme Court has repeatedly called "community sentiments" about the seriousness of different kinds of criminal acts.

The utility of such psychophysical scaling goes beyond the concern of this chapter; suffice it to say that in the allocation of police resources for the control and prevention of crime, judicial sentencing, and legislative revisions of penal codes, such seriousness scores should be of considerable value. The major reason for referring to this study within the current context is to suggest that the expected scores for various forms of behavior that previously were viewed as relatively serious and that did not involve physical injury, theft, or damage will most likely be viewed with low degrees of seriousness, thus indicating the further expansion of cultural tolerance of deviance and the contraction of what is deemed serious criminality.

The value stretch continues in a cultural pluralism that retains stability at the upper end of the continuum of the seriousness of offensive behavior and that accommodates, with a tolerant embrace, normative deviance at the lower end.

The Increase and Decrease of Crimes of Violence

Since 1930 the major method for determining the amount of crime in the United States has been the *Uniform Crime Reports* (*UCR*) of the Federal Bureau of Investigation. These annual reports are produced from the collection of police reports in departments of cities and county jurisdictions across the country. There are 29 categories of offense, but only the first 7 are used for what is known as a *crime index*, a classification analogous to the consumer price index, the cost of living index, or the index of economic productivity. These 7 categories include criminal homicide, forcible rape, robbery, aggravated assault, burglary, larceny of $50 and over, and automobile theft and are referred to as "offenses known to the police." All the remaining 22 offense categories are reported only in terms of the number of persons arrested.

There has been much critical commentary over the past 45 years about the validity of the crime index, both from traditional scholars who use the crime index reports and from Marxist criminologists who deride the data and deny the validity of a capitalist system that fails to take into account the criminogenic forces of the economic and political power of the state as it is now constructed. Putting aside those issues and admitting that except for the new series of data known as *victimization rates*, collected by the Bureau of the Census in cooperation with the Law Enforcement Assistance Administration, there is little other basis upon which scholars or public officials have for determining whether crime rates are increasing, decreasing, or remaining stable.

Using the *UCR* data, it can be said that since 1960 crimes of violence have increased 180 percent.[16] The fear of crime, as indicated in a variety of localized studies, has probably increased in even greater proportions than the recorded reality of crime. That many crimes are unrecorded, that reporting procedures have varied over time, and that more crimes may be reported now, particularly rape, than in earlier days are difficult issues to test empirically.

Nonetheless, there appears to be a consensus among the community of criminologists who examine criminal statistics that the amount of real criminality has considerably and significantly increased during the past 15 years. That there have been equally high rates of crime and crimes of violence recorded in earlier eras of the history of the United States has been asserted by such longtime series data as provided by Buffalo and Boston and recorded in the Task Force Reports of the National Commission on the Causes and Prevention of Violence.[17] Crimes of violence in the latter part of the nineteenth century were as high or higher than even the currently reported rates of crimes of violence.

The issue, however, is that within the memories of the current living population of the United States there has been such an upsurge in crimes of violence or street crimes that social concern, governmental budgets, and public policy are increasingly affected.

Explanations for the assumed increase are varied but usually embrace such issues as unemployment, broken homes, inadequate education, poor housing, racial injustice, relative deprivation, lack of law enforcement, leniency in the courts, etc. My purpose here is not to be explicative, but rather to be descriptively analytical. One thing that is known is that there have been significant demographic changes directly related to the changing crime rates. It may be that a demographic description becomes a partial explanation for change. The high fertility rates immediately after World War II, known as the "baby boom," produced a significant alteration in the age composition of the United States population, such that a swelling of the age group between 15 and 24 occurred in the early 1960s. For example, in 1940 and 1950, persons between the ages of 15 and 24 years of age constituted 14.7 percent of the total population. In 1960, 1965, and 1970, the proportions of the same age group were respectively 13.6 percent, 15.7 percent, and 17.8 percent.[18] Because this age group is the most "criminogenic," meaning that this age-specific group contributes more to the rates of crimes of violence for the total population, it has been asserted that the sheer increase in this age group has been the major contributor to the increase in crimes of violence. Studies designed to factor out statistically the contribution of this demographic change have generally supported the assertion that no matter what social interventions may have been made to control, prevent, or deter crime, the changing age composition of the population has been importantly responsible for the increase in crimes of violence.

In a detailed and statistically sophisticated econometric-type model of crime rates over time in the United States, James Fox, from the Center for Studies in Criminology and Criminal Law at the University of Pennsylvania, has shown how the 14 to 21 year age group has significantly contributed to the rising rates of crimes of violence in the United States.[19] But he has also shown with carefully controlled demographic projections to the year 2000 what changes are most likely to occur (see figure 4-1). In the United States we are now at the lowest rates of fertility ever recorded, and the reduction of fertility has already begun to be reflected in the reduced increase in crimes of violence. In 1976 we began to notice both relative and absolute decreases in crimes of violence. The rate of increase dropped and in many major cities across the country there was an absolute decrease in crimes of violence. The proportion of the youthful group in the total population has decreased and the earlier "baby boom" generation is in its late twenties and early thirties, ages at which the commission of violent crimes decreases.

We should be witnessing from now through the mid-1980s a decline or stability in the amount of crimes of violence. However, the postwar "baby boom" children now grown are getting married and will produce high fertility rates again despite the relative decline in the number of children per couple. Consequently, the 15 to 24 year age group will rise again in the 1990s, producing once more a rise in the amounts of violence. These claims are made without reference to any effect greater amounts of law enforcement activity or changes in the criminal justice system may have on the reduction of crime. As a matter of fact, the weight of empirical evidence indicates that no current preventative, deterrent, or rehabilitative intervention scheme has the desired effect of reducing crime.

Two other points need to be made about the changing rates of crimes of violence. One is related to the increase in violent crimes since the early 1960s, and the other is related to the expected decrease in crimes of violence from the late 1970s to the 1990s. First, it is not simply the increase in crimes of violence that has promoted public fear and increased expenditure of public funds to

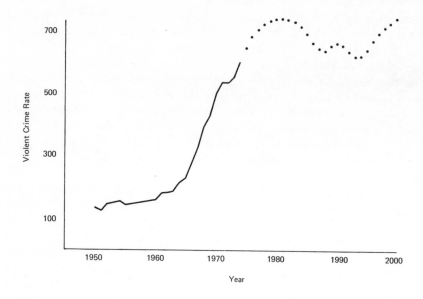

Source: James Alan Fox, *An Econometric Analysis of Crime Data* (Lexington, Mass.: Lexington Books, D.C. Heath and Co., forthcoming).

Figure 4-1. Prediction of Violent Crime Rate to the Year 2000

combat crime; it is the expansion of crimes of violence to groups that have "the power to enforce their beliefs," namely the large middle class and the upper class in American society who have increasingly become victims of crimes of violence.

The major crime-control system in Western civilization has traditionally been that of residential segregation. From the time of the ancient Greeks in Athens through classical Rome, the middle ages on the continent of Europe, and in the United States, the slaves, the "criminal classes," the beggars of society, and the lower socioeconomic classes—to use the more current traditional phrasing of social scientists—are the groups attributed with being the major crime committers of theft and physical injury and have always been residentially kept within their own densely populated, propinquitous areas. Kept on the other side of the river, the canal, or the railroad tracks, the "criminal classes" have been segregated, and crime committed among these groups has either not been well recorded or reported or it has been considered to be of relative inconsequence to the social structure that has been politically and economically powered by the aristocrats, nobility, or bourgeoisie.

In the United States, the lower socioeconomic classes, which have always included a high proportion of blacks since the days of slavery, have conveniently been residentially separated from the middle class, particularly the white middle class. Rapes, robberies, and homicides committed intragroup among the lower socioeconomic classes have been relatively unimportant to those groups in legislative, executive, and judicial power. With the increasing importance attributed to equality of opportunity, and with the breakdown of racially restrictive covenants in 1949 by a Supreme Court decision, as well as the value placed upon political equality, the traditional residential segregation crime-control system has been altered. Moreover, technological changes affording greater opportunities for physical as well as social mobility and interaction among groups have contributed to the breakdown of barriers that formerly existed. Consequently, as there has been an increase in the amount of social interaction among social and ethnic classes and groups there also has been an increase in the amount of intergroup and interclass crime, which has contributed to the greater victimization of middle and upper classes. Burglaries, muggings, rapes, and killings among the groups that define and rate the seriousness of crime and have the power to enforce sanctions have increased the concern of these groups with crimes of violence.

So long as rape, robbery and homicide were essentially an intraracial and intraclass affair, committed primarily among the poor and the blacks, the concern of the general public with crimes of violence was minimal. Public visibility of concern with such crimes has been related to the more generalized victimization as well as to the rise in the rates of such crimes.

The second point dealing with the expected stability or decrease in crimes of violence concerns the change in public perspectives about the seriousness of other kinds of crimes. For example, crimes of violence due to what some of us now call a "subculture of violence" may be replaced by cunning and corruption.[20] Cesare Lombroso foresaw some of this condition as he compared societies in the nineteenth century:

Civilization introduces every day new crimes, less atrocious perhaps than the old ones but nonetheless injurious. Thus in London the thief substitutes cunning for violence; in place of burglary he practices purloining by means of special apparatus; in place of porch climbing he uses swindling and blackmail by the aid of the press. . . . It [wealth] drives men to crime through vanity in order to surpass others, and from a fatal ambition to cut a figure in the world which, as we have seen, is one of the greatest causes of crime against property.[21]

Georges Sorel's *Reflexions sur la Violence*, which first appeared in 1906, was in a similar vein.[22] Speaking for the revolutionary syndicalist wing of the labor movement, Sorel focused his theoretical writings on the struggle for social power. He suggested that reduction of overt acts of violence in social relations is correlated with an increase in fraud and corruption, i.e., that fraud comes to replace violence as the means to success and privilege. What Sorel called *cunning* in his references to cooperation, arbitration, and "social peace" has come to replace the use of violence in many aspects of the social struggle for power. Manipulation of persons and things, especially through economic institutions and the impersonalized relationships represented by money, increasingly is substituted for force. Men become interchangeable, alienation accumulates, and minds are raped in subtle ways.[23]

With the reduction in crimes of violence, major public concern with crime will probably shift to organized and white-collar varieties. In this transitional stage we will make the trade-off of violence with fraud. Even now organized crime is using less violence than 30 or 40 years ago. Monopolies of power in service industries are gained by legal purchase or fraudulent conversion. Accounting practices and legal services constitute the backbone of organized criminal business. Loopholes in regulatory law, purposefully retained to serve a capitalist economy, are exploited by legitimate and illegitimate business. Violent liquidation of competitive persons in organized crime gives way to incorporation of the adversary through buying him out or burying him in bankruptcy.

When professional and business crime is finally viewed as corporate dysfunctionality, as an attack on the body politic, such crime will then be more carefully scrutinized and placed under the focus of stringent governmental control and public appeal for action.

Nam et ipsa scientia potestas est

Part of this change is already being reflected in a new form of information or knowledge theft that may become a major type of criminality. Computer tape theft, computer program theft, and corporate information burglary are styles of crime that may be prominent in the future. The theft of information in order to obtain positions of power will increase. The Pentagon Papers, the attempt to steal information from Daniel Ellsberg's psychiatrist, and the entire Watergate scandal are among the more dramatic illustrations of this kind of theft.

But there are many others. Recently six persons were arrested in California in what is described as a "multimillion dollar industrial espionage case" perpetrated against the International Business Machines Corporation.[24] An IBM engineer was arrested and charged with 10 felony counts: four of conspiracy, three of theft of trade secrets, two of offering or accepting inducements to steal trade secrets, and one of receiving stolen property. The principal subject of the theft was an IBM-developed direct-access storage device known as the Merlin, which comprises the data-storage portion of many computer systems.

This is not an isolated case, for many similar ones are coming to light. These, combined with consumer fraud, securities thefts, and political corruption, constitute a growing form of major crime in our postindustrial era.

The penal codes of socialist countries may more nearly represent this future condition in the United States. No inference is made that the socialist countries represent a further step in social evolution. Whether the change suggested is upward, downward, or horizontal is irrelevant. The point is that economic crime—embezzlement, theft of corporate moneys, and theft of property—is considered in socialist countries as more serious than many, or most, crimes against personalized victims. The sanctions for the former are more severe; however, the frequency of committing either is apparently lower than in capitalist countries.

The change is already occurring and will continue. The rise in the number and political and economic power of consumer interest groups and the increased perceived seriousness of political corruption, corporate criminality, and multinational bribery are already reflections of the changing emphasis in our society from crimes of violence to fraud and corruption. Pollution, bribery of public officials, and Medicaid and Medicare fraud may yet be viewed as being a serious as burglary or sexual assault.

Notes

1. This section is an expansion of some remarks I presented at the Fifth National Conference at the Institute of Criminology, University of Cambridge, England, on 5 July 1973. Portions of a forthcoming article in *Daedalus* are included here.

2. This is essentially John Louis Gillin's definition of crime in his *Criminology and Penology* (New York: Appleton-Century, 1945).

3. Thorsten Sellin and Marvin E. Wolfgang, *Delinquency: Selected Studies* (New York: Wiley, 1969).

4. Emile Durkheim, *The Rules of Sociological Method* (Chicago: Univ. of Chicago Press, 1938), pp. 67-71.

5. Ibid., pp. 67-68.

6. Albert K. Cohen, *The Elasticity of Evil: Changes in the Social Definition of Deviance* (Oxford, England: 1974), p. 6.

7. Ibid., p. 6.

8. See the Second United Nations Congress on the Prevention of Crime and the Treatment of Offenders (London: 8-20 August 1960), *New Forms of Juvenile Delinquency: Their Origin, Prevention and Treatment*, report prepared by the Secretariat, A/Conf. 17/7.

9. Gilbert Geis, *Not the Law's Business?* (Washington, D.C.: Center for Studies of Crime and Delinquency, National Institute of Mental Health, 1972), p. 261.

10. Philip Rieff, *Triumph of the Therapeutic* (New York: Harper & Row, 1966).

11. Thorsten Sellin and Marvin E. Wolfgang, *The Measurement of Delinquency* (New York: Wiley, 1964).

12. Sellin and Wolfgang, *Delinquency: Selected Studies.*

13. Robert M. Figlio, "The Seriousness of Offenses: An Evaluation by Offenders and Nonoffenders," Ph.D. dissertation, Univ. of Pennsylvania, 1971.

14. Graeme Newman, *Comparative Deviance: Perception and Law in Six Cultures* (New York: Elsevier, 1976), p. 297. See also Peter Rossi, Emily Waite, Christine E. Bose, and Richard E. Berk, "The Seriousness of Crimes: Normative Structure and Individual Differences," *American Sociological Review* 39, 1974, pp. 224-237.

15. Marvin E. Wolfgang, Robert Figlio, and Terence P. Thornberry, *The National Crime Severity Study*, forthcoming.

16. *Uniform Crime Reports* (Washington, D.C.: Federal Bureau of Investigation, 1975).

17. Donald J. Mulvihill, Melvin M. Tumin, and Lynn A. Curtis, *Crimes of Violence*, Vol. 11, Washington, D.C., staff report submitted to the National Commission on the Causes and Prevention of Violence.

18. *Census of Population: 1970*, "General Population Characteristics," Final Report PC(1)-B1, *U.S. Summary* (Washington, D.C.: Bureau of Census, 1972).

19. James Alan Fox, "An Econometric Analysis of Crime Data," Ph.D. dissertation, Univ. of Pennsylvania, 1976.

20. Marvin E. Wolfgang and Franco Ferracuti, *The Subculture of Violence: Towards an Integrated Theory in Criminology* (London, England: Tavistock Publications, 1967).

21. Cesare Lombroso, *Crime: Its Causes and Remedies* (Boston, Massachusetts: Little, Brown, 1912), pp. 57-58, 134.

22. Georges Sorel, *Reflexions sur la violence* (Paris: 1936).

23. See my earlier comments on this topic in "A Preface to Violence," *The Annals of the American Academy of Political Science* 364, March 1966, pp. 1-7.

24. *The New York Times*, 30 June 1973.

**Part II
Issues in Contemporary
Criminology**

5 Economic Crime

Simon Dinitz

Edwin H. Sutherland, one of the most inventive minds in criminology in this century, coined the felicitous phrase "white-collar crime" as the title of his presidential address to the American Sociological Association about 35 years ago. Despite his critics, Sutherland well understood the nature and impact of white-collar crime as a violation of criminal law, of interpersonal and entrepreneurial norms, and, above all, of social trust, personal virtue, and the moral imperatives. As a moralist, Sutherland coined the terms *white-collar crime* and *white-collar criminals* as a less elegant and more scholarly denunciation of the excesses of laissez faire economics than Roosevelt's "malefactors of great wealth," Josephson's "robber barons," Ida Tarbell's "oil and steel magnates," Upton Sinclair's "meat packers," the "new rich," and the "new elite," or Veblen's "conspicuous consumers." The new phrase lent criminological credence and academic respectability, to say nothing of a sociological perspective, to the study of what was after all merely the new rules of the economic game. For despite the Sherman and Clayton Acts, and other halfhearted legislative enactments prohibiting conspiratorial and monopolistic practices, gross fraud and deception, bribery and corruption, and the wholesale violations of even minimal health and safety codes, the new economic morality prescribed building empires not character. Eventually, the great economic bust, the profusion of New Deal legislation, the loss of self-confidence, a war or two, the income tax bite, and other assorted changes on the socioeconomic-political scene soon dampened, but by no means quenched, the unbridled thirst for wealth, status, and power, however achieved.

But Sutherland's goal was not moralizing alone, or even translating popular cries for economic justice into criminologic concepts. Instead, Sutherland saw in white-collar crime—concept and behavior—a vehicle for demolishing traditional perspectives about the etiology of crime and delinquency. Surely it was not poverty that drove a railroad tycoon into telling his equally famous colleagues that as men he would trust them with all his material possessions but as businessmen he wouldn't trust them out of his sight. It was not poor housing, family disorganization, and slum living, to say nothing of poor schools and unequal opportunity, which produced a Fisk, Gould, Morgan, or Musica-Coster and their ilk. It was not intrapsychic disabilities caused by maternal deprivation, early weaning, sibling rivalry, an unresolved Oedipus, a horrendous latency, or a cyclothymic crisis which made malefactors like Carnegie, old man Rockefeller, Stanford, Hill, and all the rest connive, conspire, compete, and corrupt to attain their goals. It is hard to believe that Charles Ponzi had an extra Y chromosome or that the robber barons were saddled with hyperkensis, dyslexia, or other glandular malfunctions of the limbic and autonomic systems. The odds are equally great that none of the conspirators had high F scores on the Adorno scale or could be differentiated, except for their success, on the projective pencil-and-paper or performance tests then sweeping psychology. The criminal theft, looting, conspiracies, illegal rebates, bribery, corruption, and power struggles associated with the remnants of our unregulated economy were simply targets of opportunity and not of socioeconomic status, color, ethnicity, or deprivation. White-collar crime is the conventional crime of those in positions of trust and wealth. As Geis has since suggested, the suite is the site of privileged crime.

In our industrial society, the chief and sometimes the sole constraint on the businessman is the balance sheet. Such ethical considerations as may be involved are wholly secondary to the moral imperative to turn a profit. Various segments of the economic structure, sad to say, compel criminal violations or, at least, structural and occasionally inventive types of deviousness. Economic survival and surely economic health promote manipulation and law violations which are frequently ingenious and rarely subject to social sanction. Unfortunately, the public is usually innocent of the personal costs of these depredations—a condition which hardly nullifies the cost and damage of suite crime—whether committed by economic minnows, sharks, or whales.

The demonstration of this principle—that suite crime is the street crime of the business and professional communities—was not, however, the ultimate concern of Sutherland. Indeed, by ridiculing the prevailing etiological conceptions of criminality as class-biased, he was, in fact, offering his genetic theory of crime causation—differential association—as the explanation of crime in boardroom and barroom, in street and suite, of native and naturalized, and of winners and losers. As every fledgling criminology student has read or heard, crime is a learned behavior. It is an outgrowth of contact with patterns of deviant conduct and intimate interaction or association with the carriers of these patterns. Thus, the bottom line, to be *au courant*, is that Sutherland found the concept of white-collar crime eminently useful in documenting and illustrating his differential-association hypothesis or theory.

Under these circumstances, Sutherland was never really forced to deal with the implications of his "discovery" of white-collar crime. In contrast, he was forced to wrestle with the problems of professional theft, of sexual psychopathy, and of the many other issues which his fertile mind and indefatigable efforts produced. For example, with regard to white-collar crime, Sutherland never sought to understand the political consequences of his work. He seemed oblivious to the need for comparative work to determine whether white-collar crime would surface, in what form, and to what degree in a socialist society, in newly industrializing societies, and in transactions that were personal and not simply perfunctory. It is difficult also to determine whether he saw white-collar crime as inevitable. On the control level, Sutherland called for the treatment of white-collar crime as real crime requiring the invoking of penal rather than civil sanctions. But even here, he never constructed or proposed a theory of justice, of fairness, of punitiveness, or of deterrence in dealing with the white-collar offender. Clearly he favored criminal over administrative law. He also understood the difficulties inherent in the definition and social control by regulatory agencies over what he perceived to be an occupational variant of ordinary crime involving, after all, misrepresentation and duplicity. In the final analysis, neither Sutherland nor most of those who followed in his inventive footsteps understood or fully comprehended (even today) the exquisite problems posed by the emergence of the administrative agency as a rule-making and rule-enforcing body. Nor have the arguments over the "realness" of white-collar crime been resolved.

Apart from the ever vexing issue of the definition and substance of white-collar crime, various critics have raised major objections to the very formulation of the concept. First, legalists object to the use of the word *crime*, since most cases of such violations are handled outside of the criminal justice system. Second, except in infrequent instances, an uninformed public does not perceive the activity as criminal. Neither for that matter do the perpetrators. Perhaps Musica-Coster had a finely tuned sense of the public mentality when he left a suicide note which read something to the effect that as God was his witness, he had done no wrong. Such, too, was the public view and the expressed sentiment of the participants in the electrical equipment conspiracy case and now of the Equity Funding principals. Surely, the critics contend that for crime to be crime, the public at the very least ought to view misrepresentation, duplicity, and conspirational conduct as criminal. It is, of course, a well known axiom in the field that when consensus exists, laws are unnecessary; where dissensus is characteristic, laws are ineffective. In white-collar crime, except at the lowest levels, such as in repair frauds, consumer gouging, or the misgrading and mislabeling of goods, the nature of the violation is often so complex that neither consensus nor dissensus exists but only ignorance. The third argument is that white-collar crime is so pervasive that it is the norm and not the exception. If so, how can a norm be a crime? Tax law and expense account violations and business kickbacks are a few examples of practices that are so commonplace as to defy the concept of crime and to qualify as norms of evasion. Fourth, as Clinard has implied, Sutherland's approach involved learned occupational role violations. What about all the offenses which are outside the occupational sphere entirely?

Despite these limitations, objections, and critical carping, Sutherland's pioneering conception met with widespread acclaim in the profession. In short order various research projects were initiated and yielded systematic data. Eventually, however, all led into a dead end of case histories and descriptions of this or that fraud or violation. Thus, Clinard did an excellent study of the phenomenon of the black market and violations of wartime regulations; Hartung looked at the wholesale meat industry; Cressey at embezzlers and later at respectable criminals; Newman at public attitudes; Quinney at retail pharmacists; Wilging into installment credit problems; Wraith and Simpkins into corruption in far off places; Aubert into the social structure; Bauer into truth in lending; Bernard into medical quackery; Ball into the use of criminal sanctions; J. Becker into abuses in unemployment benefits; and Bartenstein into research espionage. Reputable journals raised the issue of the ethics of the marketplace and of the honorable men therein.

Criminologists and journalists alike have had a field day with the corporate executives in the electrical conspiracy case; with Tony DeAngelis, the former soybean oil tycoon; with Sherman Adams and Bernard Goldfine and the vicuna coat caper; with Wolfson, Lowell Birrell, Billie Sol Estes; and recently with Cornfield and with Vesco. Lately, attention has been rivted on the oil cartel—both national and international—and, of course, on the implausible events of Watergate!

As a corpus of work, however, the ambiguities of the initial concept, the division between the headline case and the daily depredations of malefactors (large and small, in blue and white collars, and with wide or narrow suit coat lapels), and the 35 years since Sutherland have advanced the field almost imperceptibly. Some of our naivete is gone, but the study of white-collar crime is, if anything, more elusive than before.

Certain changes have, of course, occurred. On balance, they have reduced the muckraking element and increased the possibilities of assessing the problem of white-collar crime with greater incisiveness and specificity. Most of these changes were introduced by legally trained scholars with regulatory body experience working both ends of the prosecution-defendant adversary system. Short on etiology, a substantial blessing in itself given the history of this area, they are long on substance and procedure, on classification, and on the rules of evidence. The National District Attorneys' Association project is a case in point. When the district attorneys finally become cognizant of this special and costly problem, then we must be doing something right in this field.

Along with Geis and one or two others, the most influential figure in the field is Herb Edelhertz whose National Institute of Law Enforcement and Criminal Justice (NILECJ) monograph reads more like a legal brief than an academic criminological piece. Yet this monograph operationalizes the definition and step by step leads us through a system of classification and the entire network of decision points, including detection procedures, investigation techniques and problems, prosecutive evaluations, pleas and plea bargaining, sentencing, diversion, and necessary additional legislation. There are short detours to the cashless society, the impact of civil rights, election law reforms, environmental problems, and consumer protection. In short, Edelhertz's brief makes it abundantly clear why economic crimes are so difficult to prevent, deter, or even to process.

As defined by Edelhertz, an *economic crime* is "an illegal act or series of illegal acts committed by nonphysical means and by concealment or guile, to obtain money or property, to avoid the payment or loss of money or property, or to obtain business or personal advantage." There is nothing in this definition about occupational role requirements, respectability and high social status, or about etiology. In this sense, this legalistic conception is at once superior in being more inclusive and democratic, while it lacks Sutherland's principal point—that white-collar crime is an upper-class version of street crime and is therefore profoundly more costly in moral and social integration terms.

Edelhertz, ever the legalist in the best sense of that increasingly derogatory term, presents a four-category classificatory system of *economic crime*—a term he prefers to white-collar crime. These categories are:

1. Crimes by persons operating on an individual ad hoc basis (e.g., tax violations; credit card fraud; charity frauds; and unemployment, insurance, and welfare frauds.
2. Crimes committed in the course of their occupations by those operating inside business, government, or other establishments in violation of their duty of loyalty and fidelity to employer or client (e.g., computer frauds; commercial bribery and kickbacks; "sweetheart" contracts; embezzlement; expense account padding; and conflicts of interest).
3. Crimes incidental to and in furtherance of business operations, but not the central purpose of the business (e.g., fraud against the government, food and drug violations, check kiting, housing code violations, and other forms of misrepresentation).
4. White-collar crime as a business or as the central activity (e.g., bankruptcy, land, home improvement, merchandising, insurance, pyramid, vanity, stocks and bonds, and related frauds and schemes.

While subject to considerable overlap, this assortment of public bilking schemes and regulatory agency violations is a considerable improvement over the twin evils of misrepresentation and duplicity identified by Sutherland. Edelhertz finds a great many common elements in the panoply of economic crimes. Among these he identifies:

1. The intent to commit a wrongful act (*mens rea*) or to achieve a purpose inconsistent with law or public policy.
2. Disguise of purpose or intent.
3. Reliance by violator on ignorance or carelessness of victim. The same proviso incidentally might be stated for conventional criminality as well.
4. Acquiescence by victim in what he believes to be the true nature and content of the transaction.

5. Concealment of the crime by:
   a. Preventing realization of victimization.
   b. Making provision for restitution for small number of complainants.
   c. Creation of some type of dummy facade to disguise the real nature of the illegal activity.

This Edelhertz bread-and-butter formulation represents a quantum jump over the initial approach to the conceptualization of Sutherland. Nevertheless, it still fails to differentiate economic crimes by levels or classes. As I see it, the most manageable level, both practically and conceptually, is the consumer-fraud level. Here, one or more operatives bilk innocent clients in such things as the various repair rackets and related behaviors comparable to petty or grand larceny. The problem can be understood and managed in conventional criminal terms with the addition of restitution and public stigmatization, including a fine and or short sentence.

One level up and the picture begins to change. Conventional criminal law becomes inadequate and the regulatory and administrative agencies do not yet fully enter the picture. I suggest that local price fixing by chain stores, bank interest rates, "competitive" bidding for contracts in the construction industry, and similar economic practices are cases in point. Misgrading of goods, mislabelling, underweighting, and general misrepresentation, as described by Sutherland, are other illustrations.

At the third level are the economic practices perpetrated by larger, usually national, organizations and bureaucracies in the utility, railroad, airline, food, and just about every other industrial group. These practices, requiring years of litigation to resolve, are so totally unlike conventional criminality that it is a disservice to the discipline to speak of them in the same context as petty frauds and a butcher's fat thumb on a scale. National price fixing, rebates, legislative lobbying, bribery, corruption, securities frauds, conspiracies, pension and welfare fund raids, incredible bookkeeping practices, false advertising, cost overruns, expense fraud, tax shelters (legal and otherwise) depletion allowances, fast write-offs, expensive junkets, industrial espionage, and all the rest of the shoddy and usually illegal and unethical yet conventional methods of doing business are outside the criminal law and beyond the control of the cumbersome bureaucratic machinery designed to contain and control such willful, overt conduct. That the bureaucracies in Italy, France, Israel, and the second, third, and fourth worlds are even more unequal to the task is small comfort to all of us who are forced unwittingly and unwillingly to pay the price. My point is that individually and collectively we are unable to halt the erosion of our personal and social control. Tony DeAngelis, the toppled soybean oil tycoon, is admittedly good copy. But his conduct can be effectively stopped even if it is a bit after the fact. The more insidious problem is the cross-licensing of drugs (technically prohibited), which costs the public more dearly in every way and to which practice we are impotent to respond.

But the erosion of public control does not halt at water's edge. The national conglomerate, horizontal, vertical, or both, with or without computer rigging, is as a pygmy to the multinational organizations which are the current equivalent of the postfeudal states. National controls are no match at all for the unbridled power exercised by the multinationals, as recent events have so clearly shown.

I suggest, therefore, and with all due respect to Edelhertz, the District Attorneys' Association, the consumer advocates, common causers, environmentalists, Nader's Raiders, paper recyclers, vegetarians, friends of the good earth, and to my criminological colleagues of every persuasion, that the economic crime problem is a misnomer and a cul-de-sac. Apart from the lowest-level defrauders, the embezzlers, the schemers, and the land promoters who defraud the public, the problem of economic crime is not a crime problem at all but rather an issue of what kind of industrial and postindustrial society is to emerge, how it is to be organized and regulated, and by whom.

To reiterate, it is my contention that muckraking aside, the issue of economic crime, no matter how formulated, requires an interdisciplinary perspective now alien to criminology, law, economics, psychiatry, and the other social and behavioral disciplines. The assumptions and "taken-for-granteds" in each discipline are inadequate to cope with phenomena which go beyond conventional legal, political, economic, and sociological boundaries.

Some 10 or more years ago I offered my first seminar on white-collar crime. The graduate students were inevitably taken with the problem and with the standard works in the field. We were unable to resolve, of course, some of the issues raised earlier concerning definition, classification, and remedies. In this sense, the seminar reflected the status of the field, where most of the work being produced was of the case history—isn't that terrible—variety? Not a single publishable paper emerged from that exercise. In fact, a good investigative journalist could and certainly should have been able to do as well or better.

Nevertheless, the problem of economic crime remained, and some sort of research handle was necessary if the state of thinking about the problem was not to be fixed at a level not far removed from the initial Sutherland formulation. John Conrad of the Academy for Contemporary Problems, Herbert Edelhertz of HARC, Battelle-Seattle, and I agreed to pool our talents and knowledge and offer a continuing seminar in economic crime. As a kickoff, we (or rather they) arranged the first conference on Economic Crime on January 11 and 12, 1974. The invitees included as many of the luminaries in the field as we thought would come. Nearly all did. With proper fanfare, and graduate student interest and participation, the conference was launched with a discussion by Clinard on some of the problems of doing research in this area. As our conference tapes indicate, Geis, Cressey, Newman, Edelhertz, Kossack, Short, Frank Ray—the local prosecutor associated with the district attorney's project—and the many other participants had ample material to present on the problems of doing research, or anything else, in this field.

In sum, their laments, as expressed most cogently by Clinard and the others reduced to the following.

1. The entire concept of economic and white-collar crime is based on a nostalgic and erroneous conception of a free enterprise system in which unfettered competition is a positive good that must be preserved by law, no less than by social consensus and a congenial economic climate. Alas, such utiopian visions probably never even characterized the economic relationships in the United States. Hence our models, based on this conception, are perforce erroneous. The corporate economic structure, big labor, big government, and the agribusiness operate apart from the wisdom of an Adam Smith or a John Marshall, or even a Milton Friedman. Perhaps if we reversed the conception, namely, that unbridled competition is subject to civil and criminal sanction, the resulting new laws might be more enforceable. In sum, the Baptist born, Midwestern bred, highly ethical Sutherland confused Main Street and Wall Street in his conceptualization of the problem of economic crime. There is, of course, economic crime, but our model must be realistic rather than sentimental if white-collar crime is to be contained and managed effectively.

2. For much the same reasons, our thinking about the "malefactors" is inadequate. We apply the general principles in criminal law to them—harm, an overt act or acts, *mens rea*—as though responsibility can be pinpointed in massive bureaucracies like the conglomerates, the heavy industries, the multinationals. Occupational role behavior is, for most of us, a series of directives rather than a series of responsible judgments involving personal choice. Even the most powerful executives may be locked into their decisions by external consider-ations beyond their immediate, or even ultimate, control. This might be called the *Geraldine effect* after Flip Wilson, or "My boss made me do it."

3. Sorrowfully, even the always-tenuous line between legitimate business activity and economic crime is being obliterated. To twist Erasmus about 90 degrees: when everything is possible, nothing is wrong. What is the difference, after all, between a $300,000 fund to elect one's supporters to public office and the same amount in a slush fund to raise milk prices. The more we clarify our laws to divide legitimate from illegal activity, the less noticeable becomes the difference. The more agencies involved, the greater the confusion. Cases which take years to unravel simply do not promote criminological analysis or social control.

4. As a consequence of the complexity of the issues and the subject, we have been forced into several uncomfortable postures: an "isn't it terrible that such a thing could happen" response to an Equity Funding case which most students never even heard about; a muckraking stance of a Nader who soon exhausts public patience; the study of the new criminally processed violators, as in Cressey's embezzler or Karl Klockar's fence; or a reliance on investigative journalism. None of these approaches is designed to generate macro-level hypotheses, to test those now extant, or to provide more applicable models based on the actual operation of the marketplace at all levels. Theoretically, therefore, we have moved little since Sutherland toward an integrated theory of

violations in high and low places, in and out of occupational roles, and by all kinds of offenders—from the tax evader to the well-connected Arizona or Florida land gouger, from the electrical conspirators to the fraudulent and far from unique washing machine repair man. Just for the record, socialist society is no guarantor of the elimination or even necessarily the reduction in economic crime—only of conventional criminal prosecution and stiffer penalties.

5. White-collar crime, given these restrictions, is therefore a more or less nonresearchable area in the conventional sense of research as an analytic and not merely descriptive enterprise. The reasons, while self-evident on the whole, include some of the following.

First, it is impossible to test hypotheses which haven't been formulated. Second, quantitative analysis is well-nigh impossible. The laundering of money, the shredding of records, and the stonewalling in questioning, as well as an uncommonly high rate of amnesia for specific events, all make research a near hopeless cause. Long afterwards, when the memoirs are written, the safety deposit boxes emptied long since, and the unshredded records recovered, is it possible to reconstruct events as they may have transpired? But even history is hardly the answer. Only the more famous cases will surface. Most everything else will have passed from memory.

Third, even qualitative research is difficult at best. Stories are self-serving and contradictory, even when obtainable. Since malefactors do not conceive themselves as having offended, what is there to discuss? The two Haldeman interviews are a case in point. Only Colson has talked much recently, and he, apparently, chiefly to God! None of the Equity people have said much. Little wonder! So far the Equity Funding case has already lasted two years in the courts. There is now a $3 billion civil suit being litigated. Two states, three major accounting firms, a considerable number of other corporations and individuals, and 312 separate law firms—count them—are contesting an insurance fraud of elephantine proportions. So far, over 40,000 policy holders on Equity Funding's books have been found to be fictitious, thereby inflating the book value of the company out of all proportion to reality. No doubt the computer fraud people, despite Equity and its troubles, continue to manipulate the tapes, and even the smallest operatives are unreachable by the exceedingly short arm of the law.

Fourth, few studies (not even one comes to mind) have ever been replicated, even when such is possible, as in medical, legal, and other professional spheres. Who, for example, ever repeated Quinney's piece on the retail pharmacist? And why not?

Fifth, difficult as it is to obtain information from the subsystems in the criminal justice structure, access to the proceedings of regulatory agencies is nearly as difficult to achieve as would be the minutes of the National Security Council. Without cooperation we are left the petty stuff which resembles larceny and is processed by economic units or specialists within prosecutor's offices. To overcome this defect, a major research center like NILECJ might fill the void despite the obvious problems in creating a unit in so sensitive an area.

Sixth, by the same token but on a lower level, funding for economic crime research is almost nonexistent. Picture a "crime in the suites" bill sent up to the President*—a bill to establish a research institute to study occupational crime with a view to preventing, managing, and treating the problem; upgrading personnel; speeding court procedures; developing new correctional facilities and diversion alternatives; and specifying compensation and restitution modalities. Without doubt, the proponents of such a measure would be candidates for the National Institute of Mental Health diagnostic facilities at Bethesda. Yet there are institutes for everything from alcohol abuse to suicidology. Why not for economic crime?

Last, most criminologists with research competency are severely restricted by their traditional training, mostly in the social sciences. Nearly all lack experience in and knowledge of civil, administrative, or business law and such mundane competencies as accounting, marketing, and commercial skills. This being the case, the only hope lies in creating an interdisciplinary team, or teams, which can count on long-term funding and relative freedom of inquiry in carrying out their research mission.

I, for one doubt seriously that the next 35 years will advance this branch of criminology beyond its presently moribund state. The interest is real, the need great, the state of the art early, primitive, and the impediments insuperable. But then this description applies to nearly all of traditional criminology as well.

References

Anderson, David K. "Ambulance Chasing in Illinois: A Success Story." *Univ. of Illinois Law Forum* (Summer 1957):309-314.

Anthony, Robert N. "The Trouble with Profit Maximization." *Harvard Business Review* 38 (November-December 1960):126-134.

Apel, Hans. "The Scope and Significance of Economic Misrepresentation." *Journal of Economics and Sociology* 21 (January 1962):77-90; and 21 (April 1962):173-188.

Aubert, Vilhelm. "White Collar Crime and Social Structure." *American Journal of Sociology* 58 (1952):263-271.

Bacon, Seldon D. "Review of Sutherland, White Collar Crime." *American Sociological Review* 15 (April 1950):309-310.

Ball, Harry V., and Lawrence Friedman. "The Use of Criminal Sanctions in the Enforcement of Economic Legislation: A Sociological View." In Leon Radzinowicz and Marvin Wolfgang (eds.), *Crime and Justice*, Vol. II. New York: Basic Books, 1971, pp. 93-113.

Bartenstein, Fred, Jr. "Research Espionage: A Threat to Our National Security." *Food Drug Cosmetic Law Journal* 17 (December 1962):813-827.

*Editor's note: This text was written during President Ford's Republican administration.

Bauer, Bertrand, N. "Truth in Lending: College Business Students' Opinions of Caveat Emptor, Fraud, and Deception." *American Business Law Journal* 4 (Fall 1966):156-161.

Baumhart, Raymond C. "How Ethical are Businessmen?" *Harvard Business Review* 39 (July-August 1961):6-19, 156-176.

Bayley, David H. "The Effects of Corruption in a Developing Nation." *Western Political Science Quarterly* 19 (December 1966):719732.

Becker, Joseph M. *The Problem of Abuse in Unemployment Benefits.* New York: Columbia Univ. Press, 1953.

Bernard, Biola W. "Why People Become the Victims of Medical Quackery." *American Journal of Public Health* 55 (August 1965):1142-1147.

Black, Hillel. *The Watchdogs of Wall Street* New York: Morrow, 1962.

Bloch, Herbert A., and Gilbert Geis. *Man, Crime, and Society: The Forms of Criminal Behavior.* New York: Random House, 1962, pp. 379-404.

Bromberg, Walter. *Crime and the Mind.* New York: Macmillan, 1965, pp. 377-400.

Caldwell, Robert G. "A Reexamination of the Concept of White Collar Crime." *Federal Probation* 22 (1958), no. 1:30-36.

Caplovitz, David. *The Poor Pay More: Consumer Practices of Low-Income Families.* New York: The Free Press, 1963.

Carey, Sarah. "America's Respectable Crime Problem." *Washington Monthly* 3 (April 1971):44-47.

Carlin, Jerome E. *Lawyer's Ethics: A Survey of the New York City Bar.* New York: Russell Sage Foundation, 1966.

Cavanaugh, Karl W. "Retail Credit Sales and Usury." *Louisiana Law Review* 24 (June 1964):822-849.

Childs, Marquis, W., and Douglass Cater. *Ethics in a Business Society.* New York: Harper & Row, 1954.

Clinard, Marshall B. "Criminological Theories of Violations of Wartime Regulations." *American Sociological Review* 11:258-270.

Clinard, Marshall B. *The Black Market: A Study of White Collar Crime.* New York: Holt, 1952.

Clinard, Marshall B. *Sociology of Deviant Behavior.* New York: Holt, 1957, 2d ed., 1963.

Cohen, Sheldon S. "Morality and the American Tax System." *George Washington Law Review* 34 (June 1966):839-845.

Cook, Fred J. *The Corrupted Land: The Social Morality of Modern America.* New York: Macmillan, 1966.

Cressey, Donald R. "Application and Verification of the Differential Association Theory." *Journal of Criminal Law, Criminology, and Police Science* 43 (1952):43-52.

Cressey, Donald R. *Other People's Money: A Study in the Social Psychology of Embezzlement.* Glencoe, Illinois: Free Press, 1953.

Cressey, Donald R. "Foreword." In Edwin H. Sutherland, *White Collar Crime.* New York: Holt, 1961.

Cressey, Donald R. "The Respectable Criminal." In James F. Short, Jr. (ed.), *Modern Criminals.* Chicago: Aldine Publishing Company, 1970.

Cressey, Donald R. "The Violator's Vocabularies of Adjustment." In *Crimes Against Bureaucracy*, edited by E.O. Smigel and H.L. Ross. New York: Van Nostrand Reinhold Company, 1970, pp. 65-85.

Curran, Barbara A. *Trends in Consumer Credit Legislation.* Chicago: Univ. of Chicago Press, 1965.

Dershowitz, Alan M. "Increasing Community Control Over Corporate Crime: A Problem in the Law of Sanctions." *Yale Law Journal* 71 (1961):280.

Edelhertz, Herbert. *The Nature, Impact and Prosecution of White Collar Crime.* National Institute of Law Enforcement and Criminal Justice, Washington, D.C.: U.S. Government Printing Office, 1970.

Egan, Bowes. "Criminal Economic Law and Consumer Protection." *Journal of Business Law* (England) 26 (January 1967):26-31.

Emerson, Thomas I. "Review of Sutherland, White Collar Crime." *Yale Law Journal* 59 (January 1950):581-585.

"Ethics in America: Norms and Deviations." *Annals of the American Academy of Political and Social Science* 363 (January 1966):1-136.

"Expense Accounts." *Harvard Business Review* 38 (March-April 1960):6-12*ff.*

Farago, Ladislas. *It's Your Money: Waste and Mismanagement in Government Spending.* New York: Random House, 1964.

Findlay, Robert C., Frank J. Miele, and Robert M. Hanlon, "Consumer in the Marketplace: A Survey of the Law of Informed Buying Protection," *Notre Dame Lawyer* 38 (August 1963):556-613.

Finklestein, Louis. "The Businessman's Moral Failure." *Fortune* 58 (September 1958):116-117*ff.*

Frank, Stanley B. "Beware of Home-Repair Racketeers." *Saturday Evening Post* (July 21, 1956), pp. 17*ff.*

Fuller, John G. *The Gentlemen Conspirators: The Story of Price-Fixers in the Electrical Industry.* New York: Grove Press, 1962.

Fuller, Richard C. "Morals and the Criminal Law." *Journal of Criminal Law and Criminology* 32 (March-April 1942):624-630.

Gartner, M. (ed.). *Crime and Business: What You Should Know About the Infiltration of Crime into Business and Business into Crime.* Princeton, New Jersey: Dow Jones Books, 1971. (A collection of articles from the Wall Street Journal From 1968 to 1970.)

Geis, Gilbert. "Criminal Penalties for Corporate Criminals." *Criminal Law Bulletin* 8 (1972) no. 5:377-392.

Geis, Gilbert. "Toward a Delineation of White Collar Offenses." *Sociological Inquiry* 32, no. 2:160-171. (The journal of the Alpha Kappa Delta National Sociology Honor Society.)

Geis, Gilbert (ed.). *White Collar Criminal.* New York: Atherton Press, 1968.

Gentry, Curt. *The Vulnerable Americans.* Garden City, N.Y.: Doubleday, 1966.

Gibney, Frank. *The Operators.* New York: Harper & Row, 1960.

Goldman, M.M. *You Pay and You Pay: An Expose of the Respectable Racketeers.* New York: Howell, Soskin, 1941.

Goodman, Walter. *All Honorable Men: Corruption and Compromise in American Life.* Boston: Little, Brown, 1963.

Gross, Llewellyn. *Symposium on Sociological Theory.* New York: Harper & Row, 1959, pp. 531-564.

Grundfragen Der Wirtschafts Kriminalitat. Wiesbaden: Bundes Kriminalant, 1963.

Grygier, Tadeusz, Howard Jones, and John C. Spencer (eds.). *Criminology in Transition: Essays in Honour of Hermann Mannheim.* London: Tavistock, 1965. See especially "White Collar Crime," by John C. Spencer.

Hadden, Tom. "The Origins and the Development of Conspiracy to Defraud." *American Journal of Legal History* 11 (January 1967):25-40.

Hadlick, Paul E. *Criminal Prosecution Under the Sherman Antitrust Act.* Washington, D.C.: Ramsdell, 1939.

Hall, Jerome. "Criminology." In Georges Gurvitch and Wilbert E. Moore (eds.), *Twentieth Century Sociology.* New York: Philosophical Library, 1945, pp. 342-365.

Hall, Jerome. *Theft, Law, and Society*, 2d ed. Indianapolis: Bobbs-Merrill, 1952.

Hall, Jerome. "Criminology and Penal Theory." In *General Principles of Criminal Law*, 2d ed. Indianapolis: Bobbs-Herrill, 1960, pp. 600-621.

Harding, T. Swann. *The Popular Practice of Fraud.* New York: Longmans, Green and Company, 1935.

Hartung, Frank E. "White Collar Offenses in the Wholesale Meat Industry in Detroit." *American Journal of Sociology* 56 (1950):25-34.

Hartung, Frank E. "White Collar Crime: Its Significance for Theory and Practice." *Federal Probation* 17 (1953), no. 2:31-36.

Hazard, John N. "Soviet Socialism and Embezzlement." *Washington Law Review* 26 (November 1951):301-320.

Hazard, Leland. "Are Big Businessmen Crooks?" *The Atlantic* 208 (November 1961):57-61.

Herling, John. *The Great Price Conspiracy: The Story of the Anti-Trust Violations in the Electrical Industry.* Washington, D.C.: Robert B. Luce, 1962.

Hilt, Peter B. "Criminal Prosecution for Adulteration at Common Law." *Food Drug Cosmetic Law Journal* 15 (June 1960):382-398.

Hodges, Luther. *The Business Conscience.* Englewood Cliffs, N.J.: Prentice-Hall, 1963.

Hopkinson, Tom M. "New Battleground—Consumer Interest." *Harvard Business Review* 42 (September-October 1964):97-104.

Hurwitz, Stephan. *Criminology*. London: Allen and Unwin, (1947) 1952. (First published in Danish.)

Insalata, S. John. "Deceptive Business Practices, Criminals in Cuff Links." *Speeches of the Day* 29 (May 15, 1963):473-475.

Irey, Elmer L., and William J. Slocum. *The Tax Dodgers*. New York: Greenberg, 1945.

James, Leslie. "Bribery and Corruption in Commerce." *International and Comparative Law Quarterly* 11 (July 1962):880-886.

Jaspan, Norman, and Hillel Black. *The Thief in the White Collar*. Philadelphia: Lippincott, 1960.

Jeffery, Clarence R. "The Structure of American Criminological Thinking." *Journal of Criminal Law, Criminology, and Police Science* 46 (1956):658-672.

Jones, Howard. *Crime and the Penal System: A Textbook of Criminology*, 2d ed. London: University Tutorial Press, (1956) 1962.

Josephson, Matthew. *The Robber Barons: The Great American Capitalist, 1861-1901*. New York: Harcourt, Brace, 1934.

Kadish, Sanford H. "Some Observations on the Use of Criminal Sanctions in Enforcing Economic Regulations." *Univ. of Chicago Law Review* 30 (1963):423.

Kaleki, Michal. "An Attempt at the Elucidation of the Phenomenon of Economic Criminality." *Kulturai i Spoteczenstwo* (1962), no. 3:73-77.

Kessler, Friedrich. "The Protection of the Consumer Under Modern Sales Law." *Yale Law Journal* 74 (December 1964):262-284.

Keysor, Charles W. "Beware of Genteel Crooks." *Commerce Magazine* 52 (April 1955):20*ff.*

Kline, George L. "Economic Crime and Punishment." *Survey* 57 (October 1965):67-72.

Kossack, Nathaniel E. " 'Scam': The Planned Bankruptcy Racket." *New York Certified Public Accountant* 35 (June 1965):417-423.

Lane, Robert E. "Why Business Men Violate the Law." *Journal of Criminal Law, Criminology, and Police Science* 44 (1953):151-165.

Lane, Robert E. *The Regulation of Business: Social Conditions of Government Economic Control*. New Haven, Conn.: Yale Univ. Press, 1954.

Langer, Elinor. "Growing Old in America: Frauds, Quackery, Swindle the Aged and Compound Their Trouble." *Science* 140 (May 3, 1963):470-472.

Lasagna, Louis. *The Doctors' Dilemma*. New York: Harper & Row, 1962.

Lefkowitz, Louis, J. "New York: Criminal Infiltration of the Securities Industry." *Annals of the American Academy of Political and Social Science* 347 (May 1963):51-57.

Leonard, W.N., and Marvin Weber. "Automakers and Dealers: A Study of Criminogenic Market Forces." *Law and Society Review* 4 (February 1970):407-424.

Lever, Harry, and Joseph Young. *Wartime Racketeering.* New York: Putnam's, 1945.

Lynd, Robert S. "Our Racket Society." *The Nation* 170 (August 25, 1951):150-152.

Marecki, Yacek. "Economic Criminality: Mechanism and Remedies." *Kulturai i Spoteczenstwo* (1962), no. 3:57-72.

Mannheim, Hermann. *Criminal Justice and Social Reconstruction.* London: Routledge, 1946.

Mannheim, Hermann. *Comparative Criminology: A Text Book.* London: Routledge, 1965.

McMillen, Wayne. "Charitable Fraud: An Obstacle in Community Organizations." *Social Service Review* 29 (June 1955):153-171.

Merton, Robert K. "Social Structure and Anomie." *Social Theory and Social Structure.* Glencoe, Ill.: Free Press, (1938) 1957, pp. 131-160. (First published in the *American Sociological Review.*)

Merton, Robert K. "Continuities in the Theory of Social Structure and Anomie." *Social Theory and Social Structure.* Glencoe, Ill.: Free Press, 1957, pp. 281-386.

Meyer, J.C., Jr. "An Action-Orientation Approach to the Study of Occupational Crime." *Austr.-N.Z. Journal of Criminology* 5 (1972), no. 1:35-48.

Middendorff, Wolf. *Soziologie des Verbrechens: Erscheinungen und Wandlungen des asozialen Verhaltens.* Dusseldorf (Germany): Diederich, 1959.

Morris, Albert. *Criminology.* New York: Longmans, 1934.

Mors, Wallace P. "State Regulation of Retail Installment Financing: Progress and Problems." *Journal of Business* 23 (October 1950):199-218; and 24 (January 1951):43-71.

Mourant, Francois. *"La Criminalties des Classes Superieres." Bulletin, Societie de Criminologic de Quebec* 3 (May 1964):43-52.

Myers, Robert S. "The Rise and Fall of Fee-Splitting." *Bulletin of the American College of Surgeons* 40 (November-December 1955):507-509, 523.

Nelson, Walter II. *The Great Discount Delusion.* New York: McKay, 1965.

Normandeau, Andrew. *"Les Deviations en Affaires et la 'Crime en Col Blanc.'" Internationale de Criminologre et de Police Technique* 19 (October-December 1965):247-255.

Newman, Donald J. "Public Attitudes Toward a Form of White Collar Crime." *Social Problems* 4 (1957):228-232.

Newman, Donald J. "White-Collar Crime." *Law and Contemporary Problems* 23 (1958):735-753.

President's Commission on Law Enforcement and the Administrator of Justice. *Challenge of Crime in a Free Society.* Washington, D.C.: Government Printing Office, 1967, pp. 47-49.

_____. *Crime and Its Impact—An Assessment.* Washington, D.C.: Government Printing Office, 1967, pp. 102-115.

"Quackery in California." *Stanford Law Review* 11 (March 1959):265-296.

Quinney, Earl R. "Occupational Structure and Criminal Behavior: Prescription Violation by Retail Pharmacists." *Social Problems* 11 (1963):179-185.

Quinney, Earl R. "The Study of White Collar Crime: Toward a Reorientation in Theory and Research." *Journal of Criminal Law, Criminology, and Police Science* 55 (1964):203-214.

Radzinowicz, Leon. "Economic Pressures." In Leon Radzinowicz and Marvin Wolfgang (eds.), *Crime and Justice*, Vol. II. New York: Basic Books, 1971.

Reckless, Walter C. "White-Collar Crime And Black-Marketing." In *The Crime Problem*, 3d ed. New York: Appleton, (1950) 1961, pp. 207-229.

"Regulation of Advertising." *Columbia Law Review* 56 (November 1956):1018-1111.

Riemer, Svend H. "Embezzlement: Pathological Basis." *Journal of Criminal Law and Criminology* 32 (November-December 1941):411-423.

Riis, Roger, and John Patric. *Repairmen Will Get You If You Don't Watch Out.* Garden City, N.Y.: Doubleday, 1942.

Rising, Nelson. "Contours of Conflict: Protection of the Defaulting Consumer." *U.C.L.A. Law Review* 13 (January 1966):348-365.

Ross, Edward A. *Sin and Society: An Analysis of Latter-Day Inquity.* Boston: Houghton Mifflin, 1907.

Saden, George A. "Inquiry Into Ambulance Chasing." *Connecticut Bar Journal* 34 (June 1960):117-122.

Scavey, Warren A. "Caveat Emptor as of 1960." *Texas Law Review* 38 (April 1960):439-449.

Schur, Edwin M. "Respectable Crime." In Edwin Schur (ed.), *Our Criminal Society.* Englewood Cliffs, New Jersey: Prentice-Hall, 1969.

Sherwin, Robert. "White-Collar Crime, Conventional Crime and Merton's Deviant Behavior Theory." *Wisconsin Sociologist* 2 (Spring 1963):7-10.

Smigel, Erwin O. "Public Attitudes Toward Stealing as Related to the Size of the Victim Organization." *American Sociological Review* 21 (June 1956):320-327.

Smigel, Erwin O. "Public Attitudes Toward Chiseling with Reference to Unemployment Compensation." *American Sociological Review* 18 (February 1953):59-67.

Smith, Richard Austin. "The Incredible Electrical Conspiracy." *Fortune* 63 (April 1961):132-137; and 63 (May 1961):161164.

Sorenson, Robert C. "Review of Sutherland, White Collar Crime." *Journal of Criminal Law, Criminology, and Police Science* 41 (May-June 1950):8082.

Steefen, Thomas L. "Truth in Lending: A Viable Subject." *George Washington Law Review* 32 (April 1964):861-892.

Stern, Philip M. *The Great Treasury Raid.* New York: Random House, 1964.

Stocker, Frederick D., and John C. Ellickson. "How Fully Do Farmers Report Their Incomes?" *National Tax Journal* 12 (June 1959):116-126.

Stoddard, S.M., and C.A. Stutsman, Jr. "Income Tax Offenses by Lawyers: An Ethical Problem." *American Bar Association Journal* 58 (1972):842-845.

Sutherland, Edwin H. "Crime and Business." *Annals of the American Academy of Political and Social Science* 217 (September 1941):112-118.

Sutherland, Edwin H. *White Collar Crime.* New York: Dryden Press, 1949.

Sutherland, Edwin H. "The White Collar Criminal." In Vernon C. Branham and Samuel B. Kutash (eds.), *Encyclopedia of Criminology.* New York: Philosophical Library, 1949, pp. 511-515.

Sutherland, Edwin H. "The Sutherland Papers." In Albert K. Cohen et al. (eds.), *Social Science Series*, no. 15. Bloomington: Indiana Univ. Press, 1956.

Sutherland, Edwin H. "The Sutherland Papers." In *Crime and the Conflict Process*, edited by Albert K. Cohen et al. Bloomington: Indiana Univ. Press, 1956, pp. 99-111.

"Symposium on Consumer Protection." *Michigan Law Review* 64 (May 1966):1197-1466.

Tappan, Paul W. "Who Is The Criminal?" *American Sociological Review* 12 (1947):96-102.

"Translating Sympathy for Deceived Consumers into Effective Programs for Protection." *Univ. of Pennsylvania Law Review* 114 (January 1966): 395-450.

Vold, George B. *Theoretical Criminology.* New York: Oxford Univ. Press, 1958, pp. 245-261.

Wagner, Walter. *The Golden Fleecers.* Garden City, N.Y. Doubleday, 1967.

Walton, Clarence C., and Frederick W. Cleveland, Jr. *Corporations on Trial: The Electrical Cases.* Belmont, California: Wadsworth, 1964.

Weinberg, Arthur and Lila. *The Muckrakers.* New York: Simon and Schuster, 1961.

Weston, Glen E. "Decline of Caveat Emptor." *Federal Bar Journal* 24 (Fall 1964):558-578.

Whitman, Howard. "Why Some Doctors Should be in Jail." *Collier's* 132 (October 10, 1953):23-27.

Willets, Harry. "The Wages of Economic Sin." *Problems of Communism* 11 (September-October 1962):26-32.

Willging, Thomas E. "Installment Credit: A Social Perspective." *Catholic Univ. Law Review* 15 (January 1966):45-68.

Wraith, Ronald, and Edgar Simpkins. *Corruption in Developing Countries.* London: G. Allen, 1963.

Zirpins, Walter, and Otto Terstegen. *Wirtschaftskriminalitat: Erscheinungen und ihre Bekampfung.* Lubeck (Germany): Schmidt-Romhild, 1963.

6

A New Look at Political Offenses and Terrorism

Nicholas N. Kittrie

Introduction

The international community has witnessed in recent years a growing number of unorthodox political activists and movements. Their tactical arsenal has ranged from civil disobedience to the coup d'état, from tyrannicide to guerilla war and terrorism. Their proclaimed goals have included self-determination and human rights, but unorthodox activism need not be confused with exclusively liberal and humane pursuits. Both recent and earlier history has demonstrated that reactionary and oppressive goals may also be served by resort to extralegal or violent means.

Political activists have attracted an inordinate degree of public attention. More square inches of newsprint have been devoted during the course of a single year in America, and in many other countries East and West, to the adventures and trials of Patricia Hearst, Lynette "Squeeky" Fromme, and Sarah Moore than to any other topic in the field of criminal justice. What was uniquely common to all three was not only their gender but also the political character of their crimes. As one adds to these domestic headline leaders the coverage of such transnational violence as the South Moluccan train hijackers in Holland, the kidnapping of the OPEC oil ministers in Vienna, and the increasing worldwide speculations regarding the mysterious Carlos, it is apparent that political crime and terrorism are this decade's favorite cops-and-robbers stories.

It is not the sheer number of those killed, injured, or otherwise affected by political crime and terrorism that accounts for the widespread public attention given this phenomena. In the four worst years of domestic turmoil in America (1965-1968), a grand total of 214 were killed and 9000 were injured as a result of terrorism, protest, and ghetto riots. But this compares with a national total of 12,000 murders and 250,000 aggravated assaults annually. During the height of the aircraft hijacking epidemic (1968-1972), the number of persons who lost their lives or were injured in all domestic and international flights did not exceed 200. In the same period the number of internationally protected persons subjected to attack, kidnapping, or threat of violence did not exceed 46, with 16 meeting eventual death. The most recent statement issued by FBI Director Clarence Kelley, pointing to the growing threat posed by terrorist activities, lists 11 victims killed and 72 injured through bombings and other violence in America during 1975.[1] Worldwide it is estimated that in 1975 at least 50 people lost their lives and more than 150 were taken hostage in 17 major acts of international terrorism.[2] Thus, it is apparent that political crime and terrorism account for a mere fraction of all domestic and international crime. There are more people murdered annually in intrafamily strife or killed in automobile accidents in America alone than are killed as a result of political and terrorist activities worldwide.[3]

What then underlies the significance of the public as well as media preoccupation with terrorism and other forms of political crime? Others have commented on the political offender's denial of the very legality of the challenged system of justice and the terrorist's resort to "violence for effect," viewing a grip of panic as his ultimate goal. Some additional observations need to be made regarding the functions of political violence in modern Western societies. In the first place, political offenses—frequently reflected in highly colorful deeds and offenders—are antidotes to public apathy and boredom. They appeal to the news consumer's prurient interest in the unexpected, the unpredictable, and the adventurous.

There were times when motiveless psychopathic mass killers had the major claim to public attention. At other times the media spotlighted organized crime and its "godfatherly" management system. There are growing indications that white-collar crime and business criminality—ranging from corporate disregard for safety and ethics to the practices of the multinational corporations—might gain more attention in the future. But the current stage belongs to two major classes of political crime, posed like the obverse faces of the Roman god Janus. On one side there are the crimes perpetrated by those holding the reigns of political power. These official or quasi-official offenses range from such relatively "mild" abuses of justice as Watergate and election law frauds (what Kirchheimer terms *political justice*[4]) to such atrocities as the "reigns of terror" employed in postrevolutionary France, the Soviet Union, and Nazi Germany. On the other side are the crimes undertaken by those who view themselves as being out of power: those politically, economically, racially, ethnically, or otherwise subjected to discrimination. This second group of offenses likewise ranges from mild displays of protest and civil disobedience (at times described as "political offenses") to a full arsenal of violent tactics against authority and established institutions, sometimes labeled as a "siege of terror."

As often as not, political offenses are directed against persons who have achieved high position (heads of state, politicians, diplomatic personnel, and captains of industry), and it is the victim's status that endows the offender with identity. The loss of such leaders is likely to dramatically affect political, social, or economic conditions, nationally and worldwide, and the offender at least temporarily senses the pulse of power. In a society suffering from a high degree of alienation and individual feelings of impotence in the face of government and big business, the political offense symbolizes the little man or woman's remaining power to be noticed. He or she can at least disrupt if not direct the flow of distant and unaccountable government powers. Most political offenders thus carry the message of many others who feel aggrieved and without adequate opportunities to be heard. Moreover, when government or other established institutions are increasingly perceived to be in the wrong—when they become the dispensers of injustice—the political offender becomes a crystalization of popular discontent and opposition, much like Robin Hood, antislavery leader John Brown, or the patriots of the American Revolution.

In the councils of international affairs and law, political crime and terrorism equally have been receiving growing attention because of their adverse impact on fundamental international institutions and doctrines of international law. First, by seeking out weak links in the international air traffic system, political terrorists have been able to render not only air carriers but also governments virtually helpless in the face of blackmail demands. Not since the heyday of classical piracy has international traffic been so seriously affected. To a lesser degree letter-bombs, for a period, similarly jeopardized the flow of international mail, traditionally immune to such interferences. Second, the historical inviolability and special protection of diplomats both in peace and in war has been totally rejected, if not in theory then at least in practice, by terrorist organizations. Frequently, these agents of international communications are specifically singled out as targets for terrorist activities. Third, previous international efforts to protect the innocent and noncombatants from the ravages of uncontrolled violence through codifications of the law of war have again been contradicted both by the practices and doctrines of modern terrorism. The Hague and Geneva Conventions sought through firm standards to confine and restrain the theaters of war. Yet, modern terrorism denies the very concept of innocence and noncombatancy and seeks to make the whole globe accountable to violence.

It is not surprising, therefore, that despite evidence of relatively limited victimizations, transnational political crime and terrorism have become grave concerns to the international community. For regardless of doctrinal shadings, the security of international commerce and travel, diplomatic protection, and the safeguarding of noncombatant civilian populations are long-standing and indeed classical pillars of the international community.

To these concerns one should add the terrifying hazards posed by present-day technological progress. A shrinking world, due to the revolution in transportation, has so redefined the theaters of violence that no place is safe from terrorism. Progress in mass destruction weaponry, and its ready availability, further affords terrorists an almost boundless expansion of destructive capabilities.

Despite terrorism's challenges to the basic institutions of society, newly coupled with fears of potential exposure to nuclear or other high-risk blackmail, the community of nations has not produced a joint plan of antiterrorist action. Lack of consensus affects not only the ability of governments to agree on how to respond to these manifestations of violence but also on how to classify and differentiate among various types of politically motivated offenders.

In the face of these disagreements, the two major international attempts of the past 40 years to define and control terrorism have not proven successful. The League of Nations in 1937 prepared an international convention against terrorism, to have it ratified by one country only.[5] In 1972 the United States presented a draft convention to the United Nations where it languishes in committee. However, the prevalence of transnational violence places the topic once again on the international agenda and revives attempts to seek new and acceptable solutions.

Political Crime in National and International Law

A productive analysis of the new efforts cannot be undertaken without due attention to past political and legal traditions. It is this heritage which in part accounts for the present impasse. Yet these very traditions might help dictate fruitful future directions. Because most nations have not recognized the existence of political crime in their domestic law, the phenomenon has not been subjected to close scrutiny by courts or commentators. The significance of the political nature of an offense has been recognized primarily in the law of extradition. In this limited sphere, the framework for a conceptual analysis of political crime has been developed. Moreover, several attempts to define terrorism have been made in the context of international agreements to control transnational crimes.

The terms *political crime* and *terrorism* cannot be readily defined through a review of the standard literature of the social and behavioral sciences. Similarly, legal materials provide little assistance.[6] In the Anglo-American tradition, crimes are usually classified according to the objects of the offenses—crimes against the person (such as murder and rape), against the habitation (such as burglary and arson), against property (such as larceny), and against public order (such as disturbing the peace). Another system relied primarily upon the severity of the offenses and their requisite penalties, thus drawing a line between felonies, which almost always called for capital punishment, and misdemeanors, which merited lighter dispositions. Both English and American jurisprudence also distinguish ordinary offenses from treason, the most despised of all crimes and the one which resulted, under common law, in the corruption of blood in addition to drawing and quartering.

The United States Constitution delegated the lawmaking power to Congress. Only one crime is listed and defined in the Constitution: treason, the levying of war against the United States or the aiding and comforting of its enemies. But despite this constitutional identification of the political crime par excellence, American law retains the unusual distinction (which it shares with its English predecessor) of failing to list, identify, or recognize political crimes as a distinguishable class.[7] An offender's political motive is never to be afforded a forum or hearing.

Some legal systems specifically define political crimes in their domestic codes. In so addressing themselves openly and directly to the problems of political crimes, the laws might also decree a differential treatment for political offenders. To draw a distinction between political offenders and common prisoners, points out Alexander Solzhenitsyn, "is the equivalent of showing their respect as equal opponents, of recognizing that people may have views of their own."[8] Reflecting this respect, the German penal system in the Weimar Republic offered imprisonment in a fortress (*Festungshaft*) as a symbolic confinement when the offender's motives were considered "honorable." It was the benefit of this differentiation which permitted Adolph Hitler, after the failure of his 1923 Munich Putsch, the leisure for writing *Mein Kampf*.

Describing Czarist practices, Solzhenitsyn reported:

Criminals were teamed up and driven along the streets to the station so as to expose them to public disgrace. And politicals could go there in carriages. Politicals were not fed from the common pot but were given food allowance instead and had their meals brought from public eating places.[9]

But while a great number of countries have treated their political offenders leniently, others have responded more harshly. After the Czar came the revolution, and the pursued of the past became the new pursuers. The lenient Czarist practice gave way to a totally different and much harsher Soviet response to political crime in the name of socialist justice. Equally, the Nazi and Fascist regimes, as well as other totalitarian governments in the post-World War II era, have singled out their domestic political offenders for particularly oppressive controls and punishment.

The major recognition and differential treatment of political offenders occurred not in domestic law but in international practice. In antiquity and throughout the Middle Ages, the offender who committed a crime against the sovereign was the most despised of all criminals. For he had challenged the most sacred of all institutions–divinely ordained government.[10] In the Middle Ages political offenders, persons guilty of crimes of *lèse majesté*, thus became the most important targets of extradition to facilitate the meting out of punishments. The first known European treaty dealing with the surrender of political offenders was entered in 1174 between England and Scotland, followed by a 1303 treaty between France and Savoy. But the Age of Enlightenment and the subsequent Ages of Revolution revealed government to be less than godly. How, therefore, could all rebels against authority be labeled evil?

One commentator has noted that "the French Revolution of 1789 and its aftermath started the transformation of what was the extraditable offense par excellence to what has since become the nonextraditable offense par excellence."[11] Recognizing the nobler motives of political offenders and the growing diversity of political regimes, Belgium in 1833 became the first country to enact a law withholding the extradition of political offenders. By the middle of the century, the doctrine was widely established throughout the continent. Virtually every European treaty gave a refugee political offender protection against extradition back to the country in which his offense was committed. While a domestic political offender was often accorded no differential treatment, the offender who committed his crime abroad and sought refuge elsewhere was afforded a safe haven.

Who was this privileged offender? The term *political offense* is seldom defined in either treaties or domestic legislation. The determination of what constitutes a political offense is reached according to the laws of the haven country, and the decision is usually made by the courts of the state. Seeking to establish the proper boundaries for political crime, most courts have drawn a distinction between "pure" political offenses and "complex" or "connected" offenses. Treason, sedition, espionage, other acts endangering the external security of the state, rebellion, and incitement to civil war are all viewed as offenses exclusively against sovereign authority and are considered pure political offenses. Other offenses that endanger the life or property of individuals but are carried out in connection with and in furtherance of a crime against the state might be classified as either complex or connected to political offenses. Viewed alone the latter offenses are common crimes. But if a criminal act (such as the assassination of a head of state) was primarily the "means, method or cloak"[12] for carrying out a political offense, the act will be viewed as a complex political crime. When an act affects primarily individual life or property, yet is closely connected with other acts against the security of the state, it would be described as a connected political offense (e.g., a bank robbery by revolutionaries).

The political offense exception was not designed to accommodate the individual conscience of each malcontent or rebel. In the common law approach, represented by the classic case of *In re Castioni*, the requirement was established that recognized political offenses must be "incidental to and formed part of a political disturbance."[13] Absent a general political revolt or disturbance, the individual offender, regardless of his political or ideological motivation, was to be viewed as a common criminal. Moreover, the European, and primarily Swiss, practice further sought to curtail excessive violence by conditioning the political offense exception upon objective standards of proportionality. Accordingly, the ideological beliefs and goals of the offender must be correlated to the effect of his acts and offenses. In the *Ktir* case, Ktir, a member of the Algerian liberation movement (F.L.N.), was charged in France with the murder of another F.L.N. member suspected of treason. Ktir fled to Switzerland and contested the French request for extradition. In granting the request the Swiss court held that "the damage had to be proportionate to the aim sought; in the case of murder, this had to be shown to be the sole means of attaining the political aim."[14]

While domestic laws have found it difficult if not impossible to allow the political offender's challenge to the legal order, the international legal system has found a way to accommodate the conflicting interests. The political offender exception to extradition was certainly an innovative answer. In his own country the political offender often remained a common criminal, but the civilized world community was willing to listen to the defense of conscience. This accommodation was reached in the last century. But in recent years the old conflict between individual conscience and public order has once more returned to haunt the international arena. Once again the right to resist injustice is being heatedly debated in world councils.

Since the creation of the political offense exception, new international standards of justice have gained world acceptance. World War I ended with a commitment to international self-determination. And the movement which started with President Wilson's Fourteen Points reached its peak in the post-World War II era. Little of this commitment has been reflected in positive international law, but the climate of the world community has certainly supported the most expeditious roads to self-determination.[15] The conclusion of World War II also resulted in a renewed international commitment to the protection and promotion of individual human rights worldwide. In 1948 the General Assembly of the United Nations adopted the Universal Declaration of Human Rights. In the following quarter century a host of other declarations, conventions, covenants, and proclamations were advanced by the United Nations on such topics as economic, social, and cultural rights; civil and political rights; racial discrimination; slavery; collective bargaining; rights of children; and the right to asylum.[16] While these documents have not been uniformly accepted, nor do they share the same legal status, they have nevertheless made an indelible mark upon world opinion. Even stronger undertakings for the advancement of human rights have come into being on a regional basis. The European Convention on Human Rights and its enforcement process is a notable example.[17]

The terrible experiences with Nazi and Fascist policies and practices produced, after World War II, a special sensitivity to the rights of minorities. The Genocide Convention of 1948 sought to protect national, ethnic, racial, and religious groups.[18] It defined as an international crime the killing of members of a group, causing them serious bodily or mental harm, or deliberately inflicting conditions of life calculated to bring physical destruction. In recent past the General Assembly of the United Nations, after a discussion of the South African practice of apartheid, labeled it "a crime against humanity."[19]

The Shrinking Political Offense and the
Growth of International Crime

Despite the unwillingness of many countries to condemn acts committed under claims of self-determination and the furtherance of human rights as terrorism, there has been an evident trend in international law to narrow the traditional exception granted to political offenders. As early as 1856, Belgium, the first country to embody the political offense protection in its law, amended its requirements by excluding assassinations of chiefs of state from this safeguard. This limitation, called a *clause d'attentat*, was widely copied in both bilateral and regional treaties among European, South American, and African states. In several recent treaties, all assassinations are excluded from the political offense protection.[20]

Another narrowing of the scope of political offenses came at the end of the last century in the face of the growing threat of anarchism. The earlier tolerance toward those seeking to violently overthrow a particular regime turned into a suspicion of those viewed as a danger to all governments. The case of *In re Meunier*[21] held, in 1894, that confessed anarchists are not political offenders exempt from extradition. To constitute a political offense, the English court held, there must be two or more parties each seeking to impose the government of its own choice, but "the party with which the accused is identified . . . is the enemy of all governments. Their efforts are directed primarily against the general body of citizens."[22]

In subsequent years, domestic laws, international conventions, and judicial decisions further confined the political offense exception. The French Extradition Law of 1927 provided that the exception was not to apply to "acts of odious barbarism and vandalism prohibited by the laws of war."[23] The extradition agreement approved by the League of Arab States in 1952 likewise exempted from the exception premeditated murder or acts of terrorism.[24] Similarly, the Supreme Court of Argentina declared in 1968: "Extradition will not be denied where we are dealing with cruel or immoral acts which clearly shock the conscience of civilized peoples."[25]

In the post-World War II era an even more drastic restriction was placed on the benefits of the political offense claim. World revulsion against the Nazi and Fascist excesses resulted in the designation of crimes against humanity and war crimes as international crimes not entitled to the benefit of any political offense exception. Both the Nuremberg trial and the subsequent formulation of its principles by the United Nations General Assembly established crimes against humanity to be universally condemned.[26] War crimes, as defined by the 1912 Hague Convention and 1949 Geneva Conventions, also constitute international crimes to which the political offense exception does not apply.

The origins of international criminal law date back to the crime of piracy, long considered an offense against all civilized nations.[27] Other early international efforts concentrated on white slavery and traffic in narcotics. But in more recent years there has been a growing international commitment to limit, through international criminalization, conduct which could be viewed as political yet which threatened basic institutions of the world community. The definition of counterfeiting as an international crime after World War I was such a step.[28] Even more demonstrative of the world community's willingness to condemn universally disruptive political violence are the recent treaties making aircraft hijacking[29] and the kidnapping of diplomats (internationally protected persons) international crimes.[30] So condemned by international law, these crimes can no longer be viewed as political offenses affording their perpetrators protection from extradition. Instead, it has become the duty of all civilized nations to apprehend the offenders and subject them to either prosecution or extradition.

While the terminology of political crime has had nearly a century and a half to reach a degree of maturity, terrorism is a relatively unstable newcomer. Most commentators find the origins of modern terrorism in the "reign of terror" after the French Revolution and in the anarchist movement of the last century. But neither domestic legislation nor international treaties specify its elements. Like the political offender, the terrorist may be motivated by political considerations. He might also claim to act out of an altruistic rather than an egoistic motive and, unlike the common offender, proclaim the goal of serving humanity rather than his own baser interests.

What distinguishes the terrorist from political offenders generally is the nature of his deeds, his strategy, and his goals. The political offender is not necessarily committed to violence. Breaking censorship laws or publishing official secrets is as much a political offense as the assassination of a head of state. The political offender usually seeks to assert rights that he believes the state has improperly denied him, e.g., freedom of speech and assembly or the right to travel. At times a reactionary political offender might seek a restriction of civil rights. The offender need not be militant; he may prefer to depart for more compatible societies. The political offender's deed is usually directed against those he views as specifically responsible for the conceived ills. The terrorist, however, has a commitment to the violent process as an end, "as a catharsis not therapy." The political offense might be "a passing deed, an event. Terrorism is a process, a way of life, a dedication."[31]

While the political offender seeks to remove the specific causes of his discontent, the terrorist believes the social order to be so corrupt as to require its total destruction. For the deprived, says Franz Fanon in *The Wretched of the Earth*, violence is a purifying force. The true terrorist consciously employs terror. The goal is to spread panic by maximizing uncertainty. The final erosion of popular support for the system is to be attained through indiscriminate terrorism which produces equally brutal countermeasures. A leading nineteenth century Russian revolutionary once proclaimed that "the object is perpetually the same: the quickest and surest way of destroying this whole filthy order."[32] To the terrorist this objective can be best attained through bold actions that demonstrate the terrorist's complete unconditional and irrevocable opposition to the existing order. Frequently the strategy is to attack the masses, "the very people he wants to liberate, but to attack them in such a way that it is government which appears to be their enemy."[33]

Codes of Conduct for Political Offenders and Terrorists

Political offenses, as previously seen, may range from "pure" offenses, such as sedition, to a "siege of terror," involving random and indiscriminate violence. Political offenders may be within the confines of international legality even though in violation of domestic laws. The so-called "pure" political offense—which challenges the state but affects no innocent private rights—continues to benefit from a privileged status in international law and practice. Those who violate state laws limiting freedom of speech or assembly, those who disregard censorship and other secrecy laws, or those who break laws restricting religion or other exercises of human rights may benefit from international asylum, at the very least. Hopefully they may gain additional protective shelters, both internationally and domestically, through expanding international standards of human rights.

On the other extreme of the political offense spectrum there is a growing list of activities which have been prohibited as outright international crimes. This group includes crimes against humanity, aircraft hijacking, and the kidnapping of diplomats. Some of this conduct might be classed as complex political crime, while other acts could be described as connected political offenses. Aircraft hijacking and other offenses against innocent victims would fall within the category of connected offenses. But both assassinations and diplomatic abductions might be categorized as complex offenses. All the political offenses which have been designated as international crimes are not "pure" political offenses, but beyond that, they do not readily respond to any further classification. They do reflect, by and large, a universal reaffirmation of classical international law commitments to the preservation of transportation and communication routes.

There is an area in the center of the political offense spectrum which remains unaffected by the growing recognition of human rights on the one hand and the increasing expansion of international crimes on the other. Typical of this middle conduct are what might generally be regarded as both complex political offenses and connected political offenses. The assassination of a governmental official in the course of a political uprising, the bombing of military headquarters, and violent resistance to an oppressive arrest all come within this class. But also included in this group of behavior are such practices as bank robberies for the replenishing of a political treasury, the kidnapping of a business executive for extortion, and the taking of hostages for exchange for political offenders. It is the legal status of this wide range of conduct in the middle spectrum that has become increasingly uncertain in light of recent international developments. To these examples could be added some of the contemporary manifestations of international terrorism, e.g., when violence is used indiscriminately against innocent victims only marginally associated with an opposing political regime or party. The assault against such victims, furthermore, might increasingly take place in neutral countries remote from the battlefield. A machinegun assault against a bus carrying school children in Northern Ireland, the Munich Olympics kidnappings, and the massacre of Christian Puerto Rican pilgrims upon their arrival at Israel's Lod airport come within this category. How should these types of conduct be treated by the international community? And to what extent would the conventions previously offered in response to terrorism have affected such conduct?

The most comprehensive convention for the prevention and punishment of terrorism was proposed by the League of Nations in 1937. Following the assassination of King Alexander I of Yugoslavia at Marseilles on October 9, 1934, the French government urged the Council of the League of Nations to prepare an international agreement for the suppression of terrorism. A committee of experts prepared a draft convention which was later opened for signature at a conference held at Geneva in November of 1937. An international criminal court was also proposed, to help in the enforcement of terrorist violations. On January 1, 1941 India became the only country ever to ratify the convention.

Viewing the League of Nations convention today, from the vantage point of some 35 years of historical developments, the shortcomings of that effort are readily apparent. The document required all signatories to make acts of terrorism committed on their territories criminal offenses. Similarly, signatories were required to either extradite or punish persons who committed these offenses abroad. Acts of terrorism were defined by Article 2 to include: (1) causing death, grievous bodily harm, or loss of liberty to heads of state, their spouses, and others holding public office; (2) willful destruction of public property; and (3) acts endangering the lives of members of the public. Article 3 specified further that conspiracy to commit the above acts and incitement and assistance in performing such acts were likewise criminal offenses.

The attempted assassination of Hitler and the successful execution of Mussolini could have readily qualified as internationally condemned terrorist acts under the proposed League Convention. Many of the post-World War II liberation movements would have been defined as terroristic under it. Broadcasting to an oppressed people to encourage them to rise against an exploiting regime would have been condemned as an incitement to commit international crime. No wonder that there were few takers for the 1937 document.

The League Convention clearly attempted to perpetuate the pre-World War II status quo and manifested a willingness to label any future revolutionary or national liberation movement as terrorist. But what about the terrorist excesses of recent years? Why could international consensus not be reached with regard to the suppression of these?

A more reasonable effort to suppress international terrorism was contained in the draft convention introduced at the United Nations on September 25, 1972 by the United States. The major, and limited, intent of the proposed draft was to require countries to either prosecute or extradite those engaging in the exportation of terrorism. To come within the scope of the convention, an offender must intend to damage the interests of, or to obtain concessions from, a state or international organization. The prohibited acts include killing, causing serious bodily harm, and kidnapping. Acts are defined as international offenses if they are committed outside the offender's own country, and (1) also outside the country against which they are intended, or (2) within the country against which they are intended but against persons who are not nationals of that state.

The narrower scope of the United States' draft convention makes it much less subject to criticism for being oppressive to unorthodox political change. Indeed, the convention has been criticized for having defined its goals so narrowly as to be farfetched and irrelevant. A German terrorist acting against his own regime would not come under the draft convention. An Irish offender bombing a London cafe inhabited only by Englishmen would also be exempt. It is only, for example, when a Greek terrorist commits an act of violence against a Turkish national living in Switzerland, or against a non-Turkish national in Turkey, that he would come within the confines of the treaty. The basic principle of the United States convention is simple: Fight your enemies in your country or theirs; do not export your grievances to distant places where innocent persons are likely to be affected. But even these limited goals, which steer clear of ideological conflicts, have not assured the draft convention widespread support. In part, the American authorship had doomed it from the start. Today, any revival of this effort remains unlikely.

Despite the existence of some historical and legal insights into the nature of modern terrorism, there has been little success in reaching an internationally acceptable definition. To most Western writers, the term connotes an undiscriminating commitment to violence. In the view of third world countries, the terrorist label has too frequently and improperly been attached to "legitimate" national liberation and revolutionary movements. The misapplication of labels, however, is evident in many camps. Even nonviolent conduct has been tagged "terrorist" in socialist and other use. For example, an East Berlin court recently sentenced a West Berliner to 15 years in prison for having helped 96 East Germans flee to the West. The East Berlin City Court found him guilty of "organized human trafficking, sabotage, espionage and terrorism."[34] Similarly, South African law provides that a person who has written letters to Africans likely "to encourage feelings of hostility between the white and other inhabitants" will be presumed to have done so with "intent to endanger the maintenance of law and order." Defined by law as a terrorist, such a letter writer is subject to the death penalty.[35]

What makes the international definition of terrorism difficult is the conflict between diverse camps and ideologies in the world community. What is terrorism to some is heroism to others. The international disagreement on whether political violence should be universally condemned is not unlike the domestic debate on whether political offenders should be accorded differential treatment.

One who disobeys the law, does so at his own peril. It is a fundamental premise of most legal systems that obedience to the law is an absolute obligation of all citizens, irrespective of the morality of the legal command.[36] But while "render unto Caesar" remains the imperative, what about the individuals or groups who are bound by a conviction that the law is cruel, unjust, immoral, or plainly outdated? What about those whose conviction, ideology, conscience, or political motivation propel them to disobey or break the law? In 1849 Henry David Thoreau cried out: "Must the citizen even for a moment, or in the least degree, resign his conscience to the legislator? Why has every man a conscience, then?"[37] But despite the compelling resurgence of this question, few legal systems have found satisfactory solutions to the conflict between individual conscience and the dictates of public order. Once the law has been made, it is said, individual conscience may not override it. Indeed, no society can survive if the subjective values and judgments of individual citizens are allowed to contradict community rules.

Comparing the expanding boundaries of international crime with the narrowing perspective on political offenses, one soon confronts two central questions:

1. Within the confines of international legality, what may persons deprived of recognized human rights do in the defense of their claims?
2. In view of the recent expansion of international crimes, notwithstanding past failures to define terrorism, what are the future prospects for the regulation of terrorist excesses?

In the light of the international commitment to self-determination, human rights, and ethnic and racial survival, one must examine the acceptable tools for the enforcement of these rights. How is the international community to judge those who claim merely to assert these recognized rights? May people press for these rights through force of arms? May they protect themselves against abuse? To the "haves," to many others committed to the gradual and peaceful processes for remedying the claims of the aggrieved, to all those fearing international chaos and anarchy, the tools of violent opposition and rebellion remain unacceptable.

In the eyes of the "have nots"—and many others who believe that the international machinery for bringing about political, social, and economic justice is at best defective—the self-help approach is totally justifiable. Viewed from these diverse perspectives, those who are terrorists to some are evident freedom fighters and legitimate revolutionaries to others.

So long as these ideological and definitional schisms exist, no honest cooperation with regard to the control of terrorism can be expected in the international community. Each country might develop its own domestic machinery for the prevention and suppression of terrorist violence. It might further seek assistance and cooperation from those nations with a common mind. But as long as a significant number of safe haven countries remain for terrorists—to supply the weapons for destruction, the training grounds, and finally the escape routes—effective prevention, control, and punishment will be difficult. Recent efforts to bridge these schisms have not been successful. Typically, most efforts in the United Nations and elsewhere designed to condemn and to impose sanctions upon terrorist "sieges of terror" have resulted in third world and other countries calling for a parallel curbing of official "reigns of terror."[38]

Given the present freeze in the movement toward an international agreement for the control of terrorism, how should civilized nations respond to the problems posed by transnational and domestic political violence?

One approach would be to encourage self-policing and greater conformity by guerrillas and others with the traditional rules of war, in exchange for granting them recognition as belligerents rather than criminals. There has been considerable writing recently concerning the status of guerrillas and other irregular belligerents in international law.[39] Especially with the decline of "all out" formal wars, the movement for the regulation of military conflicts short of war has gained momentum. Attention has centered particularly on the question of whether guerrillas and other irregulars in transnational conflicts should benefit from the privileges traditionally afforded belligerents under international law, in particular, the prisoner-of-war status. By and large, Geneva Convention III of 1949 on Prisoners of War would condition the grant of those protections upon guerrilla willingness to comply with specified standards of lawful belligerency, including the wearing of insignias, the open bearing of arms, and conformity with the laws and customs of war.

Adherence by guerrillas and other irregulars to these standards might help reduce the outrages of civil war and especially the abuse of innocent parties. But apart from the reluctance of governments to treat domestic terrorists as belligerents, there is little hope of guerrilla conformity, since the effectiveness of guerrilla activities depends in great part upon departure from the traditional rules of war. An extension of the belligerency status to terrorists will therefore offer little help to governments in their combatting of excessive violence.

Another effort to infuse civilized standards into civil wars might call for greater enforcement of the requirements contained in Article 3 of all four Geneva Conventions of 1949. This article, which deals with domestic armed conflicts, seeks to protect persons taking no active part in the hostilities and applies to all parties to the conflict, governments and rebels alike. The article specifically prohibits (1) violence to life and person, in particular murder, mutilation, cruel treatment, and torture; (2) taking of hostages; and (3) outrages upon personal dignity, in particular, humiliating and degrading treatment. But the fact that these prohibitions do not require reciprocal observance by all parties, and other shortcomings, have resulted in widespread disregard of these rules in recent civil wars.[40] Moreover, it remains uncertain whether these rules for domestic armed conflicts are applicable or enforceable with regard to individual political offenders and terrorists in situations short of an "armed conflict."

A different approach with considerable following calls for an international convention that would define and outlaw all forms of terrorism and related types of political violence. The enforcement of such proposed prohibitions would be handled either through the universal jurisdiction of cooperating states or through the creation of an international criminal tribunal.[41] Not disputing the value of such goals, the likelihood of their adoption in the foreseeable future must be seriously questioned.

A fourth approach attempts to deal with the problem of terrorism by means of a further narrowing of the extradition exception. This approach was adopted by the Council of Europe in a 1974 resolution in which a Committee of Ministers pointed out correctly its conviction that extradition is a particularly effective means for the control of terrorism.[42] The Council urged member states in their response to extradition requests to consider the particular seriousness of terrorist acts which (1) create a collective danger to life, liberty, or safety; (2) affect innocent persons foreign to the motives behind them; or (3) employ cruel and vicious means. If extradition is refused in such serious instances, submission of the cases for prosecution by competent domestic authorities is required.*

Obviously, there is no single or simple solution for the control of the excessive violence posed by political crime and terrorism. The recent efforts to control these increasingly transnational threats, however, suggest several possible approaches. In the concluding section of this chapter, several principles will be advanced as a starting point for further discussion and development.

Reconciling Protection of Human Rights with World Order

Essentially, the crux of the problem of transnational political violence revolves around the fact that while the permissible spectrum of political crime and terrorism is being narrowed, at the same time, the growing international commitment to human rights tends to further legitimize political offenses. Recent international agreements have already proscribed some of the more extreme measures of political violence. At this point, if there is a need for further codification and regulation, it exists primarily with regard to the less extreme middle spectrum of political conduct, consisting mainly of complex and connected political offenses. Since these offenses are, at present, subject to the ad hoc sovereign dispositions of the various countries in extradition cases, and their substance is frequently complex and controversial, they remain resistant to international agreement. Last but not least, while a desire to protect innocent and remote victims exists, there is a fear also that international legislation will unduly assert the rights of existing regimes and overlook the needs of exploited people. This concern is crystalized in the continuing opposition, especially in the

---

*Editor's note: See the European Convention on the Suppression of Terrorism, 1977, especially Articles 1 and 6.

third world, to proposed antiterrorist conventions which might deny self-help measures to those who assert to be struggling to attain political goals. Some of these political goals, moreover, are claimed to have gained general international acceptance. Possibly, what might be required first, before more formal international developments can take place, is a clearer and more open balancing of the conflicting interests. This chapter, therefore, does not call for a new antiterrorism convention nor for the creation of an international criminal tribunal. It seeks instead to suggest, at present, a more tentative and deliberate, yet more pragmatic, step-by-step approach: further national and international studies, deliberations, discussions, and recommendations and the development of draft resolutions for action by governments and international organizations. Especially, it urges the exploration of potentials for greater consensus regarding the extradition of political offenders, including terrorists. This avenue seems most capable of support among various governments, and it promises a direct affect upon the imposition of criminal sanctions.[43]

Following the regional model of the Council of Europe, it is likely that what could be attained first, on a more global scale, is not an international convention but a less formal product, similar to the Council's Resolution on International Terrorism. Such a universal resolution could be developed and advanced at the United Nations. But a less politicized forum might be more appropriate. One of the nongovernmental organizations in the field of international justice, or a combination of such organizations as the International Association of Penal Law, Amnesty International, and the International Committee of the Red Cross, could support such a development.

However, this will deal only with one side of the problem. Seeking to maintain world order, governments should not overlook the growing international commitment to self-determination and human rights which, of course, tends to further legitimize political activism and, consequently, seeks better international protection for political offenders. While recognizing that extradition might serve as an effective measure for the control of transnational violence, one should not be unmindful of the "political offense" exception in extradition law, which reflects nineteenth century and ongoing international recognition that extralegal means are justified in political conflicts. To maintain a balance between human rights and world order, a proposed resolution could not give exclusive support to the proposition that any act is justified if supported by considerations of conscience. Neither could it take the other extreme stand that no opposition to an established regime is permissible by international standards. What could be introduced more vigorously into this arena is the principle of self-defense and a scale of proportionality.

In domestic law, the only justified resort to violence is grounded upon the concept of self-defense. Similarly, in post-World War II international law, the only legal resort to arms is justified in the case of self-defense. A modification of this principle seems to be useful also in the international response to the problems of terrorism and political crime. In essence, assertive conduct by individuals in response to denial of recognized human rights might be viewed as a class of self-defense.[44]

Drawing upon the previous observations, a number of general principles might be here advanced. Any person who deliberately commits acts against innocent persons, who uses cruel or vicious means or engages in collective violence, or who otherwise violates the requirements of any international criminal law should be subject to punishment for what might be designated "crimes against humanity." All states should have universal jurisdiction to try offenders who commit crimes against humanity. If extradition is refused in such instances, the case should be submitted to competent local authorities for prosecution, in accordance with the principle *aut dedere aut judicare.*

Those seeking the status of political offenders should be required to circumscribe their conduct. Acts of self-defense should be addressed, as directly as possible, against those exercising the overall, or the most applicable, state power and must avoid all deliberate, or careless, harm to innocent parties. The force used in such acts of self-defense should be appropriate and proportionate to the right deprived by the authorities, as well as the amount of force utilized by the authorities. States should undertake to grant asylum to all persons who commit such proper acts of self-defense, whatever the country in which such acts occurred, which means that no person should be extradited for acts that come properly within the above principles.

A resolution constructed substantially on these principles, with an emphasis upon the reformation of the extradition principles and practices, will not require new international legislation. There will be continued reliance on a long tradition of exempting political offenders from extradition, with the exception of those who use excessive or indiscriminate violence. This approach recognizes the growing field of international crimes. Yet it will also support the enforcement of international consensus in this area, and also it will permit states the ultimate decision in extradition cases, based on the facts in each individual case.

As international deliberations and experience progress and consensus grows, it may be possible, as a further step, to provide for an International Commission on Human Rights to be set up by all countries that adhere to these principles. Member states could voluntarily refer to such a Commission for advisory opinions in all cases of doubt. Through the work of the Commission a finer line of demarcation would be drawn between nonextraditable political offenses and crimes against humanity.

Needless to say, this development would constitute a major contribution toward more effective rules and a machinery for international criminal and political justice. These intermediate steps, at some future stage, might culminate in an international criminal tribunal.

One need not be a visionary to see that public interest and opinion will continue to press more and more for effective controls not only over the "siege of terror" but also over "reigns of terrors." Thus, in developing proposed principles and resolutions on political crime and terrorism, all concerned should seek to overcome the current ideological breach by dealing both with nongovernmental and governmental violence and illegality. To bridge the current gap one will have to dispel the serious concern that while "sieges of terror" are being condemned and regulated, "reigns of terror" are left free of international intervention. The outcome must reflect the growing realization that people are entitled to expect all rights enunciated in the Universal Declaration on Human Rights and in similar documents and that the exercise of such rights should not, in itself, be internationally considered a criminal act.

Some may go further to suggest that on the basis of international law, people, in given circumstances and within certain restrictions, are entitled to engage in acts of resistance and self-defense against governmental denials of basic and universally recognized human rights—including the right to life; liberty; religious, political and ethnic equality; and self-determination. Such "acts of resistance," even though utilizing extralegal means, may be indispensable as long as the international community lacks the tools for the effective enforcement of such fundamental human rights around the world.

It is to be expected that within the not too distant future growing support will develop around a call to combat governmental violence and illegality in the government's very core of sovereignty—in its relation to its own citizens. Here one should be prepared to face growing public emphasis on the need for further extension of the international recognition that any governmental official who deliberately deprives an individual of fundamental human rights is to be subject to punishment for crimes against humanity.

One cannot avoid the remaining knotty problems of jurisdiction. Who is to apply criminal sanctions against individuals and officials alike who deprive others of recognized rights or who use excessive violence? Two approaches deserve further attention. One will grant all states universal jurisdiction to try offenders in such cases. States within whose boundaries such offenders are found might be required, furthermore, to either extradite them or to submit their cases to competent domestic authorities for prosecution in accordance with the principle of *aut dedere aut judicare.* Another approach would be to explore more vigorously the creation of an international criminal tribunal. Possibly, the International Commission on Human Rights that might be set up voluntarily by the countries that adhere to these principles should be also vested with the mandate to explore the needs and to recommend whether an international criminal court should be constituted to exercise concurrent jurisdiction with the several states in the prosecution of persons turned over to it for crimes against humanity.

Political crime and terrorism are destined to remain with us in the years to come. Excesses by both those in power and out will continue. The agenda for research, deliberations, and resolution making—designed to seek a reduction in the climate of violence—is long and difficult. A number of general principles have been proposed. Once these principles have undergone more precise development by scholars or by appropriate international bodies, public or private, they could be offered to the community of nations for guidance in the operation of existing or future extradition treaties. Beyond extradition, these principles could provide guidelines for a more comprehensive response to the conflict between human rights and world order. In endorsing and adhering to these principles, states will have an opportunity to condemn those forms of conduct which are destructive of a civilized world community. At the same time, they will be able to commit themselves more effectively to support those universal human rights which they proclaimed nearly three decades ago.

Notes

1. *Washington Post*, January 14, 1976, p. 3.

2. *U.S. News and World Report*, January 19, 1976, p. 27.

3. In some parts of the world, however, political violence has developed into large-scale civil or guerrilla war and presents a major public safety problem. For example, British Prime Minister Harold Wilson claimed that 1400 political killings were committed in Ireland since 1969 (*Washington Post*, January 31, 1976, p. A17).

4. Otto Kirchheimer, *Political Justice* (Princeton, N.J.: Princeton Univ. Press, 1961).

5. See Appendix Q in *International Terrorism and Political Crimes* 546, Bassiouni (ed.), (Springfield, Ill.: Charles C. Thomas, 1975); and M. Hudson (ed.), *International Legislation* 862 (1941).

6. For a review of the status of political crime in the United States, see "Comment, Criminal Responsibility and the Political Offender," *American Univ. Law Review* 24 (1975):797.

7. American law parallels that of the United Kingdom. Thus Brendan Behan commented upon "the usual hypocrisy of the English not giving anyone political treatment and then being able to say that alone among the Empires she had no political prisoners" (B. Behan, *Borstal Boy* 271, 1958).

8. Alexander Solzhenitsyn, *The Gulag Archipelago* (New York: Harper & Row, 1973), p. 500.

9. Ibid.

10. See the Biblical account of King David's execution of the messenger reporting to him that he slew David's arch enemy, King Saul: "Thy blood be upon thy head; for thy mouth hath testified against thee, saying I have slain the Lord's anointed" (2 Samuel 1:16).

11. M. Cherif Bassiouni, *International Extradition and World Public Order* (Dobbs Ferry, N.Y.: Oceana, 1974), p. 371.

12. *In re Fabijan* (Supreme Court of Germany, 1933), *Digest of International Law* 6, (1968):802.

13. 1 Q.B. 149 (1891) at 152.

14. 34 I.L.R. 143 (1961) at 143-144.

15. For one of the few examples of an attempt to implement the international commitment to self-determination, see Declaration on the Granting of Independence to Colonial Countries and Peoples, United Nations General Assembly Resolution 1514 (xv), 14 December 1960.

16. United Nations, *Human Rights, a Compilation of International Instruments of the United Nations*, no. E. 73, XIV (1973):2.

17. See generally, Robertson, "The United Nations Covenant on Civil and Political Rights and the European Convention on Human Rights," *British Yearbook of International Law* XLIII, 21 (1968-1969); O'Hanlon, "The Brussels Colloquy on the European Convention on Human Rights," *Irish Jurist* 5, (1970):252; Comte, "The Application of the European Convention on Human Rights in Municipal Law," *Journal of the International Commission of Jurists* 4, 94 (1962-1963).

18. United Nations, *Human Rights*, p. 41.

19. G.A. Res. 2923, 27 UN GAOR Supp. 30, p. 25, UN Doc. A/8730 (1972).

20. Bassiouni, *International Extradition*, p. 410.

21. 2 Q.B. 415 (1894).

22. Ibid., at 419.

23. French Extradition Law of 1927, Act of March 10, 1927, Article 5 (2); quoted in I. Shearer, *Extradition in International Law* (Manchester Univ. Press, 1971), p. 185.

24. Extradition Agreement Approved by the Council of the League of Arab States, September 14, 1952, *British and Foreign State Papers* 159 (London: HMSO); quoted in Shearer, *supra*, p. 52.

25. *In re Bohme* (Supreme Court of Argentina, 1968), *American Journal of International Law* 62 (1968):784-785; quoted in Shearer, *supra*, p. 186.

26. G.A. Res. 177 (II) (1947).

27. For the most recent statement on piracy, see The 1958 Geneva Convention on the High Seas, in M.M. Whiteman (ed.), *Digest of International Law* 4 (1963):657.

28. Convention for the Suppression of Counterfeiting Currency, 20 April 1920; quoted in Hudson (ed.), *International Legislation* 4 (1931):692-705.

29. See 1971 Montreal Convention, USTIAS 7570 (sabotage of aircraft); 1970 Hague Convention, USTIAS 7192 (hijacking); and 1963 Tokyo Convention, USTIAS 6768 (offenses committed on aircraft).

30. Convention to Prevent and Punish Acts of Terrorism Taking the Form of Crimes Against Persons and Related Extortions that Are of International Significance, OAS/Off. Rec./Ser. p./Doc. 68, January 13, 1971; and Convention

on the Prevention and Punishment of Crimes Against Internationally Protected Persons Including Diplomatic Agents, G.A. Res. A/3166 (XXVIIII) (5 February 1974).

31. David C. Rapoport, *Assassination and Terrorism* (New York: CBS, 1971), p. 37.

32. Nachaeyeff, "Revolutionary Catechism," in Rapoport, *Assassination and Terrorism*, p. 40.

33. Rapoport, *Assassination and Terrorism*, p. 47.

34. *The New York Times*, January 27, 1976, p. 2.

35. Terrorism Act, No. 83, Sec. 2 (1967); quoted in Leslie Rubin, *Apartheid in Practice*, UN Pub. OPI/553 (1976), p. 40.

36. A. Fortas, *Concerning Dissent and Civil Disobedience* (New York: World Pub. Co., 1968), pp. 59-64.

37. Henry David Thoreau, *On the Duty of Civil Disobedience* (New York: Lancer Books, 1968), pp. 413-414.

38. See, for example, Bennett, "U.S. Initiatives in the United Nations to Combat International Terrorism," *International Lawyer* 7 (1973):753, 759.

39. See, for example, J. Bond, *The Rules of Riot; Internal Conflict and the Law of War* (Princeton, N.J.: Princeton Univ. Press, 1974); George Schwarzenberger, "Terrorists, Guerrilleros, and Mercenaries," *Toledo Law Review* (1971); "Comment, Civilian Protection in Modern Warfare: A Critical Analysis of the Geneva Civilian Convention of 1941," *Virginia Journal of International Law* 14, (1973):123.

40. Higgins, "International Law and Civil Conflict," in Evan Luard (ed.), *The International Regulation of Civil Wars* (New York: New York Univ. Press, 1972), p. 183.

41. See, for example, Dautricourt, "The International Criminal Court: The Concept of International Criminal Jurisdiction," in M. Bassiouni and V. Nanda (eds.), *A Treatise on International Criminal Law* (1973), p. 636.

42. Council of Europe, Resolution (74) 3 (January 24, 1974).

43. Since 1970 a total of 267 transnational terrorists were apprehended. Of these, 50 were released after serving prison terms and 104 were still confined in mid-September 1975. But another 39 were freed without punishment, 58 avoided punishment by getting safe conduct to other countries, and 16 were released from confinement on the demand of fellow terrorists (*U.S. News and World Report*, September 29, 1975, p. 79).

44. For discussion of such an approach, see Bassiouni, "Ideologically Motivated Offense and the Political Offense Exception in Extradition—A Proposed Juridical Standard for an Unruly Problem," *DePaul Law Review* 19 (1969):217, 254-257.

7 Women and Crime in Israel

Rita J. Simon

The major theme of a recent work on women's participation in crime in the United States is that there have been no significant increases in the overall amount of serious crime committed by women in the past two decades,[1] but that there has been, since 1967, a shift in the types of serious crimes that women are more and less likely to commit.[2] It turns out that the emerging pattern is consistent with the objectives and goals of the current women's liberation movement. By that I mean that the American data show that there has been a significant increase in the proportion of women who have been arrested for property, white-collar, and financial offenses, such as larceny, embezzlement, forgery, and fraud, since 1967 and a slight decline or absence of change in the proportion of women who have been arrested for violent offenses, such as murder, manslaughter, and assault. The argument that this trend is consistent with the contemporary movement for women's liberation is as follows.

As women become more liberated from hearth and home and become more involved in full-time jobs, they are more likely to engage in the types of crimes for which their occupations provide them with the greatest opportunities. As a result of their expanded consciousness (acquired from the rhetoric and objectives of the contemporary women's movement) and greater occupational opportunities, women's participation and involvement in crime is expected to change and to increase.

However, the increase is not likely to be uniform or stable across crimes. For example, women's participation in property offenses and in financial and white-collar offenses, of which fraud, embezzlement, larceny, and forgery are the best examples, should increase as their opportunities for employment in higher status occupations expand. But women's participation in crimes of violence, especially homicide and manslaughter, is not expected to increase, because women's involvements in such acts typically arise out of the frustration, subservience, and dependency that have characterized the traditional female role. Case histories of women who kill reveal one pattern that dominates all others. When women can no longer contain their frustrations and their anger, they express themselves by doing away with the cause of their condition, which most often is a man and sometimes a child or an unborn baby. Thus, the thesis is that as women's employment and education opportunities expand, their feelings

The author acknowledges with appreciation the help of Havatzelet Leinwand in collecting the statistics and in preparing the tables used in this article. Aryeh Lewis also helped collect some of the statistics and the author acknowledges his help.

of being victimized and exploited decrease and their motivation to kill becomes muted.

The purposes of this chapter are to describe the situation vis-à-vis the female offender in Israel and, where appropriate, to compare Israeli statistics with American and British data. Some of the specific questions this chapter sets out to answer are: How much of the crimes known to Israeli police are accounted for by women? Has this amount changed over the past decade and a half? Have the types of crimes with which Israeli women are charged changed? Do the changes follow the American pattern? Have there been changes in the proportion of women convicted and sentenced to prison over the same period?

An analysis of the available criminal statistics over a 15-year time span shows that in 1960, 11 percent of all persons charged were females; in 1965, 13.3 percent; in 1970, 14.2 percent; while by 1974 the proportion was down to 10.3 percent.[3] The years from 1968 through 1971 (which was the period immediately following the Six Day War) marked the high point in female representation, with a peak of 17.1 percent in 1968. None of the percentages in any of the years, however, are close to being commensurate with the proportion of women in the society.

Comparison was made with female arrest statistics in the United States for Index offenses[4] from 1960 through 1972 (selected years shown in table 7-1). In 1960, in both societies, the ratios of male to female offenders were the same (11.0 percent). Ten years later the ratio in Israel was one woman for every ten men; in the United States it was approximately one woman for every five men.

Table 7-1

Percentage of Females Among All Offenders Suspected/Arrested in Israel and in the United States[a]

Year	Israel	United States
1960	11.0	11.0
1965	13.3	14.4
1968	17.1	15.0
1970	14.2	18.0
1972	10.2	19.3
1973	10.6	—
1974	10.3	—

[a]The data presented in the first part of this chapter are based on figures for suspected offenders in Israel, which are compared with arrest data in the United States. Such comparison seems justified in that criminal proceedings are usually initiated in the United States by an arrest, whereas in Israel this is not necessarily so. One may add the pragmatic consideration that these were the only forms in which the data are available from the statistics published in Israel and the United States respectively—which in turn illustrates one of the problems of cross-cultural comparison in the field of criminal justice.

The figures show that in the United States there has been a steady increase in the percentage of females arrested. In Israel the figures show that the proportion of females charged begins to decline after 1971. In each society the proportion of female offenders is much lower than is their representation in that society.

The proportion of Israeli women suspects who were charged between 1960 and 1974 was also analyzed by type of offenses. Such analysis revealed that over the 15-year period, there has not been a consistent increase in the percentage of females in any of the offense categories (see table 7-2). After 1966 there was a steep increase in the percentage of females charged with "crimes against the public order"[5] —14.6 percent in 1966, 21.1 percent in 1967, 38.0 percent in 1968, with a peak of 43.7 percent in 1971. However, since 1971 the percentage has been below the 1966 level.

Detailed study of the acts for which women have been charged within that category showed that the large majority of them (64 percent in 1964, 76 percent in 1967, and 92 percent in 1970) fall into a single subcategory: disturbing the public order. Prosecuting attorneys confirmed our guess that the charge "disturbing the public order" is in fact a euphemism for "prostitution." After 1971 the percentage of women in that category declined to its pre-1967 level.

When we analyzed the distribution of offenses within separate sex cohorts, as shown in table 7-3, we found that there was no consistent increase in any of the offense categories. Over the most recent ten years, Israeli women were most likely to be arrested for crimes against the public order, followed by crimes against the person and crimes against property.

When we compared the proportion of females in the United States who had been arrested by offense categories over the past two decades, we did find that significant changes had occurred. The most striking change was the big increase in women's participation in property and white-collar offenses: notably larceny and theft, embezzlement and fraud, and forgery and counterfeiting. Thus in 1960 about 17 percent of all arrests for larceny were women; in 1972 women accounted for about 31 percent of all larceny arrests. The figures are similar for

Table 7-2
Female Suspects as a Percentage of All Suspects by Offense Categories: Selected Years, 1960-1974

Year	Against Public Order	Against Person	Against Morali- ty	Against Property	Fraud and Forgery	Fiscal and Economic	Other Offenses
1960	6.7	14.1	18.2	7.6	5.0	13.7	15.5
1965	17.9	18.6	9.9	8.3	5.1	14.3	9.5
1970	37.0	9.8	7.5	5.3	6.5	12.7	3.8
1974	13.5	12.1	5.8	6.7	12.2	6.7	6.1

Table 7-3

Distribution of Sex Cohorts by Type of Offense: Selected Years, 1960-1974

Year		Against Public Order	Against Person	Against Morali- ty	Against Property	Fraud and Forgery	Fiscal and Economic	Other Offenses
1960	M	14.4	17.6	3.0	36.2	3.5	0.6	24.7
	F	8.3	23.3	5.4	24.0	1.5	0.8	36.6
1965	M	25.0	23.6	3.6	33.3	10.3	1.8	2.5
	F	35.6	35.1	2.5	19.5	3.6	1.9	1.7
1970	M	18.2	21.6	4.0	44.1	8.4	0.6	3.0
	F	64.4	14.1	2.0	14.8	3.5	0.5	0.7
1974	M	28.1	23.6	3.6	35.9	6.4	0.4	0.6
	F	38.5	28.3	1.6	22.6	7.8	0.3	0.4

embezzlement and fraud as well as forgery and counterfeiting. The increase in those categories has been consistent over the past two decades.

In Israel, on the other hand, the statistics describing female subjects charged indicated that as of 1974 women accounted for 10.3 percent of all offenders; and while percentages from 1968 through 1971 were appreciably higher, reaching a high of 17.1 percent in 1968, the representation of females in the early 1970s was in fact slightly lower than in the early 1960s. Moreover, there was little evidence in the Israeli statistics that the percentages of women charged with property and financial types of offenses are increasing, as they appear to be in the United States. Apart from some recent increase in the fraud and forgery category, the only big increase, which lasted for a period of five years, occurred after the Six Day War, from 1967 through 1971, and only affected the percentage of females charged with disturbing the public order.

In the United States, however, not only was there a big increase in the proportion of women who were arrested for property and financial offenses, but during the same time period there was also an increase in the proportion of women (married women, especially) who worked outside their homes on a full-time basis. The thesis presented earlier about the relationship between an increase in property offenses committed by women and women's opportunities to commit such offenses is dependent upon women being gainfully employed outside their homes: in banks, insurance companies, private business, department stores, etc. These are the places in which the opportunities for embezzlement, forgery, and larceny are most likely to occur.

The female workforce statistics for the United States from 1960 through 1970 indicate that there has been a big increase in the proportion of women gainfully employed, and the increase has been especially marked since 1967. In 1970 42.6 percent of all adult women in the United States were gainfully employed, compared with 26.9 percent for all Israeli (Jewish) married women.

About the same proportion of Israeli women worked outside their homes in 1960 as did in 1970 (27.3 to 29.3 percent). In the United States 34.8 percent of the women worked outside their homes in 1960, as compared with 42.6 percent in 1970.

Thus the female crime statistics and the female workforce data in Israel both fail to show any significant shifts during a period that saw big changes in the United States. The absence of a significant women's movement in Israel is, we think, an important link in this explanatory chain.

The next stage in the criminal justice system occurs in the courtroom. From the statistics that are available, the following can be derived: (1) the proportion of women as opposed to men prosecuted; (2) among those prosecuted, the proportion of women convicted; and (3) among those convicted, the proportion of women sent to prison.[6] At each of these decision stages, we wanted to find out whether any changes occurred in the manner in which women were treated in the decade between 1960 and 1970.

The proportion of females among all persons prosecuted was 7.7 percent in 1960. This figure increased to 8.5 percent in 1962 and 1963 but declined again to between 6 and 7 percent in the years 1966 to 1970. Similarly, the proportion of females among all persons convicted was 7.1 percent in 1960, rose to 8.0 percent in 1962 and 1963, and fell again to between 6 and 7 percent in the years 1966 to 1970. Thus while females accounted for 14.2 percent of suspected offenders in 1970 (see above), they represented less than half this proportion of the prosecutions and convictions. The figure for convictions—6.4 percent—compares with 8.5 percent for the U.S. federal courts, 11.1 percent for the California state courts, and 13.2 percent for the courts in Great Britain. Moreover, the Israeli figure seems, if anything, to be declining, while those for the other jurisdictions are on the increase.

Table 7-4 compares the proportions of men and women in Israel whose cases were prosecuted and who were convicted, acquitted, or had their charges dropped.

Over the 10-year period the average differences between men and women in

Table 7-4
Among Females and Males Prosecuted Percentage Charges Dropped, Acquitted, and Convicted: Selected Years, 1960-1970

Year	Charges Dropped		Acquitted		Convicted	
	Males	Females	Males	Females	Males	Females
1960	13.7	21.4	6.3	5.8	80.0	72.6
1965	9.7	14.0	5.1	6.1	85.2	79.9
1970	9.7	12.7	4.2	5.7	86.0	81.6

the percentages convicted is 4.7 (that is, almost 5 percent more of the men prosecuted were convicted than the women). In every year from 1962 onward, the acquittal rate was higher for females than for males. On the whole, however, the differences were greater for "charges dropped," where females had relatively more of such cases in every year except 1968, when the figure for both males and females was 10.8 percent. In general, however, there was no trend which would indicate that significant changes are occurring in the judicial treatment of either males or females.[7]

The differences in the percentages of men and women convicted by types of offenses are described in table 7-5. All of the offenses shown in table 7-5 except one, crimes against morality, exhibit a common tendency. The tendency is for men and women to move closer together; suggesting thereby that the advantages women may have enjoyed at the hands of the court appear to be on the decline. That pattern prevails for all offenses except those "against morality."

We looked next at sentencing patterns and asked: Are women accounting for a larger or smaller proportion of the offenders sent to prison? The figures show that the proportion of women in Israeli prisons, which was 4.4 percent in 1960, reached a peak of 8.1 percent in 1964, and subsequently declined to 2.9 percent in 1970. A declining trend was also observed in other jurisdictions, notably New York State, but not to the same degree.

Another way of comparing the percentages of men and women committed to prison between 1960 and 1970 is by examining the proportions of convicted men and women who were committed within each sex cohort. Thus, in 1960 3.2 percent of convicted females were sentenced to imprisonment, as compared with 5.3 percent of the males; and 2.6 percent in 1965, as compared with 4.4 percent of the males. The rate of female imprisonment reached its lowest point, both absolutely and relative to the rate for males, in 1970, when 2.1 percent of the females were sentenced to imprisonment, as compared with 4.7 percent of the males. However, the changes have not been very great during this period.[8]

Table 7-5
Differences in the Percentage of Males and Females Convicted by Types of Offenses[a]

Year	Against Public Order	Against Person	Against Morality	Against Property	Fraud and Forgery
1960	+0.2	−12.5	−0.7	−4.6	−24.0
1965	−0.5	−7.1	−5.6	−5.1	−3.2
1970	−1.4	0	+8.7	0	−3.0

[a]Female percentages subtracted from male percentages.

Concluding Remarks

The major purpose of this chapter was to analyze the extent and types of involvement in serious crime of Israeli women in the period from 1960 through 1974. This was a period that witnessed the emergence and expansion of a women's liberation movement in the United States and in many other Western societies. The major thrust of the rhetoric and objectives of the contemporary women's movement is the attainment of jobs and incomes commensurate with a woman's training and ability and equal to those of men with comparable education and experience.

An analysis of crime statistics in the United States reveals that since 1967 (the period in which the women's movement expanded and gained considerable publicity) there has been a marked increase in the percentage of women committing crimes against property and other white-collar offenses and a slight decline in the percentage of women committing crimes of violence. The increase in female property offenders occurred at the time when there was also a sizable increase in the percentage of women holding full-time jobs. In an earlier work I argued that there was a connection among those three events: a movement for women's liberation, an increase in female property offenders and a decline in female offenses involving violence, and an increase in the proportion of women employed full-time outside the home. The argument was summarized briefly in the opening pages of this chapter.

The second major purpose of this chapter was to compare female crime data in Israel against data in the United States to see if the same patterns were occurring in both societies. My conclusion is that there is no evidence that the American pattern generalized to Israel. The data indicate that in both societies women's participation in crime is not at all commensurate with their representation in the society, but that in the United States the proportion of female offenders appears to be on the increase. In Israel the proportion seems to be declining. There is also no indication that Israeli women have increased their participation in crimes against property or in other types of financial and white-collar offenses during the period of the women's liberation movement in the United States. In addition, there is no indication that the proportion of Israeli women who work outside their homes on a full-time basis has increased in that same time span. The percentage in 1970 was roughly the same as it was in 1960.

Finally, there is little evidence of a nonstatistical nature that a significant proportion of Israeli women are involved in a movement for their liberation. The cry "women's lib" may be heard in Israel, but one has to listen hard, and then, it may be heard only in a few circles and among those women who have achieved for themselves many of the goals they urge upon their "less fortunate" sisters. In the absence of such a movement, there is less reason to anticipate major shifts in the amount and types of serious crimes Israeli women are likely to engage in over the next few years.

Notes

1. Rita J. Simon, *Women and Crime*, National Institute of Mental Health, Center for Studies of Crime and Delinquency, 1975.

2. The specific felony offenses in the United States for which information about women's participation was reported are murder and nonnegligent manslaughter, manslaughter by negligence, robbery, aggravated assault, burglary, larceny, and auto theft. These are the offenses that are used to establish the Index in the Uniform Crime Reporting Program that measures the trend and distribution of crime in the United States.

3. The categories of offenses that the statistics describe are: (1) against the public order and administration of lawful authority (many of the specific offenses included in this category pertain to emergency laws that were passed immediately preceding and following the 1967 War); (2) against the person (murder, attempted murder, manslaughter, assault and bodily harm, threats, and offenses connected with dangerous drugs); (3) against morality (rape, indecent acts, procuration, soliciting, and maintenance of a place for purposes of prostitution); (4) against property (robbery, breaking and entering, theft, receiving or possessing stolen property, arson, willful damage to property, and criminal trespass); (5) fraud and forgery; and (6) fiscal and economic offenses.

4. See note 2.

5. The acts included in this offense category are: (1) offenses against public order and the administration of lawful authority; (2) offenses against the security of the state (treason and espionage); (3) offenses under emergency laws (infiltration, military government, etc.); (4) offenses against a national group; (5) unlawful association and unlawful society; (6) unlawful possession of firearms, other weapons, and unlawful possession of explosives; (7) disturbing public order; (8) assault on, or foiling of, a police officer; (9) corruption or abuse of office; (10) perjury and giving false information; (11) offenses connected with Defense Service; and (12) other offenses of the above type.

6. Unfortunately, statistics concerning the percentage of females prosecuted, convicted, and sentenced to prison are not available past 1970.

7. A comparison with the California data for a few of the same years and for 1971 and 1972 shows almost the same pattern as the Israeli data, both in terms of the proportion convicted and the differences between men and women:

	California data	
Year	Male	Female
1969	86.4	81.4
1970	85.3	80.8
1971	86.8	82.2
1972	87.6	83.2

8. The Israeli ratio is similar to the California ratio in 1967, 1968, and 1969, which was 2.2. The difference between the California and Israeli figures, however, is that in California a much higher proportion of both men and women are sentenced to prison: for example, in 1967, 15 percent of the men and 7.4 percent of the women; in 1968, 13.1 percent of the men and 6.2 percent of the women; and in 1969, 11.8 percent of the men and 5.1 percent of the women.

8 The Major Dimensions of Victimology

Walter C. Reckless

It is increasingly apparent that victimology is becoming a major concern of criminologists, the public, and legislators in the United States. The long delay in focused attention was due primarily to the emphasis which postmedieval penal law placed upon the state-operated punishment of the criminal, including collection of fines. Apparently, after the Middle Ages, when modern European countries developed specific penal codes, compensation or retribution to the injured party or his family as the long historic forerunner of legally administered punishment was abandoned. Reparation to the injured party or to the victim's family or clan, besides expulsion of the offender from his community, constituted the main form of punishment in primitive (tribal) societies. And reparation by the offender for injuries done lingered on into our ancient civilizations and into the medieval period of European history.

Growing Awareness of the Problem

Some of the early criminologists in the late eighteenth century and early nineteenth century called attention to the problem of the victim of crime, and several of the international congresses on criminology made proposals to study and do something about the plight of the victim. But nothing was done. In the 1940s, criminologists began sparingly to publish books and papers on the subject. Among the outstanding contributions was the treatise *The Criminal and His Victim* (1948) by the German criminologist Hans von Hentig, which among other things emphasized the relationships between doer and victim and also described the various types of victims.

Stephen Schafer made three important contributions to the study of victimology in the sixties.[1] The last of the three, namely *The Victim and His Criminal*, published in 1968, may be looked upon as a textbook on the subject.

Although only a limited amount of actual field research has been done, victimology is now considered a major aspect of criminology, and several universities and colleges offer lectures and/or seminars on the subject.

Since the sixties, a large number of articles on different phases of the subject have appeared in various journals, and several (not many) states and countries have established programs to compensate victims of violent crimes. The First International Symposium on Victimology was held at The Hebrew University in Jerusalem in September of 1973. At the symposium a wide range of papers was presented by experts from a large number of countries. The organizer of the symposium together with a younger colleague assembled a collection of important articles and papers on victimology in a recent publication.[2]

In view of the fact that a wide range of articles and books on various aspects of victimology have been published in the last 10 years, it is apparent that the time is right for the basic dimensions of the problem to be delineated. Otherwise, the subject will soon get out of focus. The following statements will therefore concentrate not on the accumulated insights and knowledge that have been generated by study and research but rather on the phases of the problem that *need* systematic study and research. Hopefully, administrators and researchers will focus future attention on one or more of these basic areas of victimology. Hopefully also, textbooks on the subject will focus on these major dimensions of the problem.

Six Basic Dimensions

1. The Person as Victim

Crimes such as murder, assault, rape, robbery, and larceny are clearly crimes in which individual persons are victimized; and, to a greater or lesser extent, so also are fraud, embezzlement, sex offenses, and offenses against family and children. Von Hentig, in his 1948 publication, made a systematic attempt to classify victims, to call attention to the relationships between victim and doer, and to specify the psychological types of individuals who for the most part unconsciously stimulate aggression against themselves.[3] In the latter instance, the victim in a sense is the cause of crime against himself.

It was not until the special survey of householders, done for the President's Commission on Law Enforcement and Administration of Justice (ca. 1966), that important research insights into victimization were presented from a stratified sample of 10,000 householders throughout the U.S.[4] However, the kinds of offenses were limited to forcible rape, robbery, aggravated assault, burglary, larceny of $50 and over, and motor vehicle theft against members of the household during the previous year. In checking the aggravated assault, burglary, larceny ($50 or more), and motor vehicle theft interview reports with local police records, it was found that only a small percentage of the offenses were reported to the police. It should be noted also that for several years, the *Uniform Crime Reports* have indicated the relationship between victim and offenders in the instance of murder.

Subsequent to this investigation by the President's Commission, the District of Columbia Crime Commission also made a field study of victims of rape and aggravated assault.[5] Still more recently, three important field studies of victimization were conducted for the U.S. Law Enforcement Assistance Administration by the Bureau of Census as part of the National Crime Panel (NCP). The surveys covered samples of persons 12 years of age and over.

The first in this series made sample household surveys in five of the largest cities; the second, in Dayton and San Jose; and the third, in Atlanta, Baltimore, Cleveland, Dallas, Denver, Newark, Portland, and St. Louis.[6] All three studies computed rates of the reported victimization by type of crime and also cleared the householders' reports with the local police records to see the extent of nonreporting of offenses.

Whether or not NCP will cover the problem of victimology on a widespread and uniform yearly basis, as the FBI covers crime reports, is something for the future to indicate. Such a development would add greatly to basic insights into victimization.

Recently, an outstanding report of available statistical tables on all phases of crime in the United States has been published by the U.S. Law Enforcement Assistance Administration of the U.S. Department of Justice. Several tables are devoted to information on victims which was collected originally by Phillip H. Ennis for the President's Commission on Law Enforcement and Administration of Justice.[7] The Ennis data included victimization by income levels, race, and sex.

It should be noted that the biggest deficiency in available victim data is the widespread unwillingness of victims to report the offenses to the police. This unwillingness varies greatly by type of crime. The survey of 10,000 householders asked the interviewees to indicate the victim's most important reason for not notifying the police. The important reasons fell into the following categories: felt it was a private matter or did not want to harm offender; police could not be effective or would not want the report; and fear of reprisal.[8] The first two of the reasons were by far the ones most frequently indicated. The survey of 10,000 householders found that the instances of personal injury crime were almost twice as large as the number of such offenses reported to the police.[9]

2. The Relationship of Victim to Offender

Another major topic in the study of victimology is the relationship of the victim to the offender. There seems to be widespread belief that offenders are strangers to the persons they victimize, with the possible exception being in the instance of murder. Very little research has been done on this phase of the problem. But there are some indications that show this notion to be false. In sizable proportions, varying for different offenses against the person, offender and victim were not strangers but were acquaintances and relatives.

In recent years the Federal Bureau of Investigation in its annual *Uniform Crime Reports* has presented information on the relationship between victim and doer in the instances of murder and aggravated assault. The latter has been found to concentrate upon acquaintances and family members, while about two-thirds of the murders involve family members and acquaintances.[10] In the study of rape victims in the District of Columbia, the President's Commission found that two-thirds were violated by casual acquaintances, while only 19 percent of the aggravated assault victims were violated by persons with whom they were not acquainted.[11]

A study in 17 cities of the United States by Mulvihill and Tumin presented data on the sex of the victim by the sex of the offender, the age of the one by the age of the other, and the race of the former by the race of the latter in instances of five violent crimes: criminal homicide, aggravated assault, forcible rape, armed robbery, and unarmed robbery.[12] Mulvihill and Tumin also presented field-collected data (1967) on victim-offender relationships in the same 17 cities for the same five types of violent crimes. The offenses were sorted according to the following sets of relationships: husband (victim) wife (offender), wife (v) husband (o); the same two combinations for common law marriages; parent (v) child (o) parent (o), brother-sister (v or o), other family (v or o); close friend, paramour, homosexual partners (v or o); prostitute (v or o), acquaintance, neighbor, business relation, sex rival or enemy, stranger, felon, or police officer (v or o).[13]

Research into victim-offender relationships needs to be continued. It is certainly as important an aspect of the study of victimology as the type of person who gets victimized. And apparently there seems to be no greater difficulty in doing field studies on victim-doer relationships than on the personal characteristics of the victim.

Because of the gigantic aspects of doing nationwide research periodically or yearly, it seems apparent that an appropriate federal agency should undertake both tasks on a uniform basis. This does not mean that certain victims or groups of victims should not be studied in exploratory fashion by individual researchers who very likely will discover certain very important aspects of the problem.

3. Business as Victim

There is justified opinion for believing that robberies and burglaries of stores and businesses are very widespread, although infrequently reported to the police. During business hours when businesses are open, the crime is usually robbery. If after business hours, when stores, businesses, and offices are closed, the crime is burglary, since there is a breakin. During business hours, goods, valuables, and money are stolen from stores and offices not only by customers but also by employees. In retail establishments, such as department stores, grocery stores, and five-and-ten-cent stores, there is a large amount of shoplifting. But very little of the shoplifting gets reported to the police, probably a result of fear of unfavorable attitudes toward the shop on the part of the public. A large percentage of retail establishments employ store detectives and encourage sales clerks to give attention to shoplifters.

Because of the general failure of stores and offices to report theft to the police during business hours, one must surmise that shoplifting and theft from offices during business hours is greatly underreported. Likewise, the failure to report makes it impossible to indicate what available objects and valuables in shops and offices are frequently and infrequently stolen. Perhaps, coverage of losses by insurance is another reason why stores and businesses seldom report theft to the police.

The *Uniform Crime Reports* of recent years have indicated that somewhat over half the robberies in the United States take place on the streets, while slightly less than half take place in chain stores, gasoline stations, commercial places, banks, and residences. A special survey in 1967 of 5000 businesses directed by Albert J. Reiss indicated that businesses in city ghettos had by far the highest per capita number of burglaries; those in the central city (nonghetto) had less than half the ghetto rate; and those in suburban areas, still less. The rate per 100 establishments continued to decline for towns of 10,000 to 50,000 people and under.[14] Reiss's investigation (1967) also found that the rate of robberies per 100 businesses was 23 for ghettos, 6 for central city businesses (nonghettos), and 2 for suburban businesses.[15]

The Ennis study for the President's Commission on Law Enforcement and Administration of Justice 1965-1966 estimated the dollar loss from crimes of robbery, burglary, grand larceny, vehicle theft, petty larceny, auto offense, malicious mischief, counterfeiting and forgery, fraud, and consumer fraud.[16] One will notice that a few of the listed offenses represent victimization of business. Reiss's study of crimes against small businesses indicated the dollar losses according to the crimes of burglary, robbery, vandalism, shoplifting, employee theft, and bad checks. His investigation also indicated the percent of the businesses burglarized or robbed according to type of location: ghetto, nonghetto central city, suburbs, and rural.[17]

The three recently published surveys of victimization conducted by the U.S. Bureau of the Census for the so-called National Crime Panel of the U.S. Law Enforcement Assistance Administration embraced commercial establishments in its sampling of victimization. The field information covered reported burglaries and robberies during a 12-month period according to the kind of business (retail, wholesale, service, and other), the dollar amount of receipts, and the number of paid employees. Hopefully, the uniform collection of data on commercial victimization will be continued.

4. Property as Victim

Governmental office buildings, parks and playgrounds, monuments, business office buildings, private homes, churches, etc., are also subject to victimization.

The overall impression, without having comparative data, is that they are much less likely to be subject to victimization than are persons and businesses. Undoubtedly the motives behind destruction of buildings and public places are quite different from those behind theft, robbery, and burglary.

Very little research has been done on this aspect of victimology. Some insights into losses through vandalism were generated in the study of *Crimes Against Small Business* by Reiss. The damage was classified according to that done to vehicles, buildings, fixtures, merchandise, and glass.[18] The U.S. Interstate Commerce Commission collected data on the amount of loss claims paid to common carriers for loss and damage according to 63 different commodities for the 3-month period ending March 31, 1972.[19] The types of losses and damages included shortage, theft and pilferage, hijacking, concealed damage, visible damage, wreck and catastrophe, and so forth.

Buildings and property are also subject to bombings from time to time in the United States. However, it is not easy to obtain data that can indicate nationwide trends. Very little research has been done on this aspect of victimology. However, one major effort in this connection was made by the Federal Bureau of Investigation. The investigation reported on actual bombings, attempted bombings, number of bomb devices, number of bomb threats, persons killed, persons injured, and value of property damage for January to June 1972.[20] This investigation also enumerated the targets of the bombings.

The less dramatic aspect of property victimization consists of burglary and larceny of households, as well as auto theft. These three types of offenses were covered in the three sample surveys by the U.S. Bureau of the Census for the National Crime Panel of the U.S. Law Enforcement Assistance Administration. The data included race and age of head of household, number of persons in household, amount of family income, tenure of household (owned or rented), and number of units in the occupied household.

5. Collective Violence

Collective violence is probably one of the oldest social phenomena in the world. Tribal wars and family feuds seem to be just about as old as man himself. Religious conflict seems to have begun when new religious groups and forms of worship were developed. Probably the most devastating religious conflict was the Thirty Years War of the seventeenth century, which involved a large section of Europe.

America, almost from the beginning of English settlements, developed a strong tradition for violence. In the early days of the United States, feuding, especially among peoples in various sections of the Southeastern and South Central states, became very rampant. The development of organized labor in the United States was also accompanied by conflict and strife. Even families that migrated westward and southward from more settled portions of early United States developed feuds. The "gun-toting" tradition became very strong in our country. And, one should not overlook the Ku Klux Klan and its focus on assaults upon Negroes.

In recent years the United States has witnessed several upsurges of collective violence, which appear to have followed a pattern of crowd behavior. The violence seems to be triggered by some event on the part of the "establishment" (police and government), which causes spontaneous eruption of males in an urban locale that has been under increased tension. One of the more recent large-scale eruptions was the riot in the Watts area of Los Angeles (August 11, 1965), which lasted five days.[21]

Both before and after the Watts riot, the United States witnessed several different kinds of mass eruptions, such as black ghetto riots, antiwar protests, and college demonstrations. Several riots occurred in adult prisons, the most notorious one at Attica, New York. The American Correctional Association's Committee on Riots and Disturbances made a study of prison riots that took place in the prisons of the United States in two decades prior to 1970, and it classified prison riots according to general causes, institution-related causes, and non-institution-related causes.[22]

Federal commissions were appointed to study collective violence as it appeared in recent years.[23] While competent individual researchers are able to investigate certain specific aspects of localized outbreaks, a big multidisciplinary staff of researchers and investigators is usually necessary to study the overall aspects of a civil disorder. However, large-scale collective violence is not continuous enough and not dispersed enough to warrant the establishment of permanent U.S. commissions on civil disorders.

6. Compensation and Restitution to Victims

Since the leadership of Marjory Fry in England during the fifties, compensation to victims of violent crimes has become a critical issue in several modern countries of the world. New Zealand was the first country to enact the necessary law and program in 1963. England shortly after, in 1964, established a program for compensation of victims. A few states in the United States and a small number of countries in the world followed suit. According to research done by MacNamara and Sullivan, by 1973 there were only four countries in the world and eight states of the United States that had established compensation programs for victims of violence.[24] Compensation not only covers the surviving victims of violence but also the surviving members of the murdered persons' families.

Usually a state or country, under compensation law, establishes a top board of administrators and decisionmakers, with investigational staff and local offices where applications can be made for compensation. The compensation is granted after appropriate field investigation of the applicant's victimization. One should notice that victim compensation programs are separate from a related movement, which has hardly born fruit as yet, namely, the compensation for persons who are killed or injured as a result of their attempt to prevent a crime. Such proposals are usually referred to as "good Samaritan" laws, but very few have been enacted into law.

There has been a revival of the idea of restitution by the offender to the victim for damage to his person and property including theft and burglary. As is well known, restitution is one of the oldest practices in the world for dealing with local offenses, going far back in tribal history and surviving in many primitive tribes. But as was mentioned earlier, it faded out of existence with the development of state penal laws, whereby the state administered punishment and collected fines imposed by criminal courts. Schafer has led a movement to inaugurate "correctional restitution," whereby the offender pays the victim or the victim's family in money or personal services for the injuries and losses sustained.[25]

Some European countries have developed state programs to compensate the "good Samaritan," but states in the United States have resisted the proposal.

How far victim compensation laws and programs will spread in the United States is an unanswerable question at this time. Whether the proposals will ever go beyond violent crimes to the person is questionable. Whether the United States will embrace good samaritan laws is also open to question. One reason for reluctance might possibly be the widespread adoption of insurance and operation of "medicare." Another reason is the firm conviction that bystanders do not have to get involved. They can be witnesses in court and they can call the police, but they should not step in to thwart an attack on the victim according to prevailing public sentiment.

Conclusion

As pointed out above, the major dimensions of victimology consist of the person as victim, the relationship of victims to offenders, business as victim, property as victim, collective violence, and compensation and restitution in the instance of violent crimes against the person. Some scholars and practitioners will notice that victimless crimes, such as abortion, homosexuality, and drug addiction have been omitted. In such instances, the self is the doer and also the sufferer and there is no doer-victim relationship, as in crimes against the person, nor doer-object relationship, as in the instance of business and property. Victimology is primarily concerned with the projection of criminal behavior on persons and objects external to the doer. The difference between crimes with victims and crimes without victims seems to lie in the contrast of external with internal focus of behavior.

The first four dimensions in the study of victimology require studies and reports primarily by ongoing agencies of the federal government. The fifth dimension, namely collective violence, requires the establishment of large-scale temporary commissions. The last dimension (compensation and restitution) can be studied by governmental agencies or interested persons. Specific aspects of all six dimensions of victimology can be investigated by technicians at the university or administrative level.

In a university or college course, it would be wise to present available material to the student on the six dimensions, so as to give proper coverage. Undoubtedly, textbooks and books of readings on the subject will in the future have to stress the basic aspects of the problem and not wander over dubious fringes. The study of victimology, because of its recent acceptance as a subject for research and exploration, can make excellent progress by accepting the basic dimensions which clearly have arisen in the first generation of its administrative, research, and scholarly exploration.

Notes

1. Stephen Shafer, *Restitution to Victims of Crime*, London: Stevens & Sons, 1960; *Criminal-Victim Relationships in Violent Crimes: A Study in Florida,* National Institute of Mental Health, Bethesda, Maryland, July 1965 (mimeographed); *The Victim and His Criminal, A Study of Functional Responsibility*, New York: Random House, 1968.

2. Israel Drapkin and Emilio Viano (eds.), *Victimology*, Lexington, Mass.: Lexington Books, D.C. Heath and Company, 1974.

3. Hans von Hentig, *The Criminal and His Victim*, New Haven: Yale Univ. Press, 1948.

4. The President's Commission on Law Enforcement and Administration of Justice, *Task Force Report: Crime and Its Impact—An Assessment,* Washington, D.C.: USGPO, 1967, pp. 80-84.

5. *Report of the President's Commission on Crime in the District of Columbia*, Washington, D.C.: USGPO, 1967.

6. See Law Enforcement Assistance Administration, U.S. Department of Justice, *Crime in the Nation's Five Largest Cities*, Washington, D.C., April 1974; *Crimes and Victims: A Report on the Dayton-San Jose Pilot Survey of Victimization*, Washington, D.C., June 1975; *Crime in Eight American Cities*, Washington D.C., July 1974.

7. Law Enforcement Assistance Administration, National Criminal Justice Information and Statistics Service, *Sourcebook of Criminal Justice Statistics 1973*, Washington, D.C.: USGPO, 1973, pp. 169-173.

8. The President's Commission on Law Enforcement and Administration of Justice, *Task Force Report: Crime and Its Impact—An Assessment*, p. 18.

9. Ibid., p. 17.

10. Federal Bureau of Investigation, U.S. Department of Justice, *Uniform Crime Report: 1973*, Washington, D.C.: USGPO, 1979.

11. *Report of the President's Commission on Crime in the District of Columbia*, pp. 53, 76.

12. Donald J. Mulvihill and Melvin Tumin, *Crimes of Violence*, Vol. 11, National Commission on the Causes and Prevention of Violence, Washington, D.C.: USGPO, 1969, pp. 267, 271, 275, 279. These tables are readily available in the recent compilation of the *Sourcebook of Criminal Justice Statistics 1973*, National Criminal Justice Information and Statistics Service, Washington, D.C.: USGPO, 1973, Tables 3.42-3.46, pp. 195-196.

13. Mulvihill and Tumin, *Crimes of Violence*, p. 287; and *Sourcebook of Criminal Justice Statistics*, Table 3.50, p. 197.

14. Albert J. Reiss, *Crime Against Small Business*, Department of Commerce, Small Business Administration, Washington, D.C.: USGPO, 1968, p. 75. Also reported in *Sourcebook of Criminal Justice Statistics*, Table 3.20, p. 172.

15. Reiss, *Crime Against Small Business*, p. 76; also *Sourcebook of Criminal Justice Statistics*, Table 3.21, p. 172.

16. P.H. Ennis, *Criminal Victimization in the United States: A Report of a National Survey*. Submitted to The President's Commission on Law Enforcement and Administration of Justice (Washington, D.C.: U.S. Government Printing Office, 1967); also *Sourcebook of Criminal Justice Statistics*, Table 3.31, p. 175.

17. Reiss, *Crime Against Small Business*, p. 24; also *Sourcebook of Criminal Justice Statistics*, Table 3.31, p. 175.

18. Also in *Sourcebook of Criminal Justice Statistics*, Tables 3.34-3.36, pp. 176-177.

19. Also in *Sourcebook of Criminal Justice Statistics*, Table 3.37, pp. 178-179.

20. Federal Bureau of Investigation, U.S. Department of Justice, *Uniform Crime Reports Bomb Summary: A Comprehensive Report on Incidents Involving Explosives and Incendiary Devices in the Nation*, Washington, D.C.: USGPO, January-June 1972, pp. 1, 3, and 4; also in *Sourcebook of Criminal Justice Statistics*, Tables 3.73 and 3.74, pp. 260-261.

21. The President's Commission on Law Enforcement and Administration of Justice, *Task Force Report: Crime and Its Impact—An Assessment* pp. 116-120.

22. The American Correctional Association, *Causes, Preventive Measures, and Methods of Controlling Riots and Disturbances in Correctional Institutions*, Washington, D.C., October 1970.

23. See *Report of the National Advisory Commission on Civil Disorders*, Washington, D.C.: USGPO, March 1968; *Progress Report of the National Commission on the Causes and Prevention of Violence to President Lyndon B. Johnson*, Washington, D.C.: USGPO, January 9, 1969, which condensed report

was followed by 12 volumes on various aspects of collective violence in the United States; *To Establish Justice, To Insure Domestic Tranquility, Final Report of the National Commission on the Causes and Prevention of Violence*, Washington, D.C.: USGPO, December 1969; *Report of the Miami Study Team on Civil Disturbances: Miami Report*, August 5, 1968, submitted to the National Commission on the Causes and Prevention of Violence; *Rights in Conflict: The Violent Confrontation of Demonstrators and Police in the Parks and Streets of Chicago during the Week of the Democratic National Convention of 1968*, the so-called Walker Report, which was made by the National Commission on the Causes and Prevention of Violence, New York: Bantam Books, Inc., 1968; *Report of the President's Commission on Campus Unrest*, Washington, D.C.: USGPO, September, 26, 1970.

24. Donald E.J. MacNamara and John J. Sullivan, "Making the Victim Whole," *The Urban Review* 6 (1973), no. 1:22.

25. Stephen Schafer, "The Correctional Rejuvenation of Restitution to Victims of Crime," *Interdisciplinary Problems in Criminology: Papers of the American Society of Criminology*, Walter C. Reskless and Charles L. Newman (eds.), Ohio State Univ., 1965, pp. 166-167.

Part III
Clinical Perspectives:
Theory and Practice

9

Psychological Theories of Delinquency

Franco Ferracuti and
Graeme R. Newman

Psychological explanations of delinquency will be considered within three broad categories:

1. *Unchanging intrapersonal factors*, which may be defined as factors within the individual that influence the individual's behavior but are generally not subject to change by the individual himself. Although we suggest that these states are largely unchanging, this is not to say that they may not be changed by factors or circumstances outside the individual.

2. *Changeable intrapersonal factors*, which may be defined as those factors within an individual that may be subject to change, either by the individual himself or with the assistance of external agents.

3. *Interpersonal factors*, which may be defined as factors which influence the individual's behavior as a result of his interactions with others. The locus of cause may in this case shift from lying basically with the influence of others over the individual to the opposite extreme in which the individual influences others. Typical of this group are theories of social learning and imitation.

Each of these three theoretical problem areas can be interpreted as having distinctly different prevention implications. It should be understood that the same theory will very often apply to all three areas.

Apart from the empirical evidence available to support the theories, three further criteria will be used in evaluating their explanatory power. These will be the extent to which they are able to explain: (1) the rates of delinquency, including differential rates according to various population subgroups and the peaking at age 16; (2) the forms of delinquency; and (3) the individual motivation to delinquency (i.e., why one does it and another does not). Standards for prevention and control will also be considered to the extent that they may affect each of these three major questions.

The definition of delinquency is a major problem in a chapter such as this. To avoid disregarding possibly relevant theories, we have taken the broad definition used by Hirschi: "... delinquency is defined by acts, the detection of which is thought to result in punishment of the person committing them by agents of the larger society. . . ."[1] This means that the concept of aggression—so extensively studied in psychology—will also be considered as "delinquency."

Unchanging Intrapersonal Factors

Dispositional Theories

For the first half of this century, these theories were the most popular theories in explaining individual motivations to delinquency. The earliest forms of this theory suggested that there was a simple one-to-one relationship between a particular fixed state and delinquency, which led to studies of the relationship between body types and various other physical attributes and delinquency. In general, a consistent relationship has been found between athletic body type and tall-thin body type and delinquency.[2] These earlier studies have their modern-day counterpart in the attempts to display a relationship between the incidence of XYY chromosomes and the higher rate of incarceration. These studies have today been largely discounted.[3] However, the much more complicated theories of this type are those which have postulated the genetic (and usually by assumption, "unchangeable") basis for particular personality types which are subsequently more prone to delinquency. It has been argued, for example, that extroverts are less easily conditioned, less easily socialized, and thus more likely to be found in the criminal population.[4] Similarly, it has also been argued that intelligence is closely related to delinquency, mostly indirectly by its relationship to poor school performance, which in turn is shown to have an enduring relationship to delinquency. Furthermore, in a recent penetrating review of intelligence and delinquency studies, Hirschi and Hindelang concluded that the evidence was compelling that delinquents were less intelligent (as measured by IQ tests) than nondelinquents.[5] These arguments usually assume that intelligence is fixed, because of the extensive early research demonstrating that IQ remains constant over time. There are also dynamic views of intelligence which may be related to delinquency; we shall consider these in a later section.

All these theories presume that the individual delinquent is in some way a deviation from the normal, so that they lend themselves very easily to individualistic explanation as to why one individual becomes delinquent and another does not. However, they may be used to explain differences in rates of delinquency in limited cases. It may be argued that since intelligence is probably 80 percent inherited,[6] and since blacks consistently perform less well than whites on IQ tests, being black and less intelligent is likely to be more closely related to the rate of delinquency. However, although it may be argued that girls perform slightly better than boys on IQ tests, this difference is no where nearly sufficient to explain the enormous difference in rates between male and female delinquency. Similarly, since by definition, IQ remains constant with age, it cannot be used to explain the peaking of delinquency at 16 and the subsequent falling off after that period, unless considered in relation to other variables, such as school performance. Thus, the only form of delinquency which seems *directly* explainable by these theories is school-related delinquency, such as truancy, since feebleminded delinquents are probably more likely to try to avoid failure experiences at school.

It is sometimes argued that it is only the "dumb" delinquents who get caught. However, several self-report studies have shown a relatively strong relationship between low IQ and the number of self-reported delinquent acts. Hirschi and Hindelang's reanalysis of other data also suggests that it is not only the "dumb" ones who get caught.[7]

Trait theories seem unable to explain the differential rates in delinquency unless it is empirically demonstrated that females are more easily conditionable than males. In addition, Eysenck appeared unable to explain specific forms of deviance, since he used the loose term of "antisocial" behavior as his synonym for crime. Later studies concentrated upon a reasonably well-established clinical syndrome of sociopathy or psychopathy[8] and explained this by the a post facto method. Thus, these theories are too general and do not lend themselves to the explanation of the many forms of delinquency.

All the theories described in this part are, however, useful in explaining individual differences in motivation to delinquency, since it can be postulated that particular delinquents are born with particular traits or predispositions.

Instinct Theories

Unlike dispositional theories, which concentrate on individualistic explanations, instinct theories are more appropriate in explaining basic, "normal" states, in the sense that they are said to exist in everyone. Thus, these theorists postulate basic general dispositions to act and imply that *all* persons potentially are delinquents or criminals. Differential rates might be explained in that it has at times been argued that men have stronger sex and aggressive drives than women.[9] Limited research has also suggested that endocrine factors such as androgen are closely tied to male roles and that if the male hormone is absent during the formation of the hypothalamus in *utero*, male role behavior, such as dominance, aggression, etc., fails to develop in later life.[10] Thus, although it seems at first sight redundant to argue that because men are more aggressive than females they are therefore innately more aggressive than women, the evidence from endocrinology suggests that this is the case.[11]

Other theories have also compared humans with animal species, pointing to the higher destructiveness of human aggression compared to animals, especially to show that certain environmental uses may "trigger" innate sets of aggressive behavior. In addition, it has been suggested that there is also an innate instinct for territorial defense, and this has on occasion been used to explain forms of gang delinquency where the defense of "turf" is important.[12] The further significance of this approach can only be considered when seen in relationship to the individual dealing with his own aggression in some psychodynamic sense, or when his sex or aggressive drives are thwarted by some external circumstance.[13] But in the way it has been presented here, the theory can only explain one form of delinquency, namely, aggression. It may, however, be applied to explain adolescent aggression (i.e., age differentials in delinquency) if used in conjunction with another type of "static" theory.

Maturation Theories

The oldest theory of this type was that of G. Stanley Hall, who argued that child development was a "recapitulation" of man's cultural development, which went from 0 to 4 years of self-preservation; 4 to 8 years equivalent to primitive man's adventure of hunting and fishing, learning the use of weapons, etc.; 8 to 12 years, the "humdrum of savagery"; and finally, adolescence, the years of *Sturm und Drang* (storm and stress), roughly equivalent to the period of Schiller and Goethe, characterized by the usual attributes of the adolescent personality.[14] Much of this theory has been discounted by cultural anthropologists, but the importance of the concept of physiological maturation as related to adolescent behavior remains considerable. And much weight is placed upon these variables in relation to disobedience, uncontrolled passion, eruption of sex and aggression drives, and so on. However, recent research has suggested that even the physiological levels of maturity are subject to change, as the age of adolescent physical maturity appears to be decreasing in the United States. Thus, if there is any relationship between these factors, we should predict the rate of delinquent behavior in the future gradually to peak earlier than 16. These theories do not explain individual motivation to delinquency except insofar as it may be observed that there is wide variation in the age at which individuals mature. They explain the forms of delinquency only very generally in the sense that they are acts which are rebellious and expressions of uncontrolled passion (i.e., acts typical of adolescent *"sturm und drang"*). They do not explain sex differences, especially since it might be argued that the period of adolescent maturity for girls may be more traumatic than for boys. They can be useful only if we introduce other dynamic factors into the explanatory equation.

Intrapersonal Factors

Theories of Emotional Conflict

The major approach in this area, which may be called *psychodynamic*, is that of Freudian theory.[15] In this case, although certain fixed "states" or "forces" are assumed to exist within everyone (i.e., sex and aggression), it is contended that these drives or instincts must be dealt with in a particular way if the individual is to develop normally. The individual is seen as in constant conflict with his own primitive urges (the id). In order to deal with these urges, he must develop a healthy ego (the more cognitive reality-oriented aspect of mental life, including perceptions of personal worth) and a healthy superego—roughly equivalent to the conscience. Usually, what is meant by "healthy" for these aspects of the mind is a particular kind of childhood experience. For effective socialization and ego development, boys must have a stable male authority figure (the father), especially at the age of three or thereabouts. Girls, similarly, must have an effective and stable mother figure. There must be strong emotional ties between child and parents, but these must be tempered with authority, since the Oedipal complex (i.e., the boy's wish to castrate the father and sleep with the mother) must be kept at bay. In addition, according to the famous "anatomy is destiny" doctrine, the psychoanalytic approach characterizes girls as being submissive and passive, which results from the guilt they feel at not having a penis: they assume that they have been punished for wanting to sleep with the father.[16] All these "wishes," of course, are assumed to lie in the unconscious, or a level of the mind of which individuals have no, or only indirect, awareness.

Psychoanalytic theory is especially useful in explaining many different forms, rates, and individual motivations to delinquency. It explains the difference in sexes in delinquency rates by pointing to the fact that boys are more aggressive than girls and thus are more likely to commit delinquent acts. The role of the defective ego, however, in explaining sex differences in rates of delinquency is not quite clear. Work on defective egos has usually suggested that such skills as the ability to delay gratification, coping with frustration and anxiety, selective social sensitivity, and various other "defense mechanisms" are important attributes of healthy ego functions.[17] This is a mechanistic view of ego in terms of skills rather than identity. In the broader sense, therefore, it is implied in Freudian theory that women do not develop an effective ego, in the sense that they are pictured as passive, timid creatures who do not act against the world (i.e., reality testing) to the extent that boys do. The *defective* ego of girls in this case militates *against* their delinquency. Another explanation which also follows from this is the idea that boys' egos are *overdeveloped*. Thus, many theorists have suggested that the *macho* or *machismo* aspects of many Western, Latin, or other subcultures, which reward and train boys to be aggressive, rough, and unremitting, are related to various forms of delinquency and the higher prevalence of violence among boys as compared with girls.[18] Clearly, this perspective offers one of the more promising approaches toward explaining the sex differences in delinquency rates. Since women are developing a more "liberated" and stronger ego, and since, on the other hand, homosexuality among men appears to be more widely accepted as "normal," resulting in the downplay of the *macho* aspect of the male character, we should expect a gradual increase in female delinquency and a gradual decrease, or leveling off at least, in male delinquency. Recent data on female crime suggests that this may indeed be the case.[19]

Psychoanalytic theory is also able to explain the peaking of delinquency at puberty (i.e., at about 16), since the theory of psychosexual development postulates that the Oedipal conflict of age three reappears at puberty. This is not unlike Hall's recapitulatory theory, although it is a more dynamic explanation. Thus, the role of early childhood experience, especially family relationships, is seen as crucial in the generation of delinquency.

However, empirical support for this theory as applied to delinquency is somewhat equivocal. One should expect, for example, that broken homes, an indication of disturbance in family relationships, would be an excellent indicator of delinquency. Although it turns out to be the case for boys, there is a contradiction, in that just as many girls come from broken homes, yet they do not become delinquent at anywhere near the rate for boys.[20] Most of the empirical data on such causes of delinquency have been done on boys, since understandably, there are more of them to study. Other empirical data have lent general support to the theory: the absence of a stable father figure, inconsistent discipline of boys by the father, and other family attributes have been found to be related to delinquency.[21]

Since psychoanalysis emphasizes the common basic nature of all individuals (i.e., instincts and the unconscious), yet insists on treating each individual as unique, in the sense that it is only through the individual's "cooperation" in the interviews that one can gain access to and give meaning to his unconscious, and since it may easily be argued that each individual's personal history is unique, it is a simple step to claim that psychoanalysis is indeed able to explain the individual motivation to delinquency. However, since psychoanalysis is a recapitulating theory, in the sense that it takes the current "fact" of a delinquent act and works backward through the individual's history, it is largely an a post facto argument that cannot within that framework be subject to test.

Psychoanalysis is also able to explain various forms of delinquency by its ability to transpose the symbolic, unconscious images of mental life into their real-life equivalents. For example, children who light fires are expressing strong sexual urges or substituting for masturbation; children who kill or attack their parents have an unresolved Oedipal complex; children who steal have not resolved their early psychosexual stage of anality: they must collect and hoard objects, just as they retained their feces; boys who steal cars for joyriding use the car as the vagina; the juvenile gang is the primal hoard, and their exploits are to steal the "fires" of others and then to urinate on them. One could go on and on. Obviously, these highly symbolic translations are difficult to test empirically. They do offer, however, a very rich source of explanation of forms of delinquency with a specificity which few other theories are able to match.

Identity Theories

The major identity theory used to explain delinquency has been that of Erikson, which generally took as its starting point the Freudian theory of psychosexual development.[22] Erikson extended the Freudian theory into a broad cultural frame of reference, downplaying its more fixed aspects (i.e., instincts) and emphasizing the role of society and culture in the individual's development of an ego identity. This approach also improved upon the previous mechanical conceptions of ego function. For Erikson, although sexuality during adolescence was important mainly in terms of the abrupt change it brought on for the adolescent, the boy's main problem becomes one of maintaining continuity in his development: he must at this stage make a conscious attempt to make the future a part of his life's plan. But to do this, he must have developed a clear sexual identity of himself at an earlier stage. If this has not been reached, a serious identity crisis may arise, typified by "role diffusion" or an acute lack of ability to decide upon the role he should play in society. The forms of deviance which may result, according to Erikson, are "delinquency and psychosis." These are, however, too general; and from the description he gives of role diffusion, one can easily infer that the types of delinquency which may result would be those of the "retreatist" behavior, e.g., taking drugs, running away from home, leading an uncommitted "hippie" life, or heavy solitary drinking leading to alcoholism. However, Erikson notes that the peer group is crucial at this stage, since the adolescent may take refuge in the gang and thereby allow the gang with its rigid rules and intolerance of "differences" to provide him with an identity.

This, and other observations of adolescent life, have led researchers to study the peer group or gang as a generator of delinquency, which we will consider in the following section.

Other identity theories have become important in this area, especially those concerned with distorted perceptions of self and with self-esteem. Research has shown generally that delinquents have a rather low opinion of themselves, or low self-esteem, and that they often distort both explanations of their own specific behaviors and have overall distorted images of themselves.[23] A link has often been made between the distorted images that blacks have had of themselves (i.e., the attempt to see themselves as "white" because of the dominance of the while culture) and the subsequent self-hatred and interpersonal hatred of blacks of each other. Thus, using an essentially political analysis of the relationship between the individual and culture, black power theorists have been able to argue that serious psychological aberrations result, followed by a particular patterning of black delinquency, i.e., a higher rate of personal crime and those crimes heavily perpetuated upon other blacks. Although much of this remains at the level of theory, and sometimes only at the level of polemic, considerable evidence for the process of self-hatred, low self-esteem, and distorted "white" identity in black children has been presented by Robert Coles.[24] In addition, studies of self-esteem in delinquents are often conducted upon those who are incarcerated, so that it is difficult to know whether the low self-esteem existed before the delinquent was processed or whether it has resulted from the incarceration process itself.

Only in a very general sense can this theory explain our three questions. It has often been argued that girls have very low self-esteem—yet they commit much less delinquency. Therefore, the theory would appear unable to explain sex differences in delinquency, though it may be used to explain race differences. Because the theory emphasizes common stages of development along with an individualistic appraisal of personal history, it may be used to explain individual motivations to delinquency, but it is subject to all the criticisms made of psychoanalytic theory. It may explain particular forms of delinquency, such as retreatism, but even here the theory seems much too general.

Theories of Moral Development

Piaget, and others after him, have argued that the moral development of a child is directly related to his cognitive development.[25] We find here, the application of intelligence as a causal factor in moral development (and by implication of delinquent behavior) not as a static, or fixed, entity, as we discussed in the first section, but as a dynamic, changing aspect of individual behavior. Although perhaps this theoretical perspective could just as easily have been discussed under the interpersonal section, we have retained it here since the approach relies heavily on the concept of *stages* through which one must successively pass in order to reach the highest stage. Effective development of intelligence, according to Piaget, depends upon both the physiological makeup of the child, which provides various limits to development at each stage, plus an essential interaction of these physical attributes with the environment (whether physical or social). It is the process of interaction which lays the foundation for the next stage. Thus, if a child cannot manipulate certain objects at a particular age, there will be limitations upon the concepts he will be able to grasp. In addition, embedded in the Piagetian model is the idea of an objective classification of concepts, based largely on a natural scientific assessment of the successive complexities of such key scientific concepts as space, time, quantity, and so on. Theories of moral development which have spun off this approach have therefore also found it necessary to assume some kind of "natural ordering" of moral development. Although some research has found support for the hypothesis that delinquents have a defective moral development compared with nondelinquents, this is about as far as it goes.[26] These theorists have yet to address themselves to the dynamic aspects of why it is moral development that has become defective; whether it is moral development alone or the other aspects of cognitive development which are defective (i.e., "dullness"); and what factors at crucial stages in the child's development may produce defective moral development.[27] At present, the theory is at too general a level and may explain only the factors which may produce a tendency toward defective morals and not why individuals develop in this way. Psychoanalytic theory would suggest that girls develop more quickly through the stages of moral development than do boys, which may explain sex differences in delinquency. However, the little research in this area has shown no differences between the sexes in moral judgment.[28]

"Bottling" Theories

The major work in this area is that on the frustration-aggression hypothesis, which argues that if an individual is thwarted in seeking a goal or reward, frustration results, the natural product of which is aggression. Underlying most of these theories is the assumption that drives of various kinds exist in individuals and must constantly be consummated. Although this approach originated with Freudian theory, it rapidly became an important part of the experimental learning psychology as a result of the early work of Dollard et al.[29] These early works were basically experimental attempts to verify the Freudian postulate of the "damming up" of the libido. Again, this theoretical perspective could just as easily be considered as "interpersonal," but because the origin of cause is seen to reside primarily within the person, we have considered it under this section.

The frustration-aggression hypothesis may be applied to the adolescent delinquent by arguing that many cultural and societal proscriptions are placed before him, so that consummation of drives is not possible: there are strong formal and informal prohibitions upon indulgence in sexual activity of any kind, yet the sex drive is supposedly reaching its zenith at this time. There are strong prohibitions against eating various "rich" foods because of concern for facial acne, etc.; there are strong prohibitions upon mobility (i.e., driving a car) until the adolescent is old enough to get a license; and there are strong prohibitions against leaving school, although the adolescent strives for independence from parents. The list could be extended indefinitely. Thus, this theory is sufficient to explain why delinquent behavior peaks at 16. However, the theory's obvious weakness lies in its lack of specificity. The definition of aggression and the measures of aggression used in much of the research have been extremely fragmented and inconsistent.[30] In addition, it has been shown that many other different types of behaviors may result from frustration, as well as aggression, but there is nothing in the theory itself to suggest what forms the behavior should result. However, influential sociologists have attempted to explicate this relationship.[31] The theory also lacks specificity in defining which drives, or which goals, are important.

Some would argue that girls are frustrated more than boys, since girls have traditionally been kept close to the household longer than boys and have had vocational choices considerably delimited compared with those of boys. If they are more frustrated, this certainly does not show up in the delinquency statistics. It might be argued by women's liberationists that girls have not formerly realized their restricted roles in society, so they are not frustrated at adolescence but rather are pleased to continue a dependent relationship within the family. However, the newly liberated image of women in society is encouraging women to seek more goals, but their "imprisonment in the family" will thwart their satisfaction of such goals and delinquency may result. In this case, one would predict the peaking of the rate of female delinquency to be much later than for boys.

Finally, the theory seems unable to explain individual motivations to delinquency, although it has been reformulated to explain group motivations to delinquency.[32] One must reformulate the theory into one that takes into account the individual's perceptions of his own drives or affect, his perceptions of external goals, and of what (to him) is thwarting the attainment of these goals. However, once one begins such analysis, the theory becomes no longer a frustration and aggression theory but rather a different model for examining personal causation. This model is currently termed *attribution theory*, with which we will deal in the following section.

Interpersonal Theories

Social Learning Theories

Social learning theories can be thought of as being middle of the road in the nature/nurture dichotomy. They reject the notion that man's behavior is the result of inner drives or instincts operating below the level of consciousness. On the other hand, they reject the opposite extreme of man as a passive creature acted upon by the external conditions surrounding him. Thus, behavior is seen not simply as a result of the two extreme independent influences, the individual and the environment, but rather it is formed in the interaction of these factors.[33]

Various systems are utilized to explain how behavior is learned, regulated, and maintained.

Stimulus Control: To function effectively an individual must have an idea of the possible consequences of a course of action he is contemplating. This information is transmitted to the person in the form of environmental stimuli, verbal communication, or knowledge of past events and their outcomes. Knowing that a certain course of action will be punished tends to inhibit the person from acting in that manner.

Reinforcement Control: Once an individual decides to act in a certain manner, he waits to see what consequences follow. Future action will be fashioned by the degree to which the individual's clues about the environment were accurate. Behavior which is positively reinforced will be repeated. While reinforcement is commonly envisioned as material gains, it also includes symbolic reinforcement, praise from others, or a feeling of accomplishment in one's self.

Cognitive Control: Cognitive control refers to one's ability to judge an act's consequences without ever performing that act. In this way, social learning becomes more than trying out courses of action and suffering the consequences. Most of the alternatives are worked out symbolically before ventured.

Modeling: Modeling is the process whereby an individual gains new behavior patterns and modifies existing ones by observing others whom are regarded as influential models. Learning through modeling requires that the individual view the other person as a model. In this way the individual is not at the mercy of all the influences surrounding him. He discriminates as to which influences will be important. It is probable that those with whom the individual associates most frequently will be seen as models. In this way, individuals who associate with people displaying delinquent modes of behavior will incorporate these patterns of behavior into their repertoire. In general, this area is probably the most systematically and thoroughly researched approach to the study of aggression in juveniles, and much of the theory is well substantiated empirically.

One may explain sex differences quite easily by postulating that boys learn aggressive behavior from the male role models of their fathers and those represented on television. This approach does not seem able to explain the peaking of delinquency rates at age 16, however, unless hooked into an additional theory which emphasizes adolescent development in relation to influential role models. Forms of delinquency may perhaps be learned through watching television, but generally the research on the effects of television upon the learning of aggression has been unable to resolve the contradiction between watching violence as letting off steam and watching violence as a stimulus to aggression.[34]

Individual motivation may easily be explained post facto by pointing to the patterns of the individual's social learning history.

Family Dynamics

The family has for many years been assumed to play a major role in socializing a child. Research has suggested that those who feel a strong attachment to their parents are more likely to feel bound to conform to the norms of society, and thus they commit less delinquent acts.[35] This holds irrespective of the parents' views of the conventional rules of society. However, in contrast to psychoanalytic theory, it has recently been argued that attachment to either parent has similar effects in preventing delinquency—just so long as a strong attachment is maintained.

Historically, a number of factors have been studied as causing inadequate child-parent attachment and, thus, inadequate socialization of the child, leading to delinquent activity. As was mentioned in a previous section, broken homes have often been regarded as a factor leading to delinquency. Research on the subject suggests that the relationship is not quite that simple. In fact, it has generally been found that it is various kinds of family discord which are related to delinquency, not broken homes per se.[36] In addition, some limited research has also linked certain familial breakdowns with specific types of delinquency, such as homosexuality, sociopathy, and aggression.[37]

Discipline in the parent-child relationship has been related to a child's tendency to criminality. The important consideration is not whether the discipline is punitive or love-oriented, but the consistency of its application. Punishment meted out in a random or arbitrary fashion has been correlated with all crime except traffic violations.[38]

In explaining the differential rates of delinquency, this approach seems to have some difficulty. Since it has never been shown that girls experience families in less discord than boys, it is difficult to see just how the family discord hypothesis can be used to explain the sex differences in delinquency rates. It seems necessary to superimpose a theory about the quality of family relationships, as does either social learning theory or psychoanalysis, before the family discord hypothesis can be used to explain differential rates. Indeed, it might also be argued that girls display a stronger attachment to home and to school and, thus, have a lower tendency to delinquency, but this hypothesis has yet to be researched.

Individual motivations to deviance might be explained by pointing to common maladjusted patterns of family relationships, but it is difficult to apply this approach to individual cases.[39]

Attribution Theory

Recent developments in social psychology have placed emphasis upon the locus of cause of the individual's behavior as perceived by that individual and, in addition, as perceived by others.[40] Although no formal application of this theory has been made to delinquency, one may interpret some existing theories within this framework. A number of theorists and researchers have pointed to the misperceptions of self and others which delinquents hold.[41] Since, as we have seen, the peer group is often considered an extremely important mechanism through which the adolescent may achieve identity, the mutual perceptions between the peer group and the delinquent would seem to be crucial. So far, no specific research has been conducted to investigate the delinquent's perception of the "locus of cause" of his own behavior, although it is easy to interpret some research which suggests that delinquents will "explain away" their delinquent behavior by using "neutralizations" or "rationalizations" (i.e., "other people do it"; or "why me"; or today more commonly in the rhetoric, "it's the political oppression and economic conditions that made me do it").[42] Research on the role of this aspect of interpersonal perception with the delinquent group in producing delinquency is inconclusive, mainly because it is not clear whether in fact delinquent individuals share the same perceptions of (a) themselves compared with the delinquent group, (b) each other, or (c) the dominant adult cultural values.[43] Nor is it clear whether attachment to the peer group promotes or prevents delinquent activity.[44]

Another recent field of research in social psychology may also have special application to the explanation of gang delinquency. This is the study of "risky shift."[45] A typical experiment is to provide an individual with a series of choices, each graded according to risk. It has been consistently found that individuals will choose a much riskier option after they have discussed the options with a group, rather than if they made the decision on their own.

An original explanation for the falling off of delinquent behavior after 16 is provided by one researcher within this model. The argument is that adolescents hold to conventional values but perceive their friends as belonging to a delinquent subculture. To gain approval they strive toward this fictitious peer-group value system. It is only in later adolescence when they form closer relationships with people that they realize their error. Thus, they no longer feel it necessary to perform delinquent acts.

Differential attributions as to the perceived causes of behavior by family members also provide a rich field for the study of incipient delinquency. However, no substantial research has yet been conducted in this area, although the move toward family therapy for delinquents may anticipate such research.[46] Although not specifically designed according to attribution theory, a classification system based entirely upon the delinquent's perception of self and others and the causes of his behavior has been developed which also offers specific treatment alternatives.[47]

Prevention Strategies

Although we will suggest some treatment measures that are preventive in the sense that hopefully they prevent further commission of delinquent acts, we see this only as a "last resort" measure or a preventive measure which is most often "too late." We will therefore concentrate more upon general measures that may be applied to prevent delinquency before it occurs. Naturally, such an approach virtually rules out the serious considerations of "clinical" or "psychiatric" treatment, since it would require massive treatment of many individuals only a few of whom would be likely to turn out delinquent—assuming that our predictive measures are still only very rough. In addition, much of these intrapersonal theories, if they are to be used for treatment or prevention, require the intervention by an outsider into the family of the potential delinquent. This also, as a large program, seems infeasible in our society in terms of cost, politics, and ethics.

Unchanging Intrapersonal States

Although it was implied in the survey of these theories that these states were largely unchangeable by the individual on his own, much research has suggested that basic "instincts" of sex and aggression may indeed be controlled by various drugs.[48] However, there are two very serious criticisms of such a prevention strategy. First, the range of behaviors controlled by these drives is extremely broad, when only a small aspect of such behaviors might be delinquent. Thus, if these drugs are to be used, they should be used only upon the most serious, clearly identifiable cases, where a large portion of the individual's behavior is indeed of a delinquent character. Second, side effects from long-term use have not yet been established. However, it should be said that in cases where prolonged incarceration is the only possible disposition for a juvenile (and this must surely be an extremely rare case), one might argue that the use of such drugs might be more humane and less costly to society if the individual could be treated in the community.

In our opinion, the role of fixed intelligence as a causal factor in delinquency should be reevaluated, especially as it relates to poor school performance, which in turn is clearly related to delinquency. A number of policy implications are raised by this theory. If intelligence is fixed, dull children will not reach the levels of school performance of normal children. Since, in theory at least, special educational services have been provided in schools for failing children for some years now without appreciable statistical effects, strong consideration should be given to lowering the school leaving age. This could be achieved in three ways. First, the leaving age could be arbitrarily lowered for all children by a margin which would need to be decided upon according to the comparative incidence of failure in the upper school years. Second, children, regardless of age, if they have not progressed appreciably in, say, any two-year period, could be excused from school attendance. Understandably, other community resources and institutions may be necessary to take the place of the school for these children, and this would need to be researched; viable alternatives to schooling need to be developed. And third, a more radical policy might be to abolish compulsory education. However, this may not be warranted at this stage, since only a small fraction of children become delinquents. Naturally, other factors besides the incidence of delinquency would need to be considered for such a radical move.

Finally, one further recommendation of what *not* to do comes from these studies. It is clear that the male/female difference in aggressive behavior has a strong physiological base;[49] and although it has been shown that variation in social environment may affect this physical base, we should nevertheless be wary of introducing social programs to change sex role behaviors. Such changes, if they are to occur, it seems to us, will occur over a long, evolutionary process.

Changing Intrapersonal Factors

Given the structure and values of the society we live in, there is little one can do as a general preventive mechanism within the framework of these theories. There are two main reasons for this. First, the crucial variables involved are clearly those which lie within the domain of the family, the dynamics of which administrators, officials, and policymakers can do very little to affect. Second, the effectiveness of treatment programs that have used such assumptions about the cause of delinquency have been notoriously unsuccessful.[50] Some considerations may be of use, however.

1. Early detection of potential delinquents, using the factors found predictive of delinquency by these studies, could be used to identify those children who could be excused from school at an early age, provided they were also not showing progress in school.

2. Counseling programs, instead of being provided by a school counselor, should be developed within the community and conducted along the lines of family therapy, rather than treating individual delinquents.

Since the "bottling" theories have been applied without success (e.g., channeling the adolescent's sex drive into sport), there seems little point in advancing such programs. However, the theory underlying the notion of moral development suggests that children should be provided with structured experiences with other children so that they can develop the concepts necessary for healthy intellectual development. By this view, intelligence is seen as a changing process rather than a fixed state, so that should the earlier recommendations be adopted concerning exclusion from school of children who fail to progress, constant review of such cases would be strongly recommended.

Interpersonal Theories

Two important points may be taken from the social learning approach. First, children learn to inhibit performance of aggression by either punishment or reward (administered directly or to a model); and second and most important, they must recognize the reasons or justifications for this process. This may be interpreted to mean that the authority of the administrator of rewards and punishments must be seen as legitimate. If it is not, then punishments and rewards will be fruitless.

Since we cannot do much about the authority of parents in the family because this is generally a private domain insulated from outside prevention programs, the school presents itself as the logical place to develop this approach. The permissive or "free school" era has militated against the teacher's role of authority in the school. In fact, the introduction of school security guards has spit away completely the teacher's authority functions. Therefore, steps should be taken to strengthen the authority structure of the school. This may be done in several ways, although once again, we perceive a serious need for research in this area:

1. The use of separate disciplinary "police" or guards with quasi-police function in schools should be discouraged. All authority should rest with the teachers.

2. Present teaching methods which downplay the role of the teacher's authority over knowledge, as well as discipline, should be abolished.

3. A clear hierarchy of authority among the teachers of a school should be outlined, and the children should be clearly appraised of this.

4. The system of punishments and rewards for various delinquent or "anti-school" behaviors should be clearly and specifically laid out, so that children can calculate what the costs and/or gains of delinquent behavior will be.

5. Data on the actual administration of punishments (no names) and rewards should be made available to students so that they may be made aware of the certainty of punishments and/or rewards.

6. The introduction of ceremonial school functions which enhance the teachers' authority may be worthwhile.

7. This may also imply a certain insulation of the teacher from the student, on the grounds that "familiarity breeds contempt." Essentially, the authority of the teacher needs to be reestablished.[51]

Some aspects of attribution theory may be used as techniques in the school setting. Since it seems likely that adolescents in general and delinquents in particular are confused about perceptions of both their own and others' behavior, periodic sessions could be conducted in which students would attempt to "guess" other students' values, practices, etc. A variety of "party games" could be invented with a view to providing the students with more feedback about interpersonal values.

Since the peer group may be a major factor in "risky shift" of adolescents to delinquent behavior, ways of defusing this group process could be developed. Strategies might involve:

1. Develop a "mapping" of the peer group composition of the school. This could be done easily by the use of sociometric techniques.

2. Relate the number of antischool incidents to the membership of the various peer groups; i.e., this is on the assumption that not all peer groups are delinquency-prone.

3. Break up the predelinquent groups.

Of course, these procedures relate only to what could be done within the school. As is well established, of course, much delinquency occurs out of school or by dropouts. This is why viable community alternatives must be developed at the same time as the strategies within schools are put into effect. Recent reports suggest, however, that delinquency within schools is dramatically increasing.

Conclusions

1. Prevention strategy should be leveled toward the school, since this is the only social institution that has, in theory, near total control of children for

at least 5 to 6 hours a day, and since unhappy school experience appears to be a central causal factor in delinquency.

2. A major strategy should be to reduce the proportion of school failures, and this may best be achieved by excluding seriously failing children from school and/or reducing the school leaving age.[52]

3. Research is urgently needed into viable community alternatives to schooling.

4. Strategies should be developed for use within the school to (1) reestablish the teacher's role as authority figure and (2) increase the accuracy of students' perceptions of themselves and other's behavior.

5. Radical measures, such as the use of drugs to control behavior, should only be used when the ill effects of their use would be outweighed by the ill effects of prolonged incarceration.

6. If "treatment" of delinquents is to be provided, it should be along the lines of family therapy.

7. As for the future development of psychological theories, it is obvious that a multifaceted, integrated model should emerge from the present fractured, and often conflicting, landscape. Theories, as models of reality, are limited in time, and, essentially, the *better* they are, the *sooner* they are replaced by other, more comprehensive constructs. Disciplinary divisions are crumbling, and this should carry over in the psychological approach to crime and deviance. The hard tests of usefulness and applicability will also shorten the life expectancy of some of our most ambitious theoretical explanations. The future lies, as in other fields, in the unity of science.

Notes

1. T. Hirschi, *The Causes of Delinquency*, Berkeley: Univ. of California Press, 1969, p. 47. In general, the controversy over definition of delinquency between "official" as against "self-report" is only marginal in relation to psychological theories, since most have traditionally assumed that any antisocial behavior is potentially delinquent and often these terms have been equated. The distinction does become important in one area, where it is hypothesized that "only the dumb ones get caught." This is considered below.

2. These studies have all been seriously criticized for their methodology, especially the matching delinquent-nondelinquent design. However, the findings of three studies have been very consistent. See W.H. Sheldon, *Varieties of Delinquent Youth*, New York: Harper & Brothers, 1969; J.B. Cortes and F.M. Gatti, *Delinquency and Crime: A Biopsychosocial Approach*, New York: Seminar Press, 1973; and S. Glueck and E. Glueck, *Physique and Delinquency*, New York: Harper & Brothers, 1956. On the other hand, these findings were not supported by the extensive multifactorial study of F. Ferracuti and S. Dinitz, *"Analisi Multifattoriale Della Delinquenza Minorile,"* Rassegna dell'Arma dei Carabinieri, 1975, 1:1-43.

3. S. Shah, "Biological and Psychophysiological Factors in Criminality," in D. Glaser (ed.), *Handbook of Criminology*, New York: Rand McNally, 1974, pp. 134-139. The main flaw in many of these studies was the failure to control for excessive height, which appears to be closely related to existence of the XYY chromosome.

4. H.J. Eysenck, *Crime and Personality*, Boston: Houghton Mifflin, 1964. This work has led to suggestions that there is a constitutional predisposition to psychopathy. In general, the findings of two major series of research under-takings have suggested that sociopaths are able to learn as well as anyone else under positive reinforcement, but they show a marked inability to learn under conditions of pain avoidance. See D.T. Lykken, "A Study of Anxiety in the Sociopathic Personality," *Journal of Abnormal and Social Psychology*, 1957, 55:6-10; S. Schecter and B. Latane, "Crime, Cognition and the Autonomic Nervous System," in D. Levine (ed.), *Nebraska Symposium on Motivation*, Lincoln: Univ. of Nebrasks Press, 1964.

5. Early studies assumed a simple one-to-one relationship between feeble-mindedness and delinquency. See, for example, E. Goring, *The English Convict*, Mont Clair, New Jersey: Patterson Smith Reprint, 1972 (first published in 1913); H.H. Goddard, *Feeble Mindedness: Its Causes and Consequences*, New York: Macmillan, 1914. Hirschi and Hindelang now argue that much of the empirical evidence in support of intelligence as a causal factor in delinquency has been ignored by modern researchers in favor of the more popular causal factors of race and social class. They demonstrate that intelligence is at least as equally an important variable in explaining delinquency as are the usual sociological variables. They conclude, however, that the relationship is not direct, but essentially through poor school performance, which in turn produces a lack of attachment to school, and thus is explained by Hirschi's control theory. See Hirschi and Hindelang, "Intelligence and Delinquency: A Revisionist Review," unpublished paper, School of Criminal Justice, 1975. Some of the many studies which have found a relationship between low intelligence and official delin-quency are: W. Reckless and A.L. Rhodes, "The Distribution of Juvenile Delinquency in the Social Class Structure," *American Sociological Review* 26 (October 1961):720-732; T. Hirschi, *The Causes of Delinquency*; M.E. Wolfgang, R. Figlio, and T. Sellin, *Delinquency in a Birth Cohort*, Chicago: Univ. of Chicago Press, 1972; D.J. West, *Who Becomes Delinquent?* London: Heinemann, 1973; J. Short and F. Strodbeck, *Group Process and Gang Delinquency*, Chicago: Univ. of Chicago Press, 1965; J. Toby and M. Toby, "Low School Status as a Predisposing Factor in Subcultural Delinquency," New Brunswick, N.J.: Rutger's Univ., (mimeographed). Hirschi and Hindelang report that they could locate no studies which presented counterresults.

6. This point is the bone of much argument at present. This proportion of intelligence said to be inherited was first put forward by Burt, and the evidence was reviewed in an article by him in 1966: "The Genetic Determination of

Differences in Intelligence: A Study of Monozygotic Twins Reared Together and Apart," *British Journal of Psychology* 57 (1966), 1/2:137-153. The extensive research on twins studies and the methodologically strong work of A.R. Jensen since his landmark piece, "Environment, Heridity, and Intelligence," *Harvard Educational Review*, reprint series no. 2 (June 1969) add strong support to Burt's claim.

7. This evidence is again advanced by Hirschi and Hindelang, "Intelligence and Delinquency," 1975, in a reanalysis of Hirschi's Contra Costa data. They point out that this hypothesis presumes that intelligence has a direct effect on delinquency. When the intervening variables were removed from intelligence and delinquency in the Wolfgang, et al. study, *Delinquency in a Birth Cohort*, the effects of intelligence disappeared. Similarly, self-report studies have also found a weaker though significant relationship between intelligence and delinquency; see West, *Who Becomes Delinquent?*

8. It is, of course, often argued that psychopathy is a residual category, inconsistently defined by clinicians. See, for example, E.H. Sutherland and D.R. Cressey, *Principles of Criminology*, 7th ed., Philadelphia: J.B. Lippincott, Co., 1966.

9. Most of this evidence comes from research on infrahuman species. See R.W. Goy, "Reproduction Behavior in Mammals," in C.W. Lloyd (ed.), *Human Reproduction and Sexual Behavior*, Philadelphia: Lea and Febiger, 1964; and J.A. Gray, "Sex Differences in Emotional Behavior in Mammals, Including Man: Endocrine Bases." *Acta Psychologica* 35 (1971):29-46. In addition, administration of estrogen (female hormone) to men generally leads to a rapid decrease in sexual drive and potency. R.V. Norris and C.W. Lloyd, "Psychosexual Effects of Hormone Therapy," *Medical Aspects of Human Sexuality* (1971), 5(9):129-146.

10. Evidence for this is provided by: R.L. Conner, and S. Levine, "Hormonal Influences on Aggressive Behavior," in S. Garattini and E.B. Sigg (eds.), *Aggressive Behavior*, New York: Wiley, 1969; and J. Money, "Influence of Hormones on Psychosexual Differentiation," *Medical Aspects of Human Sexuality* (1968), 2(11):32-42.

11. It is also important to note, however, that hormone levels may be affected considerably by environmental factors; see, for example, H.F. Harlow, and M.K. Harlow, "Developmental Aspects of Emotional Behavior," in P. Black (ed.), *Physiological Correlates of Emotion*, New York: Academic Press.

12. The basic work on releasing or triggering mechanisms has been conducted by K. Lorenz, *On Aggression*, New York: Harcourt, Brace, 1966; and on the "territorial imperative," R.A. Ardrey, *African Genesis*, New York: Atheneum, 1963. They have, however, been extensively criticized by various theorists on the grounds that they have indulged in extreme anthropomorphism; see, for example, J.P. Scott, *Aggression*, Chicago: Univ. of Chicago Press, 1958; and J.T. Tedeschi, R.B. Smith, and R.C. Brown, "A Reinterpretation of Research on Aggression," *Psychological Bulletin*, in press.

13. This formulation of drive or instinct theory is discussed below under Intrapersonal Factors.

14. G.S. Hall, *Adolescence*, Vol. 2, New York: Appleton, 1916.

15. For a general review of this approach, see: K. Friedlander, *The Psychoanalytic Approach to Juvenile Delinquency*, New York: International Univ. Press, 1947.

16. This doctrine has been severely questioned both by orthodox and "radical" psychoanalytical theorists; see J.B. Miller, *Psychoanalysis and Women*, New York: Pelican, 1973.

17. The most extensive treatment of the role of defective ego is provided by F. Redl and D. Wineman, *The Aggressive Child*, Glencoe: The Free Press, 1952. Redl treats the ego largely as a mechanism, as do most Freudians, including Anna Freud ("The mechanism of defense"), although he does consider the "synthetic" role of ego function.

18. Although this syndrome was emphasized by T. Parsons and R.F. Bales, *Family, Socialization and Interaction Process*, Glencoe: The Free Press, 1955, in relation to American culture, it has been found especially relevant to Mexican families. See A. Aramoni, *Psicoanalisis de la Dinamica de un Pueblo, Mexico, Tierra de Hombres*. Mexico: B. Costa-Amie, Editorial, 1965; and E. Fromm and M. Maccoby, *Social Character in a Mexican Village*, Englewood Cliffs, New Jersey: Prentice-Hall, 1970.

19. See R.J. Simon, "Women and Crime," *Annals of the American Academy of Political and Social Science*, January 1976, in press. See, also, the contribution of Professor Simon to this volume.

20. See M.R. Haskell and L. Yablonsky, *Juvenile Delinquency*, Chicago: Rand McNally, 1974, pp. 95-101, for a review and comparison of "broken home" studies in relation to sex.

21. For example, S. Glueck and E. Glueck, *Predicting Delinquency and Crime*, Harvard Univ. Press, 1959; D.R. Peterson and W.C. Becker, "Family Interaction in Delinquency," in H.C. Quay (ed.), *Juvenile Delinquency: Research and Theory*, Princeton, New Jersey: Van Nostrand, 1965; W. Slocum and C.C. Stone, "Family Culture Patterns and Delinquent-Type Behavior," *Marriage and Family Living* 25, (1963):202-208; R.G. Andry, *Delinquency and Parental Pathology*, revised edition, London: Staples Press, 1971; F.I. Nye, *Family Relationships and Delinquent Behavior*, New York: Wiley, 1958. All these studies support the psychoanalytic emphasis upon early childhood experience within the family as being closely related to later delinquency. Within female samples, similar findings have been made: C.E. Climent, A. Rollins, F. Ervin, and R. Plutchik, "Epidemiological Studies of Women Prisoners: Medical and Psychiatric Variables Related to Violent Behavior," *American Journal of Psychiatry* (Sept. 1973), 130(9):985-990.

22. E.H. Erikson, *Childhood and Society*, New York: W.W. Norton, 1950.

23. See, for example, W.C. Reckless, S. Dinitz, and B. Kay, "The Self-Com-

ponent in Potential Delinquency and Potential Non-Delinquency," *American Sociological Review* 22, (October 1957):566-570.

24. See R. Coles, *Children in Crisis,* Boston: Little, Brown and Co., 1964. The major theoretical statement is that of Franz Fanon in *The Wretched of the Earth,* New York: Grove Press, 1968. It has also been considered as an explanation for the intracultural nature of black crime by F. Ferracuti and G.R. Newman, "Assaultive Offenses," in D. Glaser, (ed.), *Handbook of Criminology,* p. 197; and J. Davis, "Blacks, Crime and American Culture," in G. Newman (ed.), *Crime and Justice in the American Republic, 1776-1976,* Annals of the American Academy of Political and Social Science, 1976.

25. J. Piaget, *The Moral Judgment of the Child,* New York: The Free Press, 1965; and L. Kohlberg and E. Turiel (eds.), *Research in Moralization: The Cognitive Developmental Approach,* New York: Holt, Rinehart and Winston, 1972.

26. See E.M. Fodor, "Delinquency and Susceptibility to Social Influence Among Adolescents as a Function of Level of Moral Development," *Journal of Social Psychology* (1972), 86:257-260; and in relation to the positive relationship between conformity and moral development, H.D. Saltzstein, R.M. Diamond, and M. Belenky, "Moral Judgment Level and Conformity Behavior," *Developmental Psychology* (1972), 7:327-336.

27. Some research has shown that early childhood experience may affect moral development; M.L. Hoffman, "Father Absence and Conscience Development," *Developmental Psychology* (1971), 4:400-406.

28. See C.B. Keasey, "The Lack of Sex Differences in the Moral Judgments of Pre-adolescents," *Journal of Social Psychology* (1972), 86:157-158.

29. J. Dollard, L.W. Doob, N.E. Miller, O.H. Mowrer, R.R. Sears, C.S. Ford, C.I. Horland, and R.T. Sollenberger, *Frustration and Aggression,* New Haven: Yale Univ. Press, 1939. In general, the theory has been largely discounted, or is seen as at least a gross oversimplification; see M.E. Wolfgang and F. Ferracuti, *The Subculture of Violence,* London: Methuen, 1967 for a balanced review of the current status of this theory.

30. See Tedeschi, Smith, and Brown, "A Reinterpretation of Research on Aggression."

31. Merton's theory of anomie assumes essentially a "bottling" theory, as does Cloward and Ohlin's opportunity theory; see Ferracuti and Newman, "Assaultive Offenses," p. 188. However, empirical tests of the frustration-aggression hypothesis in relation to homicide have produced equivocal results. See A.F. Henry and J.F. Short, *Suicide and Homicide,* Glencoe: The Free Press, 1954; and S. Palmer, *A Study of Murder,* New York: Crowell, 1960.

32. For example, R.K. Merton, *Social Theory and Social Structure,* New York: The Free Press, 1968; and R.A. Cloward and L.E. Ohlin, *Delinquency and Opportunity,* New York: The Free Press, 1960.

33. "Behavior partly creates the environment and the resultant environ-

ment, in turn, influences the behavior," A. Bandura, *Aggression*, New Jersey: Prentice-Hall, 1973, p. 43. Behavior is seen as a *process*, similar to that described by George H. Mead (*Mind, Self and Society*, Illinois: Oniv. of Chicago Press, 1934), whereby the person acts, which incurs a reaction from the environment and in turn adjusts to it. By this process, consistent behavior patterns are acquired.

34. It is reasonably established that children do learn aggressive response repertoires from watching television, as shown in the several studies reviewed by Bandura, *Aggression*, pp. 85-86 and 139-148. However, the question as to whether it may lead to actual aggressive behavior is unresolved.

35. This theory has been put forward and tested in various forms, but the most cogent of these is T. Hirschi, *The Causes of Delinquency*, 1969.

36. See W. McCord, J. McCord, and I. Zola, *Origins of Crime: A New Evaluation of the Cambridge-Somerville Youth Study*, New York: Columbia University Press, 1959, found that the existence of tension and intrafamily quarreling, irrespective of whether it was a broken home, was seen as of primary importance. The absence of the father has also been correlated to high rates of delinquency. W.C. Kvaraceus, *Delinquent Behavior: Culture and the Individual*, Washington, D.C.: National Education Association, 1959, concluded that the high levels of aggression in lower-class males was a result of anxiety due to role anxiety caused by inadequate male role models. Again McCord, McCord, and Zola, *Origins of Crime*, found that the detrimental effects of no male model could be offset by a strong relationship with the mother that includes love and consistent discipline.

37. On sociopathy, see L.E. Robins, *Deviant Children Grown Up*, Baltimore: Williams and Wilkins, 1966; on homosexuality, see B. Glueck, "An Evaluation of the Homosexual Offender," *Minnesota Law Review*, (1957):41; and on aggression, see M.E. Wolfgang and F. Ferracuti, *The Subculture of Violence*, for an extensive review of these studies. See also, S. Steinmetz and M.A. Straus, *Violence in the Family*, New York: Dodd, Mead and Co., 1974.

38. These studies were reviewed in note 20 above.

39. See, for example, D.H. Stott, *Thirty-Three Troublesome Children*, Harpenden, Herts: National Childrens Home, 1964.

40. Redl and Wineman, *The Aggressive Child*, have described the highly selective process of perception by which the aggressive child perceives himself and others. Anna Freud's "mechanisms of defense" are essentially a description of the selective modes which individuals use to perceive themselves and others.

41. See E.E. Jones, D.E. Kanonsen, H.H. Lelley, R.E. Nisbett, S. Valins, and B. Weiner, *Attribution: Perceiving the Causes of Behavior*, Morristown: General Learning Press, 1971.

42. The work of D. Matza, *Delinquency and Drift*, New York: Wiley, 1964, has investigated this area.

43. Matza, *Delinquency and Drift*, has hypothesized that adolescents view

their own acts as wrong and mistakenly think that the delinquent group views the acts approvingly, when all the time they do not. Hindelang has conducted research which has discounted this hypothesis; see M. Hindelang, "Moral Evaluation of Illegal Behavior," *Social Problems*, 1973.

44. Hirschi, *The Causes of Delinquency*, argues that any form of attachment promotes the control of delinquency. Most sociological theories of delinquent gangs and subcultures hypothesize the opposite view.

45. See Dion, Baron, and Miller in L. Berkowitz (ed.), *Advances in Experimental Social Psychology*, Vol. 5, New York: Academic Press, 1970, pp. 306-372.

46. See, for example, the application of systems theory to the study of the family in S. Minuchin, *Families and Family Therapy*, Cambridge, Mass.: Harvard Univ. Press, 1974. The work of R.D. Laring has also looked at this problem, although from a somewhat narrow perspective.

47. M.Q. Warren, "Classification of Offenders as an Aid to Efficient Management and Effective Treatment," *J. Criminal Law, Criminology and Police Science* (1971), 62(2):239-258.

48. For a review of these studies, see Shah, "Biological and Psychophysiological Factors."

49. Ibid.

50. L.T. Wilkins, *The Evaluation of Penal Measures*, New York: Random House, 1969.

51. The role of authority in the school deserves much further study. Its current state of flux most likely contributes considerably to problem behavior in the schools, and possibly to recent increases in school violence and vandalism. For a discussion of authority in the school, see G.R. Newman and L.T. Wilkins, "Sources of Deviance in the Schooling Process," *International Review of Education* (1974), 20/3:306-321. The Europeans have long been aware of the possible crucial roles of the school in preventing delinquency: *The Role of the School in Prevention of Juvenile Delinquency*, Council of Europe, Strasbourg, 1972.

52. This, and related suggestions, are not as radical as they sound. In various forms, this policy has prevailed in parts of Europe for some time. See Tunley and Roul, *Kids, Crime and Chaos: A World Report on Juvenile Delinquency*, Scranton, Pennsylvania: Harper & Row, 1962. One might also note that, in general, the delinquency rate in Europe has been lower than that in the United States.

10 Temporal Experience and the Criminal

Simha F. Landau

I. Introduction

Man has always had a feeling that there is a basic difference between the dimension of time and the physical dimensions which he encounters in his daily life. On the one hand there are many linguistic examples dealing with time as if it were a concrete object: time you can save and waste, gain or lose, borrow or invest. Sometimes we work under "pressure of time," etc. On the other hand, time has two unique qualities that differentiate it from other physical objects:

1. Time is unidirectional: it moves only in one direction and is irreversible.
2. Time units, unlike other concrete objects, cannot exist alongside each other.

For philosophers time has always provided a challenge. Among the problems that have occupied them especially are the definition of the concept of time (Aristotle, 1968; Efron, 1967; St. Augustine, 1968) as well as the problem of dividing time into past, present, and future (Feld, 1967; Findlay, 1968; McTaggart, 1968; and others).

From the behavioral point of view, the dimension of time is of great importance in that a proper sense of orientation on this dimension is one of the most important prerequisites for an individual's adjustment to his surroundings. This is particularly true in Western society, which puts special emphasis on such qualities as punctuality, long-range future planning, self-control, and preference for delayed greater rewards over immediate smaller ones.

Despite the importance of this topic, it has been relatively neglected by researchers and scholars in the behavioral sciences. One of the significant expressions of the recognition of the dimension of time was the organization of a special symposium on psychological problems of time and space perception at the 18th International Congress of Psychology in Moscow in 1966. One year later, the New York Academy of Sciences organized a special meeting devoted entirely to various topics related to time. On the same occasion, the International Society for Research on Time was founded (Fisher, 1967).

In the present framework I shall concentrate on those studies on the dimension of time which are relevant to criminological research and practice. My main aim is to analyze the process of institutionalization and to demonstrate the effects of imprisonment on various aspects of the temporal experience of inmates.

129

II. The Delinquent and His Time Perception

The Delinquent and the Psychopath: Some
Personality Characteristics

A number of psychologists and psychiatrists have developed several concepts through which they describe the personality of the delinquent. Friedlander (1947), representing the psychoanalytic approach, talks about the "antisocial character," describing him as a person with a strong drive for immediate satisfaction of his impulses without consideration of the external circumstances and future consequences. This defect is caused, according to her approach, by an inadequate transition from the pleasure principle to the reality principle. Friedlander mentions three main factors as contributing to the structure of the "antisocial character": (1) strong instinctual impulses that have not undergone any sublimation; (2) a weak ego; and (3) lack of independence of the superego. Redl and Wineman (1951) also connect delinquent behavior with an "ego defect," which among other things is characterized by the inability to delay immediate gratification.

A concept that has been used widely among psychologists and psychiatrists dealing with the problem of delinquency is the "psychopath." The psychopath is viewed by most investigators as antisocial, impulsive, lacking in guilt feelings, aggressive, unable to initiate and maintain close interpersonal relationships, and lacking in anxiety. Since the fifties, there has been a considerable increase in the scientific research conducted in this area. Many studies on psychopathy have used delinquents (defined on a legal basis) and not subjects diagnosed as psychopaths. However, it should be emphasized that these two concepts—of the psychopath and the delinquent—are far from being identical or interchangeable.

Wright (1971) arrives at a typology of three main types of delinquent: (1) the neurotic delinquent; (2) the unsocialized, aggressive delinquent; and (3) the pseudosocial delinquent. According to Wright:

Unsocialized, aggressive delinquents have sometimes been called psychopathic and this group certainly includes psychopaths. But to equate the two is to dilute the concept of psychopathy unnecessarily. The true psychopath is not so much antisocial as *a*social. His central characteristic is a near total incapacity for affective ties and sympathy for others. *Life is lived exclusively in the present*, and behavior is in no way directed by long-term purposes.(p.91)

However, in spite of this theoretical distinction, even today there is a tendency to infer from studies on delinquents about the characteristics of psychopaths, and vice versa. Frequently there is also no distinction made between the two terms in their linguistic usage. There are several reasons for this. First, to this day there are differences in opinion as to the exact diagnosis of psychopaths. Second, here, as with many other diagnostic groups, one rarely or hardly ever can find in practice a "pure psychopath." In addition, one cannot fail to see the overlap between the behavioral characteristics of the psychopath and those of certain other types of delinquents. The close connection between psychopathy and delinquency is also mentioned by Eysenck (1970), who emphasizes that

... the psychopath presents the riddle of delinquency in a particular pure form, and if we could solve this riddle in relation to the psychopath, we might have a very powerful weapon to use on the problem of delinquency in general. (pp. 55-56)

Two main approaches in studying the etiology of psychopathic behavior are identifiable in recent years. The dominant approach has focused on learning deficiencies in psychopaths and underlying constitutional factors that might account for such deficiencies. This approach stems from frequent observations showing that the psychopath does not learn from experience and that punishment and reward do not have the expected effect on him. The second approach focuses on the temporal orientation, or time perspective, of psychopaths. However, whereas in most studies on learning deficiencies, comparisons were made between psychopaths and nonpsychopaths, in most studies on time perception comparisons were made between delinquents and nondelinquents without trying to accurately identify psychopaths. Hare (1970), in summarizing the research on learning and psychopathy, states:

It appears that psychopaths do not develop conditioned fear responses readily. As a result, they find it difficult to learn responses that are motivated by fear and reinforced by fear reduction. The fact that their behavior appears to be neither motivated nor guided by the possibility of unpleasant consequences, particularly when the temporal relationship between behavior and its consequences is relatively great, might be interpreted in this way. There is some evidence that psychopaths are also less influenced than are normal persons by the relationship between past events and the consequences of their present behavior. (pp. 93-94)

As to the orientation of the psychopath (and the delinquent) on the time dimension, several researchers stress certain basic deficiencies in this respect. Gough (1948) characterizes the psychopath, among other things, as a person overevaluating immediate goals, as opposed to remote or deferred ones, and as having poor judgment and planning in attaining defined goals. Frankenstein (1959) mentions the

weakness of the time concept so typical of psychopathic behavior.... The discontinuity, in the life of the psychopath, between past experience, present behavior and planning for the future (which we tend to interpret as inability to learn from experience, positive or negative) often strangely contrasts to his intelligence. (p. 8)

Cleckley (1964) has said, "The psychopath shows a striking inability to follow any sort of life plan consistently, whether it be one regarded as good or evil. He does not make any far goal at all" (p. 400). McCord and McCord (1964) talk about the psychopath as a man for whom "the moment is a segment of time detached from all others. His actions are unplanned and guided by his whims" (p. 16). Quay (1965) relating to delinquents has said,

In view of the frequently expressed notion that delinquents are more impulsive and less concerned with the future consequences of their actions than are non-delinquents, it seems reasonable to assume that some differences might be demonstrated in the area of temporal experience. (p. 140)

As can be seen from the above descriptions, deficiencies in temporal perception are considered to be essential components in the personalities of both the psychopath and the delinquent. Our analysis and discussion of research on time will concentrate mainly on delinquents in general. The term *temporal perception* can be divided into several more specific aspects. A great deal of the research in this field is devoted to two aspects: (1) time perspective, indicating mainly the range of a person's future planning; and (2) the estimation of short time intervals, as an indicator of a person's "internal clock."

Various studies have aimed at relating each of these aspects to delinquency, either separately or in combination. In the following pages these studies are analyzed.

The Delinquent's Time Perspective

Among the various concepts related to time, the one most commonly related to delinquency is the concept of time perspective. Frank (1939) was the first to stress the importance of future time perspective and its influence on human behavior. However, this topic was made a subject of modern psychology by Lewin (1948, 1951), who viewed time perspective as a framework that includes the psychological past and future on the reality and various nonreality levels. Thus, Lewin defined time perspective as "the totality of the individual's views of his psychological future and his psychological past existing at a given time" (Lewin, 1951:75).

One of the first studies on this subject was conducted by Barndt and Johnson (1955), who compared a group of institutionalized delinquents with a group of high school boys. Subjects were asked to tell a story in response to a stimulus situation provided by the experimenter. The stories were recorded and subsequently analyzed in terms of the time span they encompassed. It was found that the stories produced by the delinquents covered shorter time periods than did the stories of the controls. The authors' conclusion was that delinquents are more present oriented and the range of their future time perspective (FTP) is shorter and more limited than that of nondelinquents. These findings were confirmed in the study of Davids et al. (1962).

Brock and Del Giudice (1963) studied elementary school pupils in a lower-class neighborhood. During the experimental session, the subject was given an opportunity to steal change that had spilled out of the experimenter's purse. The experimenter asked the subject to pick up the change for her while she rushed out of the room on the pretext of having urgent business to attend to. The original amount of change was known, so that the "stealers" could be identified after the session. In the second part of the session, after the experimenter had returned, two measures of temporal orientation were obtained from the subject. One measure was based on the story completion technique, while the other involved having the subject choose some words from a list. Half the words in that list were time related (e.g., hour, week, yesterday). It was found that "stealers" told stories with shorter time duration and chose fewer temporal concepts than "nonstealers." "Nonstealers" were also more future oriented and emphasized (more than "stealers") words denoting long duration rather than short duration. The authors' interpretation of these findings was that "stealers" cannot take into account the negative consequences of their actions, since to do so implies an elaborate temporal perspective.

However, the above findings could be interpreted as representing situational effects rather than personality differences: it is very possible that the "stealers" were tense as a result of their transgression, and this might account for the differences between them and the "nonstealers." This interpretation could be ruled out if the temporal measures had been administered *prior to* the stealing experiment rather than following it.

Matulef (1967), comparing a group of adolescent delinquents in a rehabilitation school with nondelinquents at a public school (both groups were composed of Negro subjects), found that delinquents were able to tell fantasy stories with shorter action-time spans than nondelinquents. However, the author raises the possibility that the constricted future time perspective of the delinquent group may have been a function of their state of institutionalization rather than representing a real difference between delinquents and nondelinquents.

An important study in this field is that of Stein et al. (1968). Comparisons were made between adolescent delinquents (most of them institutionalized) and a matched group of high school students. Future time perspective was measured by a test composed of 36 structured events. Each subject was asked to estimate his age at the time that each event would occur in his life, his score being the mean of the estimated future ages. It was found that nondelinquents had significantly higher future time perspective scores. It should be noted, however, that here again there was no adequate control on the factor of institutionalization. As will be shown later, this factor is very relevant to the study of time perspective among delinquents. Kroth (1969) compared teenage delinquents with nondelinquents in the Unites States and Costa Rica. Utilizing the story completion technique, he found that in both cultures the future time perspective of delinquents was shorter than that of nondelinquents. There was no information in this study on the factor of institutionalization.

Schneiderman (1964) compared institutionalized delinquent youths with noninstitutionalized controls utilizing the same story completion technique. Contrary to his hypothesis, delinquents did not have a shorter future time perspective and were not more present oriented than nondelinquents.

The findings of Howenstein (1969) were even more surprising. Utilizing both the story completion and the future events techniques, he found that there was a trend "for delinquents to have a slightly *longer* future time perspective, contrary to expectations and prior research." In this study, again, there was no adequate control of the factor of institutionalization.

Is the Delinquent's Internal Clock Fast or Slow?

A number of studies have tried to find a relationship between the delinquent's time perspective or temporal orientation (as described above) and the "speed" of his "internal clock."

Siegman (1961) was one of the first to study simultaneously both time perspective and time estimation of delinquents. He claims that the range of one's future time perspective is a significant source of variance in the experience of duration. The longer the range of one's future time perspective, the faster one's internal clock. His hypothesis was that delinquents' future planning would be shorter and their internal clock slower than among nondelinquents. Utilizing institutionalized subjects for both delinquent and nondelinquent groups, the findings supported the hypothesis. The results as to the range of future planning are in accordance with those of several other studies. However, the finding that delinquents experience time as passing slower than do nondelinquents contradicts the various theoretical and empirical approaches about the delinquent, all of which view the delinquent as having an impulsive and impatient personality. Therefore, it is only logical to expect that the internal clock of an impulsive person to be *faster* than that of a more relaxed and patient person. Some later studies (Siegman, 1966; Howenstein, 1969; and others) did in fact find that the internal clock of delinquents was faster than that of nondelinquents.

The review of studies provided in the present and previous sections shows quite clearly that in most studies there was inadequate control of the factor of institutionalization while studying various aspects of the time sense among delinquents and nondelinquents. It is our basic assumption that this is the main reason for the frequent inconsistent and contradicting findings in studies on the time perception of delinquents. The significance of institutionalization and its relevance to the study of temporal experience among delinquents will now be discussed.

III. Institutionalization: A Neglected Factor in the Study of the Delinquent's Temporal Experience

The Prison as a Total Institution and What This Implies

Institutionalization can be defined as a state of deprivation on the dimension of time. Viewing it from this angle, it is surprising that studies on the time perception of delinquents have neglected this important variable.

Prison is one example of a wider group of organizations called *total institutions* (Goffman, 1968). Besides prisons, Goffman includes within this framework hospitals and monasteries, as well as army camps.

The transition from the outside world into the total institution is followed by a complete reorganization of the individual's life. Detailed descriptions of this process are provided (among others) by Goffman (1968), who analyzes the mortification of self the inmate has to endure, and by Sykes (1958), who lists the various deprivations experienced by the prisoner, such as those of liberty, goods and services, heterosexual relationships, autonomy, and security.

These deprivations, together with other features characterizing the prison, create special social norms and behavioral dynamics affecting the relationships between prisoners and fellow inmates and between the prisoners and the staff.

However, in spite of all these deprivations and hardships that the inmate encounters in prison, very frequently his release from enforced incarceration is a problematic process. Usually, after a relatively short time in prison the inmate undergoes a process of "prisonization." Clemmer (1940), who coined this term, used it to indicate "the taking on in greater or lesser degree of the folkways, mores, customs, and general culture of the penitentiary." Obviously, the inmate waits very impatiently to be released and regain all the privileges and services he was arbitrarily deprived of while in prison. However, frequently, a short while after release (and sometimes even prior to it), a great deal of the suffering and humiliation is forgotten, and while facing the daily life struggle in the free society he sometimes longs for the protected and carefree life in prison. Life outside is made particularly difficult because of the stigma the ex-prisoner carries on him. Goffman (1968), who deals with this problem, speaks about the "proactive status" taken on by the ex-inmate:

Not only is his social position within the walls radically different from what it was on the outside, but, as he comes to learn, if and when he gets out, his social position on the outside will never again be quite what it was prior to entrance. . . . When the individual has taken on a low proactive status by becoming an inmate, he finds a cool reception in the wider world. . . . Furthermore, release is likely to come just when the inmate has finally learned the ropes on the inside and won privileges that he has painfully learned are very important. In brief, he may find that release means moving from the top of a small world to the bottom of a large one. (pp. 70-71)

The stigmatization and the hardships it causes may be even sharper when release is accompanied by various limiting conditions (such as release on parole, obligation to report regularly, etc.).

The purpose of the above short descriptions and citations is to demonstrate the deep effects and changes experienced by the inmate at the different stages of the imposed institutionalization in prison. Thus, the lack of consideration of the factor of institutionalization by most studies on delinquents' time perceptions becomes even more striking.

The Effect of Institutionalization on Time Perception: The Case of Imprisonment

The number of empirical studies investigating the various effects of institutionalization is rather limited. Even more limited is the number of those studies which have focused on the effects of institutionalization on the time perception of those confined within these types of organizations. These studies, although mostly descriptive and impressionistic, do make us aware of this factor and its important effect on time perception.

The effect of mental hospitalization on the time perception of patients was investigated by Wallace (1956), Rizzo (1967-1968), Calhoun (1969), and Foulks and Webb (1970), among others. Roth (1963) and Calkins (1970) studied this subject among patients in hospitals for physical illnesses. Other institutions in relation to which this topic was investigated were homes for the aged (Fink, 1957; Kastenbaum, 1963) and the army (Uyeki, 1960).

As to prisons, virtually all writing about experience in prison have focused the reader's attention on the problem of experiencing time within this imposed framework. These kinds of subjective accounts help us to understand the feelings of the prisoner but nevertheless possess the disadvantages of all subjective reports.

The first study that tried to study objectively the effect of institutional conditions on time perspective was that of Farber (1944). His important finding was that there is no relationship between an inmate's suffering and the total length of imprisonment or the length of time already spent in prison. The degree of a prisoner's suffering is related to the amount of time still left to be spent in prison. However, this relationship is not linear but curvilinear; i.e., the suffering is less among those about to be released within a period of less than two years or more than five years. On the other hand among inmates whose distance to release is between two to five years, the suffering is the greatest. Farber's general conclusion is that behavior in prison is dictated by the need to get out of there and the perceived ways of attaining that goal. The critical factors are those including time perspective, mainly the outlook toward the future, as well as other factors related to the inmate's "milestones" on his way to the goal: the release. According to Farber, the date of release represents the upper limit of the efficient future time perspective, and the date of incarceration is the main temporal limit of the past. It is rather surprising that this study, which showed so clearly the importance of systematic investigation of the inmate's temporal concepts at the different stages of institutionalization, was not immediately followed by other investigations in the field. Only about two decades later did a systematic empirical interest in this topic emerge again.

Galtung (1961) analyzes the concept of time in prison on the basis of his personal experience as a prisoner:

Thus, time becomes essential and so important that it is almost considered a thing, concrete and materialized. Detailed calculations as to amount of time left, and meditation on how that time could have been spent with the other identity, certainly do not constitute bedtime reflections only or once-an-hour thoughts. Concern for time seems to be an almost constant and painful *state of mind*. (p. 113)

In this context Galtung raises two relevant questions. (1) How much of a time-span forward into the future represents reality to the prisoner? According to his observations, some inmates live entirely in the present, lacking any projection even into the near future. Others, on the other hand, have their future structured as an integral part of their plans and dreams. (2) How do inmates equalize time intervals? This question, which remains unanswered by him, raises a related one: Does the person who can plan well ahead also attach value to small intervals of time?

One of the basic characteristics of a prison that makes the experience of time there so difficult, according to Galtung, is the fixed routine. Regularity, which is so important from the point of view of bureaucratic efficiency, is the real enemy of the prisoners. The total predictability of life in prison causes the future to be but a replication of the present, which is itself a copy of the past. Accordingly, Galtung assumes that one of the major (if not *the* major) functions of disturbances brought into the regularity of the prison is the decrease in predictability and thus the alteration of the inmates' time scale until order is restored. He found that prisoners had two ways of manipulating time and breaking the routine:

First, prisoners tried to change the signposts already there by conscious interference with prison routines, especially by infractions of the rules and by conscious or unconscious provocation of illness. Second, they tried to introduce new and private signposts by interaction with the prison officials and by exploring all possible or impossible avenues to new statuses in the penal system through pardon, conditional release, transfer within or between institutions etc. (p. 117)

One of the central questions in this respect is whether it is possible to find systematic changes or clear stages in time perception along the period of institutionalization. This topic is dealt with by Gibbens (1961), who spent five years in Germany as a prisoner of war during World War II, and for the last two years had charge of a psychiatric section of a hospital for prisoners. Despite the basic difference between a POW camp (in which the length of institutionalization is not known) and a prison, Gibbens, on the basis of his observations in a depot camp and his experience in criminology and penology, comes to the conclusion that there are four stages that each imprisoned person undergoes. First, there is the period of shock, bewilderment, depression, etc., which lasts for a few months. The second period is a very constructive one, marked by a conscious determination of the prisoner to make "the best of it." During this period they decide to study, participate in various courses, in psychotherapy, etc. This stage lasts between one and two years. The third period is the crisis stage. It is marked by a decision to give up, by restless depressions, by minor psychosomatic illnesses or disciplinary offenses, and often by attempted or actual escapes. This phase marks the onset of the following one. The fourth period is the chronic phase of "barbed wire disease." It is not characterized by depression, as one would expect, but rather by an inappropriate and superficial cheerfulness which is characteristic of long-term prisoners. Gibbens views this reaction as a kind of a defense or cynical refusal to hope or be disappointed.

This last period means actually that the prisoner becomes detached from the outside reality and adjusts himself to the prison as if he is going to live within this framework forever. Basically, this state is similar to the process of "prisonization" described by Clemmer (1940), but Gibbens stresses rather the pathological aspect of this phenomenon. A similar approach in emphasizing the negative and the pathological is expressed by Morris and Morris (1963) and Barton (1959), who writes about "institutional neurosis," which does not differ very much from the "barbed wire disease" described by Gibbens. The institutional neurosis syndrome is not characterized by a disturbance of the sense of reality but is rather a state of passivity, apathy, and lack of interest in events that are not directly related to the inmate, and sometimes even lack of response to harsh and humiliating treatment. Morris and Morris (1963), during their study in a prison, observed in several prisoners marked signs of mental deterioration— they made fewer and fewer jokes, their appearance became increasingly untidy, and they became less and less interested in anything about them. One inmate a few months before his release stated it clearly: "I think if I stay here I shall go mental."

Passivity may be of some help to the inmate in adjusting to the reality of prison, but at the same time it will make his readjustment to the outside world after release much more difficult. Institutional neurosis may develop according to Barton in those inmates upon whom the destructive characteristics of imprisonment have had most effect but who have not built up active responses to the situation they are in. Gibbens (1961) speaks of "the immediate release syndrome," describing it as "the sense of strangeness, agoraphobia, sometimes attacks of panic with coarse tremor and sweating, seen within hours and days of release." This syndrome is familiar, and special prerelease programs are designed to anticipate and treat it. He continues:

What is still not understood is that there are important time relations in this. The immediate difficulties are not very important, and wear off in 2-3 months. It is often 6 months or so, after return to normal, that secondary more chronic and persistent reactions occurred in military psychiatry, when prisoners had been rehabilitated and returned to duty. The majority of offenders are reconvicted in 6 months if they are going to recidivate. This is usually interpreted, especially by the courts, as a simple refusal or inability to avoid crime; but there is a proportion, so far unknown, in which the additional release reaction plays a major part in the relapse. (p. 49)

An interesting account of the time concepts of the prisoner is found in a short article by Zietz (1961), who was himself sentenced to life imprisonment. The lifer's attitude to time varies at the different stages of incarceration. It becomes for him an important factor only at the beginning of his sentence and when he feels his time for release is near. He says:

At the four-year mark, time is practically meaningless. The adjustment period is long past, there is no hope—and consequently no thought—of release. At the nine-year mark comes the realization and casual thought that the sentence (according to the Pennsylvania average) is about half or possibly more than half served. Time once again begins to take on meaning. At the twelve- or thirteen-year mark time again becomes an important factor, for at this point the lifer figures he has some hope, and with this hope comes new life. Time drags very slowly until he feels ready to apply for commutation of sentence. Time again drags while awaiting the outcome of his clemency appeal. If clemency is refused, he knows he must then wait another year before applying again. This one year period, for the first time since the beginning of his incarceration, seems like an extremely long time. (p. 51)

This author also emphasizes the fact that attitudes toward time differ according to the length of sentence. To a prisoner sentenced to two years, this period seems extremely long. To the lifer on the other hand, this period looks just like a weekend. As to future-oriented thinking, Zietz states that for the average prisoner the distant future is considered more in terms of fantasy than reality. This fantasy can become reality if the inmate has the motivation and initiative to achieve his goals and if the authorities give him the opportunity to move more rapidly toward release.

Cohen and Taylor (1972) discuss extensively the subject of experiencing time faced by long-term prisoners in a maximum security block. One of the main problems these inmates have is marking time. These inmates have to build their own subjective clock in order to protect themselves from the terror of "the misty abyss." This is rather difficult, since there are few achievements that can be used to mark the passage of time. They usually engage either in mind-building (reading or studying) or in body-building (usually weight lifting). The authors quote a conversation between two inmates in relation to this subject:

When Ronald arrived in E-Wing he turned to Paul for advice on the structuring of time. "How am I going to do twenty years?" Paul, on the basis of three years' experience of an equally long sentence, provided the only reassurance he knew: "It's easy, do it five years at a time." (p. 97)

These prisoners live mainly for the present:

In prison, one also has to find ways of increasing the content of the hours, [but] mastery of the impinging moment has a very different meaning for those who—unlike explorers or even short-term prisoners—do not have a clear conception of the future after one survives the treacherous environment. . . . The long-termer has only the choice between surrendering himself to this meaningless world as a life project or obsessionally thinking about the future—a near certain way of doing hard time. (p. 92)

The effect of imprisonment on the planning ability of the inmate is reflected in the words of one prisoner in the study of Morris and Morris (1963):

"Your mind dulls and you live in a false reality. You make quite unrealistic plans for the future, and going outside and finding out how unrealistic they are is the terrible moment." (p. 166)

The authors raise the possibility that this approach to the moment of truth may cause, three or four months before release, the breakdown of prisoners who up to that time were well adjusted to prison.

The above observations and personal accounts provide us with important information about the effects of imprisonment on the temporal experience of inmates. However, what is still lacking is more accurate and precise research on the measurable effects of this variable. This type of information is particularly needed if authorities are to improve conditions within the prison and facilitate the readjustment of the ex-inmate in the free society. Several studies in more recent years have provided us with some of this required information.

Some Recent Research

The first study known to me which investigated systematically the effect of length of imprisonment and distance from release on future time perspective and time estimation of prisoners was conducted by myself (Landau, 1969). In this study, prisoners sentenced to long terms (4-34 years) were utilized. Time estimations were measured by two methods (verbal estimation and production) on intervals ranging from 5 to 40 seconds. The range of future time perspective was determined by a method similar to that used by Siegman (1961). The subject was asked to enumerate 10 events referring to things he may do or which may happen to him in the future, and he was then asked to indicate the age he thought he would be at the time of occurrence of each of the events. For time estimation, it was found that the nearer the inmate is subjectively to his release, the faster his internal clock, which means that his subjective feeling is that objective time passes slowly. This finding was statistically significant among prisoners serving sentences of four to seven years. Among those sentenced to longer periods, the results were in the same direction but did not reach statistical significance. For the range of future time perspective, it was found that the date of release is the most significant boundary for the future planning of the prisoner: the nearer he is to release, the shorter his future time perspective. This finding provides empirical support to the findings of Farber (1944) and to the impressions reported by Zietz (1961), and Morris and Morris (1963), as well as many others. It was also found in the above-mentioned study that one of the consequences of long distance to release is a complete inability for future planning. This happened mainly in the first stages of institutionalization.

In general, the findings of this study point at significant developments in the prisoner's time sense at the various stages of incarceration. Thus, they provide empirical proof of the need of adequately controlling the factor of institutionalization while studying the time perception of delinquents.

Megargee et al. (1970) explored the affective attitudes toward the past, present, and future of youthful prison inmates. Utilizing the Roos time reference inventory (TRI) (Roos, 1964), they found that these subjects were oriented primarily toward the future and past rather than the present. Attitudes toward the future were positive, while the past and present were viewed negatively. No differences in temporal orientation were found among inmates at the beginning, middle, and end of their sentence. However, in the two above-mentioned studies (Landau, 1969; and Megargee et al., 1970), as in many others in the field, a combined effect of delinquency and institutionalization is measured, and it is virtually impossible to tell the specific effect of either of these factors on the dependent variables.

Two more of my recent studies (Landau, 1975; 1976) investigated the relationship between delinquency and several aspects of temporal experience, while adequately controlling the factor of institutionalization. For this purpose, four groups took part in these studies: institutionalized delinquents (prison inmates), institutionalized nondelinquents (soldiers), noninstitutionalized delinquents (delinquents on probation), and noninstitutionalized nondelinquents (vocational students).

In the first of these two studies (Landau, 1975) the range of future time perspective was investigated, utilizing the same unstructured future events instrument as in the previous study (Landau, 1969). It was found that both delinquency and institutionalization have a limiting effect on the range of future planning of the individual. The prisoners showed the shortest future time perspective (FTP), while the vocational students showed the longest. The soldiers' and the probationers' FTP was longer than that of the prisoners but shorter than that of the vocational students. Within the institutionalized groups (prison inmates and soldiers) a consistent pattern was found: the closer the subjects were to release, the shorter was the range of their future time perspective. This finding indicates that it is not just imprisonment as such that limits the range of future planning (as the findings of the previous study (Landau, 1969) could have been interpreted), but this is an effect of other types of total institutionalization (such as the army) as well.

The second study (Landau, 1976) investigated the relative salience of the past, present, and future in the daily thinking of delinquents, as well as their affective attitudes to these three temporal aspects, while controlling the factor of institutionalization, as in the previous study. The relative salience of the three time categories was measured by having the subject enumerate 10 items about which he had thought or talked during the week or two previous to the experiment and determine for each item whether it was related to the past, present, or future. For measuring the affective attitudes toward these three time categories, an abridged form of the TRI (Roos, 1964) was utilized (15 statements which the subject must assign to the past, present, or future, five being affectively positive, five negative, and five neutral). Here again, as in the other study, both delinquency and institutionalization proved to have an effect on temporal experience. It was found that while all subjects were basically future oriented, the institutionalized subjects (mainly prisoners) were more present oriented than their noninstitutionalized counterparts. However, as the prisoner approached release, there was a decrease in the salience of the future in his life space. Delinquents (both in and out of prison) perceived their past as more negative and their future as more positive than did nondelinquents. Institutionalized subjects perceived their present as more negative than their noninstitutionalized counterparts; and this perception among prisoners was more negative than among soldiers. The affective attitudes of the nondelinquents toward the past, present, and future were much more balanced and realistic than that of the delinquents.

IV. Implications for Future Research and Penological Policy

The few studies that have investigated the temporal experience of delinquents, while adequately controlling the factor of institutionalization, are of both theoretical and practical significance. From the theoretical-methodological point of view these studies have demonstrated the great influence situational factors may have on characteristics and behaviors that are very frequently considered as stable and situation-free personality traits. More specifically, in my studies (Landau, 1969; 1975; 1976) it was shown very clearly that total institutions in general, and prison in particular, constitute such "situational factors." Thus, my findings raise serious doubts about the findings of any study on behavioral or personality factors conducted on incarcerated delinquents without adequate control of the important situational factor of institutionalization. The recent findings of Culbertson (1975) as to the relationship between decline in self-concept and length of being incarcerated provide additional support to the above-mentioned conclusion.

The implications from these findings to future criminological studies are quite clear. Incarcerated delinquents are the most accessible population for criminological empirical research and experimentation. Too frequently, however, comparisons are made between institutionalized delinquents and noninstitutionalized nondelinquents, thereby contaminating the findings. Future research should further the study of the effects of imprisonment on other personality and behavioral characteristics related to delinquency, such as the ability to delay gratification, etc. Another aim of future research in this field should be the further clarification of the effect of different variations of total institutionalization (e.g., prisons with various emphases on the security-treatment continuum) on a variety of behavioral and so-called personality traits of their inmates.

On the practical penological level the findings described above would seem to have considerable value. The importance and problematic nature of time in prison has been acknowledged by many students of this social institution. These studies have pointed at specific crucial results: The closer the prisoner is to his release, the weaker his ability for future planning; he is preoccupied with his present situation; he views his past and present in a very negative way, coloring the future with extreme positive and unrealistic bright colors. Provided that our aim is to prepare the prisoner adequately toward his reentrance into society, several treatment implications follow from the findings:

1. One of the important goals of prerelease counseling or treatment should be the enlargement of the inmate's future time perspective. This means bringing more of the outer reality into his life space. This is of great importance mainly in the last stages of incarceration when the prisoner is most anxious about the future.

2. Another aim in counseling programs for inmates should be to make these subjects look more realistically toward their future rather than encourage their existing extremely positive (and unrealistic) coloring of this temporal aspect. In such programs, emphasis should be put on the probable negative experiences and crises with which they will have to cope in the future. This may, undoubtedly, make the inmate perceive his future in a less positive way, but at the same time it may also increase his ability to see things more realistically and therefore be better equipped to overcome difficulties and frustrations, thus improving his chances of positive readjustment to society.

3. Apart from adequate counseling, frequent and prolonged leaves should be granted to the inmate, thus enabling him to experience the outside reality while still serving his sentence. In the same line, granting him furloughs throughout his sentence (as a reward for good behavior or as part of a grade system) should help him to cope with the pains of imprisonment. Work furloughs may also be very instrumental in improving his chances for positive readjustment to society after release.

As it looks now, prisons will continue to exist in the foreseeable future. The aim of this chapter has not been to discuss the necessity of this social institution but rather to focus attention on some negative effects that imprisonment has on the temporal experience of inmates. I am convinced that the application of the theoretical and practical conclusions put forward in this chapter would improve both criminological research and the successful treatment of offenders.

References

Aristotle. "Time." In R.M. Gale (ed.). *The Philosophy of Time*, (London: Macmillan, 1968), pp. 9-23.

Barndt, R.J., and D.M. Johnson, "Time orientation in delinquents." *Journal of Abnormal and Social Psychology* 51 (1955):343-345.

Barton, R., *Institutional Neurosis* (Bristol, 1959).

Brock, T.C., and C. Del Giudice. "Stealing and temporal orientation." *Journal of Abnormal and Social Psychology* 66 (1963):91-94.

Calhoun, M.K. "The effects of age, psychiatric institutionalization and institutional environment on dimensions of time perspective." *Dissertation Abstracts* 30 (1969):2413.

Calkins, K. "Time: Perspectives, marking and styles of usage." *Social Problems* 17 (1970):487-501.

Cleckley, H. *The Mask of Sanity* (St. Louis: C.V. Mosby, 1964).

Clemmer, D. *The Prison Community* (Boston: Christopher Publishing Co., 1940).

Cohen, S., and L. Taylor. *Psychological Survival* (Harmsworth: Penguin Books, 1972).

Culbertson, R.G. "The effect of institutionalization on the delinquent inmate's self concept." *Journal of Criminal Law and Criminology* 66 (1975):88-93.

Davids, A., C. Kidder, and M. Reich. "Time orientation in male and female juvenile delinquents." *Journal of Abormmal and Social Psychology* 64 (1962):239-240.

Efron, R. "The duration of the present." *Annals of the New York Academy of Sciences* 138 (1967):713-729.

Eysenck, H.J. *Crime and Personality* (London: Paladin, 1970).

Farber, M.L. "Suffering and time perspective of the prisoner." *University of Iowa Studies in Child Welfare* 20 (1944):153-227.

Feld, J. "Opening remarks." *Annals of the New York Academy of Sciences* 138 (1967):369-370.

Findlay, J.N. "Time: A treatment of some puzzles." In R.M. Gale (ed.). *The Philosophy of Time* (London: Macmillan, 1968), pp. 143-162.

Fink, H.H. "The relationship of time perspective to age, institutionalization and activity." *Journal of Gerontology* 12 (1957):414-417.

Fisher R. "Introductory address." *Annals of the New York Academy of Sciences* 138 (1967):371-373.

Foulks, J.D., and J.T. Webb. "Temporal orientation of diagnostic groups." *Journal of Clinical Psychology* 26 (1970):155-159.

Frank, L.K. "Time perspective." *Journal of Social Philosophy* 4 (1939): 293-312.

Frankenstein, K. *Psychopathy* (New York: Grune & Stratton, 1959).

Friedlander, K. *Psycho-analytic Approach to Juvenile Delinquency* (London: Kegan Paul, 1947).

Galtung, J. "Prison: organization of dilemma." In D.R. Cressey (ed.). *The Prison: Studies in Institutional Organization and Change.* (New York: Holt, Rinehart & Winston, 1961), pp. 107-145.

Gibbens, T.C.N. "The prisoner's view of time—by a former prisoner of war." *The Prison Journal* 41 (1961):46-49.

Goffman, E. *Asylums* (Harmsworth: Penguin Books, 1968).

Gough, H.G. "A sociological theory of psychopathy." *American Journal of Sociology* 53 (1948):359-366.

Hare, R.D. *Psychopathy: Theory and Research* (New York: Wiley, 1970).

Howenstine, R.J. "Future time perspective and its relation to the effects of external stimulation and activity upon time estimation in delinquent and non-delinquent male adolescents." *Dissertation Abstracts* 30 (1969):848.

Kastenbaum, R. "Cognitive and personality futurity in later life." *Journal of Individual Psychology* 19 (1963):216-222.

Kroth, R. "A study of three aspects of time among normal and delinquent school age males in Costa Rica and the United States." *Dissertation Abstracts* 29 (1969):2094.

Landau, S.F. "The effect of length of imprisonment and subjective distance from release on future time perspective and time estimation of prisoners." *Scripta Hierosolymitana*, 21, *Studies in Criminology* (Jerusalem: Magness Press, The Hebrew Univ., 1969), pp. 182-223.

Landau, S.F. "Future time perspective of delinquents and non-delinquents: the effect of institutionalization." *Criminal Justice and Behavior* 2 (1975): 22-36.

Landau, S.F. "Delinquency institutionalization and time orientation." *Journal of Consulting and Clinical Psychology* (1976), 44, 745-759.

Lewin, K. "Time perspective and morale." In K. Lewin. *Resolving Social Conflicts* (New York: Harper & Brothers, 1948), pp. 103-124.

Lewin, K. *Field Theory in Social Science* (New York: Harper & Row, 1951).

Matulef, N.J. "Future time perspective and personality characteristics of male adolescents, delinquents and non-delinquents." *Dissertation Abstracts* 28 (1967):1204-1205.

McCord, W., and J. McCord. *The Psychopath: An Essay on the Criminal Mind* (Princeton: Van Nostrand, 1964).

McTaggart, J.M.E. "Time." In R.M. Gale (ed.). *The Philosophy of Time* (London: McMillan, 1968), pp. 86-97.

Megargee, E.I., A. Cooper-Price, R. Frohwirth, and R. Levine, "Time orientation of youthful prison inmates." *Journal of Counseling Psychology* 17 (1970):8-14.

Morris, T., and P. Morris. *Pentonville: A Sociological Study of an English Prison* (London: Routledge & Kegan Paul, 1963).

Quay, H.C. "Personality and delinquency." In H.C. Quay (ed.). *Juvenile Delinquency* (Princeton, N.J.: Van Nostrand, 1965), pp. 139-169.

Redl, F., and D. Wineman. *Children Who Hate* (Glencoe, Ill.: The Free Press, 1951).

Rizzo, A.E. "The time moratorium." *Adolescence* 2 (1967-68):469-480.

Roos, P. *Time Reference Inventory* (mimeographed, 1964), Austin State School, Austin, Texas.

Roth, J.A. *Timetables* (New York: Bobbs-Merrill, 1963).

Schneiderman, D.F. "The Time Sense of Delinquents." Unpublished doctoral dissertation, Boston Univ. Graduate School, 1964.

Siegman, A.W. "The relationship between future time perspective, time estimation and impulse control in a group of young offenders and in a control group." *Journal of Consulting Psychology* 25 (1961):470-475.

Siegman, A.W. "Effects of auditory stimulation and intelligence on time estimation in delinquents and non-delinquents." *Journal of Consulting Psychology* 30 (1966):320-328.

St. Augustine. "Some questions about time." In R.M. Gale (ed.). *The Philosophy of Time* (London: McMillan, 1968), pp. 38-54.

Stein, K.B., R.T. Sarbin, and J.A. Kulik. "Future time perspective: Its relation to the socialization process and the delinquent role." *Journal of Consulting and Clinical Psychology* 32 (1968):257-264.

Sykes, G.M. *The Society of Captives* (Princeton, N.Y.: Princeton Univ. Press, 1958).

Uyeki, E.S. "Draftee behaviour in the cold-war army." *Social Problems* 8 (1960):151-158.

Wallace, M. "Future time perspective in schizophrenia." *Journal of Abnormal and Social Psychology* 52 (1956):240-245.

Wright, D. *The Psychology of Moral Behaviour* (Harmsworth: Penguin Books, 1971).

Zietz, H. "Prisoner's views of time—by a lifer." *The Prison Journal* 41 (1961):50-52.

11 Treatment of the Dangerous Offender

Sigmund H. Manne

Introduction

After more than two decades of attempting to diagnose and treat an essentially sociopathic population, I have been requested to put some of my thoughts concerning treatment down on paper. I must, as I start this article, state that I am still not sure of exactly what a sociopathic offender is. However, I can say, with some degree of certainty what the sociopath is not. He (or she) is not what is found in the textbooks, or in the monumental work of Hervey Cleckly, *The Mask of Sanity*. I must admit also that my work may have put me in touch with a special group of sociopaths, those who are failures, those who have been caught for breaking the law. Therefore, I can candidly admit that I do not know what a sociopath is.

Such an admission appears to bode ill for someone attempting to write of treatment for the sociopath. Traditionally, our training has been that in order to treat correctly, we must have a diagnosis. This determines the course and direction of treatment. Perhaps we have followed this medical model too long, and in the case of treating the offender, we do not really need a diagnostic workup to set the direction of therapy. Although in the course of my work at Patuxent Institution I do have the benefit of a diagnostic workup (the court insists that it be done), I use it infrequently in the treatment of the offender.

The setting in which a major portion of my experience has occurred is a unique setting in the world. Patuxent Institution is loosely patterned after the Institution at Herstedvester, Denmark. We deal with convicted dangerous felons who are remanded to the Institution on an indeterminate civil sentence, with appropriate legal safeguards. The legal test each patient must meet is embodied in Section 5, Article 31B, Annotated Code of the Public General Laws of the State of Maryland as follows:

> ... a defective delinquent shall be defined as an individual who, by the demonstration of persistent aggravated antisocial or criminal behavior, evidences a propensity toward criminal activity, and who is found to have either such intellectual deficiency or emotional unbalance, or both, as to clearly demonstrate an actual danger to society so as to require such confinement and treatment, when appropriate, as may make it reasonably safe for society to terminate the confinement and treatment.

Discussion of Patuxent Institution may be found in Boslow et al. (1961); Boslow and Manne (1966); Manne (1967), (1969), (1973); and Manne and Rosenthal (1971).

In dealing with those individuals who fit the above definition, three factors became apparent. The first is the patient is poorly, if at all, motivated to make any changes in his personality. He is essentially comfortable in his mode of adjustment and obtains enough gratification of infantile or hedonistic needs to fight to maintain this form of adjustment. In the absence of an internal drive for change, it is obvious that an external motivating factor is necessary to institute any changes. This motivating factor is the indeterminate sentence, which makes the patient responsible for his length of stay in the Patuxent Institution.

Secondly, since there is no internalized drive for personality change and the patient has generally displayed a propensity for avoiding stress-provoking situations, outpatient treatment is basically doomed to failure. Inpatient treatment is necessary so that the patient's ability to manipulate and run from therapy is limited.

The third factor is that treatment of choice is group psychotherapy. I do not consider that dangerous offenders will involve themselves in an individual therapy experience other than superficially. With their low frustration tolerance, as well as their inability to withstand stress, the intensity of the relationship required in individual therapy is generally beyond them. In group psychotherapy, the relationship may not be as intense, and the insights offered by peers are less threatening than an interpretation offered by the authority figure, the therapist.

The focus of this chapter, therefore, will be the course of group therapy with an allegedly intractible, nonmotivated, sociopathic offenders' group who are confined under the special conditions imposed by Patuxent Institution. When I started group psychotherapy I was highly involved in the need for balancing the groups. I did initial interviews, weighed the pathology, determined the personality, and tried to meld all the various factors into a harmonious group. Shortly afterward, under pressure to add another group from the expanding pool of nontreated patients, I was forced to choose patients literally at random, using intellectual level as my sole criterion. Subsequent investigation indicated that both groups did equally well in the treatment situation. From that point on all my groups were open-ended. The only contraindication I found was not to have a single sex offender in a group composed of non-sex offenders. Generally, the lone sex offender was too inadequate and immature to permit exploration of his underlying problems by others.

Since I consider group psychotherapy as the treatment of choice for the sociopathic dangerous offender, I would like to explore this modality in some depth, recognizing that it is only a part of a total therapeutic milieu and that the method of group psychotherapy I use is not the only successful method employed at Patuxent Institution. As noted earlier, no attempt is made to balance a group, other than the criterion of intellect. I have found it useful, at times, to have one patient of borderline intelligence in a group of otherwise normal subjects. Such a patient frequently acts as a catalyst in the group, cutting through manipulative or intellectualized verbalizations with concrete but insightful comments. At the same time, he is forced to use his own resources maximally in order to remain an accepted member of the group. Benefits, thus, accrue to both the borderline defective and the normally endowed group members.

I have found that the optimal number of patients I can work with in a group is 10 and, therefore, will start a new group with that number. There is recognition that the group will, by attrition, reduce in number. However, I have also found that if a group falls below five members it ceases to function as a group and the process becomes individual therapy in a group setting.

The Initial Group Meeting: Limit Setting

In the initial group meeting, the anxiety level is quite high. No attempt is made to directly allay anxiety. Specific rules and regulations are set out to the group members as follows:

1. The group members *will* attend the group sessions.
2. There will be *no* acting out physically.
3. The duration of the therapy session will be one hour.
4. The hour is the patient's, he can speak of anything he wishes or not speak if he so desires.
5. The therapist will write reports on every patient in the group, not relating the substance of group discussion but indicating problem areas and the patient's attempts to work through problems.
6. Confidentiality is to be observed by all group members. Failure to comply will result in expulsion from the group.
7. The therapist reserves the right to break the confidentiality of the group if information is obtained concerning possible escapes, or if someone is to be physically hurt.
8. The therapist will not do anything for the patient when the therapist is functioning in any of his other administrative roles.

These limits are rigidly adhered to and appear to allay some of the initial group anxiety by providing structure to an essentially unstructured situation.

Each limit is imposed for a reason. The first is to be sure that the patient is available for the meeting. Failure to appear is initially explored with the patient in the group when he returns after his first absence. Repeated failure to appear results in the patient not being promoted in the unit tier system, not being given better job assignments, and ultimately, expulsion from the group, which is tantamount to not being considered for any form of conditional release. Therefore, the patient has the choice to make, knowing the alternatives.

The second limit, not acting out, is self explanatory; while the third limit, duration of therapy, is something that is constantly tested in the initial phase of therapy. Our patients have not previously been able to remain within the limits of a situation. Setting this limit and adhering to it despite the offer of juicy insights in the last moments of therapy once again forces the patient to take responsibility for his own actions and to utilize the total therapeutic hour, rather than manipulating for a more favored status.

The therapist at no time knowingly attempts to control the stream of verbalization. He does attempt to focus on the underlying affective content or interpersonal functioning of group members. Frequently, the group will focus on the nonverbal member by itself, but also will ultimately bring the monopolist, who is hiding behind his verbiage, to a halt by talking over him, by not accepting his verbalizations, or by direct verbal attack.

Item five is self explanatory, while item six is vitally important. Confidentiality of sensitive verbalizations and feelings must be maintained by all if the group is to function. Too often the patient has been mistrusting of others, with good reason. Suddenly he is being asked to divulge heretofore hidden, painful, or strongly defended thoughts and feelings to a group of people who have the potential to add to his store of hurt. Since he has been hurt by others all his life, there is a real need to be sure that his innermost thoughts and feelings will not be broadcast through his community.

Item seven is necessary in order to be completely honest with the patient and to indicate that breaches of security that are potentially dangerous to him or to his community will not be tolerated. In many respects this relieves the patient of anxiety, in that knowing the therapist is a secure anchor, the patient knows where the therapist stands. Frequently the patient is fearful of revealing such information, but does so in a tangential manner, thereby protecting himself, or his self-image, and finding in the therapist someone who is as good as his word.

Limit eight is designed to reinforce the patient's self-image. Too often a group will disintegrate into a series of infantile requests of the therapist. The patient has learned that he must remain in a dependent situation from past incarcerations. Under this rubric, the patient must think and act for himself. He is placed in a novel position: his own behavior, thoughts, and feelings are *his* responsibility. He will not be forced into a particular mold by someone telling him how to behave, think, or feel. Any changes that occur are the result of the patient's efforts and can be used to bolster his self-esteem. This limit also serves to focus the areas in which the therapist can be manipulated. Requests, for example, to phone relatives are properly directed to others than the therapist and only serve to block group functioning.

Problems in the Initial Phase of Group Psychotherapy

In common with beginning groups, those containing the dangerous sociopathic offender have difficulty in getting started. Initially, group interaction is held to a minimum. Questions are directed to the therapist, who is perceived (correctly or incorrectly) as the source of all knowledge, as holding the key to the patient's release. The therapist holds strictly to the concept that all such questions must be referred back to the group or that the patient must have some reason for posing the question. Frequently, the patients become frustrated and angry at the therapist for not answering their questions. They take refuge in the perception that nothing is wrong with them, they do not need or belong in therapy, and that the therapist is no good. At this stage in treatment the therapeutic aim is to accept and encourage the expression of affect. Hostile affect *must not* lead to hostile responses on the part of the therapist, since the patient is highly capable of handling hostility from authorities. He has done this all his life. Acceptance of the patient's right to express hostility, or any other emotion, is a new experience for the patient. He cannot bring into play older, previously learned modes of adapting to, or defending against, hostility from others which he has engendered.

Along with the aim of accepting displays of affect (which are quite rare) is the attempt to develop group cohesiveness as a prerequisite for a therapeutic group. Other group members are encouraged to respond to the patient, even if on only an intellectual plane. Group interaction is pushed, with the attempt being made to provide support to those patients showing a willingness to verbalize. Confrontations and interpretations are generally avoided at this time in the group's progress. Clarification and acceptance of underlying affect are sought. In the case of a patient who distorts, or who responds that he wouldn't have to do this in another institution, reality is brought into play, constantly bringing the patient back from flights of fancy. It is most important to continually base the patients' comments in reality.

Support is given to patients' comments that have affective components. The therapist must be skillful and careful to indicate, through his responses, that he can accept the patient's affect, that the patient is entitled to his feelings, and to move the patient and the group to further explore such feelings. Sensitivity to the patients' needs are paramount, and the therapist's response must be multidimensional, incorporating awareness of the manifest content as well as the latent and affective components of the patient's remarks. Responding in this manner is difficult to master but has the value of not frightening the patient who is making his first tentative steps toward dropping some of his pathological defenses and moving toward maturity. The therapist must be careful not to make a frontal assault on the patient's defenses (whatever they may be), no matter how well the therapist has analyzed these defenses.

The initial phase of therapy is critical. The therapist must be consistent in his responses to the patient, and essentially probing but nonthreatening. Patient defenses, such as projection, denial, hostility and withdrawal, among others, must be accepted by the therapist as being part of the patient, but also as behavior that can be changed. For many patients, with their poor self-concept, support is required to indicate that such defenses are not unique but are shared with most other human beings. Although sociopathic offenders often verbalize that they are like "normal" people, too frequently they really feel they are completely different from others. They try very hard to maintain their "difficulties," since they provide them with the justification for their acting out. Often they defensively express their feelings of uniqueness and their distrust of others when they state that the therapist cannot understand them since he has not experienced their life experiences and is therefore incapable of empathizing with their feelings.

Phase Two: The Group Process Begins

It is at this point in the therapeutic process that the second phase of therapy commences. Group members begin to challenge or support each other and bring up life experiences in therapy. There is a beginning awareness of the commonality of experiences, and the therapist must gently nudge the group toward the awareness of the feelings underlying such experiences. When I feel the timing is right, I will frequently use a "here and now" approach. I will intervene in a spirited group discussion and force the patients to focus on what is occurring right now. The focus is on the feelings being expressed, how these feelings are perceived by the others in the group, and the distortions of perceptions of group members. From this an attempt is made to determine when such feelings were experienced earlier in life, who the significant figures were when such feelings were aroused, and how the patient handled or experienced them. Minimal advances in understanding and insight appear to occur in this phase of therapy, but to the patient they are perceived as monumental. It is my experience that therapy with the sociopathic offender has now begun.

Phase Three: From Plateau to Insight

We now enter the third phase of treatment. Trust and rapport have generally been established and the patient has reached a plateau. He considers that he is "cured." His minimal insights are perceived as major gains, and he therefore is ready to return to society. Resistance and hostility are directed toward the therapist, with the patient being alternately anxious and/or verbally hostile. Ambivalence is a major factor in the sociopathic personality at this stage of treatment. He is apparently strongly involved with the therapist, is seeking to work through underlying dependent needs, but at the same time is most reluctant to give up the facade he has established as a lifestyle. In short, the patient wants to move forward in understanding himself, but the pain involved in further investigation of his repressed feelings holds him back.

The therapist, at this stage, is frequently the patient's bedrock in a world that is perceived as changing rapidly. Acceptance of the patient's hostility without rejecting the patient is initially important. The patient is working through previously unresolved conflicts using the therapist as the focal point. At this time the therapist is using the relationship built over a number of earlier sessions to clarify the feelings underlying the patients' behavior. The group becomes supportive of the patient and, at times, impatient with his resistance. However, if the therapist should make an interpretation for which the patient is not ready, it is not unusual for the group to express their hostility toward the therapist in an obvious attempt to defend the patient from the interpretation. An unskilled therapist may often see this as a regressive move by the group, when it is actually a warning to the therapist to slow down and not press too much. It becomes a major step forward in developing group cohesiveness and in dispelling the group's prior view of the therapist as omnipotent. The group self-concept is enhanced as the patients become more comfortable in dealing with emotionally charged material. They become much more at ease in dealing with hitherto taboo feelings, and the group process takes over. Group members begin to act as therapists for each other, they become impatient with manipulative behavior and new alliances are formed. Therapy becomes a high priority item, and the new toy of introspection is generalized for the first time to situations outside therapy.

It is not infrequent that at this point in therapy, one or more of the group members will frequently develop somatic symptoms. There can be much speculation as to the causation of the somatization, but I lean toward the concept that the earlier avenues of expression of anxiety and guilt are blocked by the therapeutic gains the patient has made. He is unwilling to give up these gains but has not moved to the point where he is truly aware of the close relationship between his affect and his actions. I perceive the somatizing as the beginnings of an integrative process. Though it is physically and emotionally painful to the patient, it represents an opportunity for the patient to make the connection as to how his feelings can affect him. In one group I had a patient who developed migraine-like headaches accompanied by pain in the shoulders and back of the neck. Group discussion revealed these symptoms occurred when he spoke glowingly about the sister who raised him. It was obvious that he harbored strong hostile, aggressive feelings toward this sister, feelings which he could not allow to come to awareness. The group drew the relationship to his attention and focused on the underlying hostility. Headaches increased in frequency and severity until the patient began to express some hostility and, more importantly, to accept his right to feel hostile. As he came to grips with his feelings, headaches and tension disappeared. The patient slept well and remained free of headaches all day. The effect on the patient was to permit him to delve more deeply into other conflict areas with a greater degree of confidence. For him, and for the group, emotionally charged areas were not as anxiety-provoking as they had been. They developed confidence in their ability to change their lives through introspection and proceeded to use this tool with themselves and others.

It takes only one dramatic leap forward to create an atmosphere of cohesiveness within a group. The fear of an "us against authority" or "the group versus the therapist" is lessened. The group and the therapist are perceived as working toward a common goal, and the patients frequently become overly dependent upon the group and the therapist. Such feelings are initially useful in that they permit the patients to verbalize freely in the group. Group interaction is facilitated, and patients discover they can help others and can themselves be helped by others. Others are not as threatening and the patient is able to test out some of his new-found insights and behavioral changes without overwhelming anxiety. Changes can be explored, and new ways of behaving concomitant with the emerging new self-concept can safely be expressed. It is almost as though the patient is experiencing preadolescence or adolescence, with its trials and errors, in the group situation. He is growing and maturing emotionally in a climate which nurtures such growth.

For the therapist, this is an exhilarating time. Group interaction moves rapidly, and it is difficult to keep pace. The therapist can fall into the trap of accepting his own omnipotence, though at times the group will jar him from this stance. His role is multiple at this point. He must be cognizant of the dynamics of the group, individual dynamics, as well as his own internal dynamics and needs. There is the need to avoid becoming overinvolved with the group (which is all too easy at this stage) so that he becomes subject to manipulation. For some therapists, the dependency relations formed are so satisfying they find it difficult to aid the patient to further growth. It is necessary for the therapist to continually examine his own role vis-à-vis the patient and the group. One of his prime roles is to be the stable, reality-oriented agent in the group. Reality must be stressed, since the patients can create a new reality to coincide with their new perceptions.

Though the patients are moving and growing at this time, regressive phenomena are also present. Hostility and aggression which the patient formerly held in check can now be expressed verbally. The expression of hostility and aggression by one patient can create the climate for other patients to express like emotions. Frequently the therapist, who accepts and attempts to clarify the real object of aggression, becomes the focal point for these feelings. Many therapists are threatened by the abuse heaped on them during this phase of therapy. They tend to try to stem the expression of these threatening feelings. In so doing, they perform a disservice to the patient, since the patient is testing the therapist. I consider that the patient is reliving earlier experiences with the authority figures in his life and is looking for the same responses to the feelings that were aroused earlier. If the patient receives the same responses, he feels justified in avoiding change. The therapist is perceived as no different from others in his life and is just another person not to be trusted.

When the therapist has the self-confidence to accept the patient's expression of hostility and aggression without responding in kind, he creates healthy confusion for the patient. He also provides a stable model of adult behavior on which the patient can rely. The therapist can use his own feelings to advance therapy by indicating that although he is angry with the patient, he can still accept the patient's right as a human being to express feelings verbally. Evaluation of the latent focus of the patient's feelings, and the source of these feelings, by the group and the nonthreatened therapist helps ease the patient's underlying anxiety. Equally important is that the patient is taken seriously and his feelings are valued, thus enhancing the patient's picture of himself.

At the proper time (and the patient will provide the cues), the irrationality of his behavior can be hinted at. The sensitivity of the now relatively sophisticated group is involved in the amount of pressure brought to bear on the patient. Therapists must be sensitive to the level of group anxiety and tension, as well as to the individuals' anxiety and tension level. He must also determine how much his own anxiety and tension enter into his analysis of what the group is doing.

The group is the prime vehicle for establishing a reality base for feelings. It is alternately probing and supportive, but the therapist must constantly reinforce the relationship between feelings and perceptions of reality. His involvement may then serve to increase the individual patient's feelings of dependency on the therapist. This can lead to the working through of earlier crippling dependency relationships, as well as the patient's development of a new relationship with authority. The patient's underlying fear of being a small, helpless creature who has no control over his destiny in his dealings with a powerful authority are eased in the healthy dependency relationship formed with the group and the therapist.

This is a critical stage in the therapeutic process. For some therapists, the movement from hostility and aggression to the expression of dependency on the therapist comes as such a relief that he strives to maintain this relationship. It is pleasant to have an ally in the group. The dependent patient frequently is supportive of the therapist, believing in the therapist's omnipotence. For the patient, he is reliving his early parental relationship with a "good" parent at this time. When the therapist supports the dependent patient against the probing of the group to maintain the therapist's new-found sense of security, the patient ceases to mature. He is safe and protected by the omnipotent power, the therapist. When this occurs, the therapist finds that for some inexplicable reason the group stops functioning. It takes courage on the therapist's part to look at his own role in the halting of group function. He has to be willing to give up this period of relief to aid the patient in becoming more mature and independent.

The patient will do all he can to resist further growth. Manipulation becomes one of the prime defenses to achieve this aim. Having reached a point where he has obtained gratification for needs that have long been unfulfilled, the patient is content to remain in this dependent relationship. He does not wish to encounter additional pain by looking further into himself. His feelings of comfort and satisfaction are new and exciting, and the patient likes these feelings. At the same time he is convinced that he has changed radically, and in the flush of such change, he is sure he will be able to go into society without committing additional crimes. The group will often support the patient in his assertions, seeking to maintain a prisoner code and to identify with the therapist's perceived favored sibling. If the therapist accepts these statements uncritically and moves toward releasing the dependent patient, almost invariably the patient will act out in some manner in the Institution. Should such behavior be ignored by the therapist because of his overinvolvement with the patient, two possibilities exist. First, the patient may return to the community and soon get into difficulty again. Second, he will continue to act out within the Institution until the therapist no longer threatens him with the possibility of the loss of the valued dependency relationship. If the therapist persists in overvaluing the patient's progress, the effect on the group is almost catastrophic. The group loses whatever trust it has been willing to place in the therapist. It regresses by expressing even more hostility or displays passive resistance by refusing to probe into significant areas.

Early in my career as a group therapist with offenders I was prone to be manipulated in this manner. Though I still have needs to help patients, and to be depended on, I am no longer manipulated into such a position as frequently as in the past. My own method of dealing with the dependent patient is to accept his dependency for a short period of time. I cannot be specific as to how long, since I rely on my experience, the patient's behavior, and the group response to cue me. With an enhanced self-percept, the patient can accept the therapist's statement that the patient is the one who has made the effort and has understood himself. The hostile group member unwittingly becomes a therapeutic ally in this process. His anger at the therapist forces him to agree with the therapist. The group then supports the concept that the patient has moved by looking into himself and coming up with his own answers. Omnipotence on the therapist's part is belittled. I use the point I made in the initial group meeting (point 8) of not doing anything for the patient to further reinforce the percept that he has made strides through his own efforts. At the same time, where necessary, I indicate that I will not desert the patient. I make every effort to support steps toward independence in a nonthreatening manner.

Consolidation of Insights: Final Phase

The final stage of group psychotherapy occurs when the patient recognizes his identification with the therapist. He begins to be a junior therapist, a phase which frequently indicates a consolidation of gains. Discomfort is noted, and to me, the process reaches its final point when the patient verbalizes his inability to accept his former friends. Frequently, the patient is anxious that he is different from those with whom he used to be friendly. He states that he can no longer relate to them, or to what they stand for. There is no longer a commonality of interest. The patient no longer thinks as his peers wish him to think. He makes his own decisions. Support from peers and the therapist is accepted but is not vital for his function.

A further aspect of this final stage is the so-called parole jitters. I think it is a classic case of separation anxiety. The patient looks for support in facing a new and unknown future. He tries to postpone leaving the security of the Institution, the group, and the therapist. Old, nonproductive behavior and ways of dealing with feelings surface briefly. It is the therapist's responsibility to continue reinforcing the newer learning while he provides the patient with the luxury of verbally regressing in the group. Additional support for the patient comes from the group. Many of the group members will have experienced this anxiety and are sensitive to it. They support the therapist in his attempts to allay the patient's anxiety and to point out the reality of the situation, as well as the improved self-image the patient has displayed. Fortunately, this phase is quite transitory in my experience, provided the therapist has allowed enough time to elapse that the new learning has become part of the character structure.

This phase is completed when the patient is conditionally released by the Patuxent Institution Board of Review. I am fortunate in that conditional release is also indeterminate, and treatment continues for the patient in our Out-Patient Clinic. He is treated by the same treatment team that worked with him while he was physically in the Institution, guaranteeing continuity. I think this is one of the more important aspects of the total treatment program with dangerous offenders. Although the treatment provided may not be as intensive, it does serve to reinforce the new learning developed in group psychotherapy. It further serves to keep the process of self-examinagion of feelings in the forefront of the patient's perceptions.

Some Words of Caution

The foregoing exposition of group treatment of dangerous offenders displays the process as almost a linear progression from entrance into a group to conditional release. I have been working with offenders too long to make that assumption. Therapy for the offender, as for any other patient, does not follow a linear progression toward emotional stability. All therapy, and particularly therapy with offenders, is composed of false starts, plateaus, and steps backward. These are interspersed, hopefully, with a gradual movement toward perceiving the self and the environment in a less confused manner. This movement can only be seen over time and must be corroborated through observation of changed behavior.

I must also offer another word of caution. Since I run open-ended therapy groups, the position of any patient in the process I have outlined may be varied. One patient may be at the beginning of the process while another group member may be nearing its end. The demands made on the therapist are thus almost overwhelming. He must be aware of where each patient is in the treatment process at any given moment. The therapist must be aware of the group dynamics and interrelationships, as well as those of the individuals. It is incumbent on the therapist to guide the group so that the group probing is done at a level that can be tolerated by the patient who is being probed. The therapist's comments, clarifications, and interpretations must be well thought out and directed toward all members of the group, regardless of the stage at which they are in their treatment. It is all too easy to direct a response to one individual in the group and, ultimately, to do individual therapy in a group setting. The therapist must constantly guard against this. If he does fall into this trap, he loses a most powerful therapeutic tool, the group itself.

I am not so naive as to think that group psychotherapy alone is the panacea and will "cure" the dangerous offender. At Patuxent Institution the therapist is also responsible for involving the patient in vocational training, furthering his education, and restructuring his relationships with the significant figures in his life. We try to view the total patient and his relationship to his environment. In effect, we use the concept of "total-push therapy." My point is not to attempt to restructure the personality but rather is more pragmatic. I try to aid the patient in making such changes as are necessary for him to live in the greater society without such conflict as would cause him to transgress the law and require future confinement.

As a final word, I want to state that I am convinced that change cannot occur with the dangerous offender in the program I have set forth unless there is an indeterminate sentence. I have explained my position extensively in other writings. Briefly, I feel that most repeat offenders have reduced anxiety when they are serving a sentence. Without anxiety, there is little other motivation for change. Therefore, the indeterminate sentence provides the wedge for creating the anxiety which in turn can aid in developing a modified lifestyle.

Future Directions

Attempting to divine the future is at best a parlous process filled with unseen hazards. Nevertheless, everyone does it every day, so I shall attempt it.

Notwithstanding the grim pronouncements of the former Attorney General of the United States, supported by the head of the United States prison system, that rehabilitation is just a myth, I am still optimistic that offenders can change. I think the mental health professional has oversold or overestimated his own capacity to create change in the dangerous offender. When he entered the criminal justice system, it was with high hopes and expectations, but they were focused in only one direction, psychotherapy.

My years of experience working in the penal system have led me to the conclusion that change is possible, under the conditions I have set forth earlier. I feel that society in general will no longer tolerate merely warehousing the dangerous offender. This is a waste of human resources and an unnecessary expense. It is my contention that we must learn that a fragmented approach to the dangerous offender will result in a fragmented human being let loose in society. I have high hopes that we will soon move to the use of all the tools we have at our disposal in an integrated manner to develop an integrated human reentering society. There is a need to develop a plan that is constantly reviewed and revised for each patient. The resources of vocational training, education, psychotherapy, training in social skills, and reaching out to troubled families must be interrelated in a unified whole.

It is my impression that the future direction for the treatment of the dangerous offender will be that of a unified whole. This will occur in fits and starts as each segment involved in this unity vies for power. Ultimately, there will be a recognition that power is not the answer; change in the patient is the answer. What may work for one patient may not work for another. I think the future will see us treating every person as the unique individual he is.

Corrections will give up the monoliths that are cost effective but expensive in terms of human lives. Smaller rehabilitation-oriented institutions will be used to protect society. The goal will be to integrate offenders into the community rather than to isolate them. First steps are being taken in this direction through the use of halfway houses and community corrections.

What I believe will not change in the future is the rush for the sake of political expediency into implementing new concepts that appear to have face validity. I feel the social scientist has a duty to carefully investigate and evaluate new programs and concepts in a scientifically controlled manner before they are adopted as treatment modalities. It is by using his scientific expertise in this manner that the social scientist may in the future make his greatest impact in the treatment of the dangerous offender.

References

Boslow, H.M., D. Rosenthal, A. Kandel, and S.H. Manne. "Methods and Experiences in Group Treatment of Defective Delinquents in Maryland." *Journal of Social Therapy* 7 (1961).

Boslow, H.M., and S. H. Manne. "Mental Health in Action." *Crime and Delinquency* (January 1966).

Defective Delinquent Statute, Article 31B. *The Annotated Code of the Public General Laws of Maryland.*

Manne, S.H. "A Communication Theory of Sociopathic Personality." *American Journal of Psychotherapy* XXI, no. 4 (October 1967).

Manne, S.H. "Some Comments on Hedblom's 'The Dangerous Offender (Preliminary Considerations)'." *The Pennsylvania Association of Probation, Parole, and Corrections* XXVI, no. 1 (Spring 1969).

Manne, S.H., and D. Rosenthal. "I.Q. and Age of First Commitment of Dangerous Offenders." *Correctional Psychologist* 4, no. 6 (May-June 1971).

Manne, S.H. "A Response to an Attack on Maryland's Defective Delinquent Law." *Corrective Psychiatry and Journal of Social Therapy* (April 1973).

12 Reeducation and Rehabilitation of the Criminal

Noël Mailloux

Introduction

Among researchers and practitioners working in the field of criminology, some are mainly interested in the reeducation of the criminal, while others are more concerned with his rehabilitation, or his reintegration into society. This dichotomy can be explained by the fact that some specialists feel better prepared through basic training either to come to the help of the young delinquent or adult criminal on the psychological level or to approach the problem from a social point of view. Unfortunately, one tends to work in almost complete isolation and one thinks of a possible interdisciplinary collaboration when this remains simply tangential. The situation will remain the same as long as proposed remedies are inspired by theories based on abstract conjectures or ideologies that tend to ignore almost entirely the inner difficulties facing the delinquent. So instead of taking into consideration what we have learned from indepth observations about the psychogenesis of criminal conduct and about the dynamics that underlie its various modes of expression, one tends to be satisfied with establishing an imposing array of superficial correlations, which draw our attention away from the essential to turn it to circumstances and conditionings mainly of a contingent nature.

Of course, for prevention and police supervision purposes it can be useful to know that certain crimes are committed more often at a certain time of the day, of the night, of the week, or of the year, or that they are committed more often by individuals coming from such or such a social or cultural background; but it is obvious that this knowledge teaches us nothing about the criminal mind. Independent of this confused mass of statistics, one fact remains which requires an explanation: wherever you go, there have always been people who appear to be without scruples, who are capable of the most horrible crimes, and who lead a life totally contrary to all divine or human laws. Moreover, those people may be civilized or rough, coming from the best or the worst families, belonging to the highest and most prosperous class in society as well as the most modest and underprivileged one. Should not such a fact encourage us to devote less time and money to the study of those accessory aspects of criminality and rather to try to understand fully the particular mentality that considers crime the only way of life?

This is the goal we set for ourselves almost 20 years ago and have never

161

stopped pursuing within the Boscoville establishment, situated within the borders of Montreal. Experience has told us that the more we understand the genesis and the dynamics of that particular pathology, the more precise, efficient, and lasting become our methods of reeducation. However, it is not my aim to present here the detailed results of those confirmed observations; this has been done in a number of previous publications. I would simply like to remind you briefly of a few essential points that will throw light on all the implications of reintroducing the delinquent into society and the conditions essential for success in this delicate venture.

Social Alienation and Narcissistic Regression
in the Recidivist Delinquent

The delinquent placed by a judge into the reeducational establishment of Boscoville very often is just under 18 years of age. It is usually not his first offense, and his compulsion to relapse into crime labels him a young criminal, who cannot be set free again without serious risk to himself and to others.

Besides, without admitting it explicitly, the young offender sees himself as a *black sheep*, reflected in his surroundings as in a mirror. This image (he never could understand why) was given him by the other members of his family who, as far as he can remember, always made him responsible for anything that was done wrong in the house. He finished up by seeing himself as a bad egg from birth, for whom it was quite right to foresee a black future. Once such a conviction was firmly established in his mind, it seemed to him quite natural to justify it in fact by committing all the worst tricks that were suggested to him by people who thought that he was capable or even responsible for doing them. So all his actions went more and more against the normal behavior standards that people claimed they wanted to teach him, for the simple reason that nothing else was expected of him. Every day he conformed more and more with this image of the criminal that people expected to see him become and which he felt he would most certainly ultimately turn out to be.

Overwhelmed by the degrading identity from which he could never see himself escaping, he could not possibly avoid becoming more and more alienated from society. Soon not only his own family mistrusted him, but the whole neighborhood was affected by his attitude. Upon their parents' suggestion, his friends soon came to look upon him as a little "good for nothing" and abandoned him one after another. The same was true at school, where not only was he ostracized, but he received severe reprimands from adults who were important people in his eyes and who were prejudging his intentions and his fate in terms that were as inexorable to him as those he was used to hearing at home. Hardly had he reached the age of adolescence when his reputation was already too compromised for well-brought-up girls to pay attention to him or to tolerate his company. When, a little later on, he let himself be prematurely attracted to the work world in the hope of certain recognition and the satisfaction of the chimeras which resulted from his earlier humiliations and failures, he discovered very quickly that his incompetence reduced him to the simplest of tasks receiving the lowest pay. On the other hand, for a long time already he had not been feeling at ease in church, in youth movements, and recreation centers where all the others liked to gather. In order to avoid being isolated from the rest of society, he felt obliged to seek refuge in a gang made up of his former friends, whom he considered no better than himself, and who were to lead him into a life of crime.

One day, however, following too spectacular a misdemeanor, the representatives of justice were to intervene vigorously and put an end to these exciting activities by means of a fairly long period of imprisonment, to allow for a serious attempt at reeducation. Still under the impact of this shock, which gives him the feeling that he has made an unfortunate blunder just at the moment when his narcissism (inflated by a whole series of all too easy previous successes) is prompting him to believe himself to be all powerful and invulnerable, the boy often shows the signs of a serious regression, which he will strive to overcome by resorting to obvious compensatory reactions. The opportunity of a self-reeducation offered him by an understanding judge had appeared to him, after his failure, as a welcome means of avoiding harsher punishment. But when such threat is passed and he becomes more conscious of the situation into which he has put himself by naively agreeing to be sent to an institution where his readiness to improve will be taken seriously, often he has the impression that he has made a mistake and that he is entangled in an extremely ambiguous situation. How could he become a normal individual, he whom people have always tried to convince of the contrary and who has always been looked upon as *incorrigible*? Moreover, for a long time now a painful feeling of helplessness has led him to consider as futile the faint hopes of changes that he may have entertained during his better moments. Now this disheartening feeling, which the momentary success of his delinquent activities had allowed him to stifle, once again has been emerging in his consciousness since the enormous failure he just suffered. Regretting not having been put in an ordinary prison where he could "do his time" quite peacefully without being asked to question his former mode of existence, he nevertheless wants to shut himself up in this defensive attitude. Out of fear that he will see trouble in his consciousness, conflicts that would drive him back into a state of anxiety, he has recourse to all kinds of tricks to avoid the demand of an attempted reeducation, which would force him to look himself straight in the face. Most frequently, this means escaping from a reality from which he does not yet dare risk fleeing physically, as he may well in fact do later on, by giving in to the ideas of grandeur. Certainly, if he imagines himself capable of committing the perfect crime, he can believe himself clever enough to play a part for his educators, while preparing himself for a career in crime immediately after his liberation, which he considers he has begun already and which the police certainly are not aware of.

Sometimes also, as a first effort to heal as quickly as possible the unbearable wound to his own pride that the recent failure has opened, the young delinquent boldly tries to join the ranks of his educators by showing off as the "good prisoner." Disavowing his past errors, without the slightest hesitation, he declares that he is completely in agreement with the aims of reeducation, as it appears to him in the institution, and he firmly believes that he has already attained these aims and recovered his original innocence. Assuming a moralizing and detached tone, he expresses himself with the sort of wisdom and assurance that attracts skeptcial rebuff from those of his friends for whom reeducation already seems like a living experience, and who in their own expression are beginning to "understand" its sense and more and more demanding implications. Soon with his back against the wall but still feeling himself incapable of giving up the imaginary omnipotence which makes him believe that he has complete control over his impulses and destiny, he tries to keep the feeling of his personal self-esteem intact by giving himself an assurance that is as fictitious as it is unshakable. Such a defensive reaction is quite easily understandable if one remembers that at this level of regression, any differentiation between impulse, thought, and actions tends to be obliterated. From then on, one can immediately see why the slightest solicitations from the outside world formerly led the young delinquent to act out almost automatically. On the other hand, in a milieu where demands work in the opposite direction and where delinquent acting out is curtailed, must not we expect the process to work in the opposite direction? Now that he cannot perform the same gestures as he could before, the delinquent soon ceases to see himself as such and manages to convince himself that he would have no difficulty in behaving as normally as anyone else if only people would agree to let him free. When he is reminded of his past offenses, he speaks about them as if he were talking about someone else's offenses or as if they had been committed in a moment of forgetfulness that could never again occur. Also, he obstinately repeats that he has no place in a reeducation establishment, and that he is just wasting his time, because he is ready to lead an exemplary life as soon as he is allowed to return home. In the meantime, naturally, it is not for him to take part in the reeducation program, which has value only for those who have lost all control of themselves or do not wish to change their past habits.

In spite of the fact that it is schematic, the description that we have just given of the typical recidivist—such as he often appears to us when, after having exhausted all other options open to them, the courts send him to Boscoville for an indepth and long-term reeducation—makes it possible for us to state the degree to which he has become alienated from the society. Likewise, as soon as he sees himself forced to make an effort at personal reeducation, which might bring about a transformation in him and make him capable of once more taking his place in society, his resistance will be fundamentally the same and just as difficult to overcome, whether it takes the form of a violent rebellion and the glorification of his delinquency or is disguised under the appearance of an easy, almost miraculous, conversion. Such observation should help us realize how ambiguous is the usual starting point of the whole process of reeducation or treatment of the criminal.

Two Decisive Turning Points in the Reeducation of the Delinquent

The first decisive turning point in the reeducation of the delinquent coincides with the moment (at the end of a relatively brief period of getting used to discipline and the various formative activities of the institutional life) he feels prepared to become integrated in a group whose members have already accepted their own reeducation under the guidance of a team of educators. The educators, like his new friends, are usually idealized by him out of all proportion, whereas, for his part, he feels quite incapable of participating in equal terms in the numerous activities, whether they be scholastic, manual, social, artistic, or athletic, that the others are constantly talking about as if they have been familiar with them for a long time. Doubting his natural abilities and aptitudes, he again feels himself invaded by a depressing feeling of impotence that makes him want to keep himself apart from the others. Not daring to take pleasure in fantasies of the great deeds of hardened criminals, he still has secret ambitions that lead him to claim the right not to waste time in common activities that "would be of no use to him" or would be contrary to his personal tastes. So he sometimes abandons the group to play the guitar in order to become a concert artist, to write a novel or poems that will make him famous, or to devote himself entirely to working out plans for the future.

In spite of all this, under the influence of an understanding group of people who are constantly seeking his collaboration and offering him encouragement and assistance, he finally gives way to the increasing desire to respond to the invitation being made to him, assuming once and for all the role and responsibilities that are allocated to him. Gradually, as the neutralization of part of his narcissistic impulses takes place, and as he becomes more and more capable of interest in methodical and sustained effort, he abandons his fantasies and turns toward concrete achievements that can soon be compared with the achievements of others. With repeated successes he manages to find a place for himself in the group, where he is soon recognized as one of the full-fledged members. In this way he gets an opportunity to discover his aptitudes and talents, and even perhaps a taste for effort and perseverance, which were foreign to him previously and which now open unexpected and more and more attractive prospects for the future. At the same time, in his innermost conscience, he feels some normal self-esteem, which gives him a fair amount of assurance when faced with the external world. So once more he wishes to come into contact with society and one day, hopefully, to find his place in it.

Obviously a very important stage has just been reached, and there is no doubt at all about the presence of a solid starting point for the work of indepth reeducation. Certainly, these alternating moments of discouragement and narcissistic exhaltation will return whenever the young delinquent finds himself forced to learn a new activity, whether he has to become part of a sports team, learn algebra, prove his artistic talent in the ceramic workshop, or work in theater workshop. However fragile the confidence born in him from the unforgettable experience of a *real* success may be, it is sufficient to slow down his tendency to belittle himself as well as to make him aware of the vanity of dreams of grandeur. Even if he still entertains many doubts as to the range and extent of his abilities, he at least knows that he is *good for something* and that, in this respect, he still has a lot to discover. So taking more and more seriously the suggestions of his educators and more advanced friends, he begins to progressively widen the scope of his interests and to work in new directions. For the first time in his life, he has the comforting impression that his efforts are really effective and that his development is advancing at a pace that both surprises and fascinates him. From now on, his creativity fascinates him to such an extent that he, who was formerly so apathetic and nonchalant, can be seen applying himself to long and difficult tasks with a determination that often astonishes us.

However, in spite of this productivity, which is proof of authentic talent, clear aptitudes, and recognized ability, the delinquent, even if he gives way to the dangerous temptation of not pursuing any further the work of his reeducation, is very conscious that for him the real problem is in no way solved. In fact, a better educated thief who has also become more conscious of his abilities, even if he has at the moment of his liberation no intention of returning to his interrupted career, represents for society an even greater risk than before. Simply because he now realizes that he is good for something, he is not thereby assured of becoming good, i.e., a fundamentally righteous man. Even if he has evolved a great deal and he believes himself capable of controling his impulses, an extremely threatening doubt remains a source of anxiety in the depth of his mind. At the point he has reached, he feels satisfied at having discovered what he is capable of doing and he has retrieved a certain self-esteem by realizing that fullest potential to which people like him can still aspire. However, in his eyes, a more radical change is quite impossible; he remains firmly convinced that the delinquent he has always been could not become an honest man without having a *nature* quite different from the one he received at birth.

Moreover, this is what leads us to speak of a second turning point in reeducation, one no doubt more decisive and possessing much greater consequences than the first. It takes place precisely at the moment at which the delinquent is beginning to free himself from the dreadful illusion of the perversity of his nature and is beginning to envisage the possibility of a change that will end in the progressive awakening of his moral conscience and make him capable of meeting the demands of life in society. It is not difficult to imagine the alternations of anxiety and hope the vicissitudes of this new stage will inevitably entail, both in the delinquent who accepts to become involved in it and in those whose duty it is to guide and encourage him in this most difficult of enterprises. In the case of the delinquent boy, now that he has learned to make constructive use of his aggressiveness, he cannot avoid measuring the extent of the disaster he has made of his past life and counting the ruins he has continuously accumulated along the way and, even more alarming, within himself. Scared, he now wonders through what miracle of courage and ingeniousness he will manage to rebuild his future with the reduced resources remaining.

Moreover, with growing lucidity, but without yet possessing sure enough moral judgment to make it possible for him better to control his conduct, he clearly perceives that he now cannot return to his former ways without accepting much more responsibility, without deceiving those he feels love him deeply, and without running directly to his ruin. On the other hand, for those who wish to help him complete his reeducation, the task does not really appear neither less demanding nor less heavy in responsibility. They are well aware that in his disturbed state, this young man sees them as models from which to construct his new ideal of the ego capable of counterbalancing the still oppressive influence of an unforgiving superego. They know also that at times of temptation and doubt he will never stop turning toward them for help in defining values that will become for him a rule of life and help him form an honest and lucid conscience. Finally, they know that the evolution and fate of this "rebel without a cause," which they have managed to turn away temporarily from his aberrant projects, are now going to depend upon the authentic quality of the human relationship they will establish with him.

In the context of this rapprochement, in which intimacy is associated with profound respect for liberty and develops in the course of more and more yearned for communication, one is not long in observing obvious signs of internal changes. In the case of a boy, for example, coarse speech is replaced by politeness, his mistrust becomes friendliness, lies are replaced by frankness, the exploitation of others gives way to generosity, meanness becomes devotion, from egocentricity he moves toward a concern for the common good, until one would find it very difficult to recognize him if such a change had not taken place before one's very eyes. Very happy to have been able to get rid of this defensive armor, he admits candidly in the presence of his friends that he wants to change and is determined to take advantage of any assistance offered him so as to bring this change about as soon as possible.

A very experienced educator knows very well that this evolution, although so gratifying and fruitful, is beset with too many obstacles and risks for it not to encounter difficulties. The risks of an outing, an unexpected relapse or an alluring provocation, will often bring about once more the temptation toward discouragement and escape. But the desire to win back the esteem and confidence of an educator will soon bring about a recovery, sometimes slow and painful but sometimes spectacular and decisive.

However, we must stress that at this final stage of reeducation, a difficulty arises in the mind of the former delinquent the importance of which has for too long escaped us and which does not fail to evoke in him a vague anxiety that from time to time disturbs his conscience but not perceptibly enough for him to be able to come to grips with it.

Now that he has been able to have frequent contact with the outside world, he casually manages to tell us, without giving any more details regarding his thoughts, that "people on the outside are very different" from those he has met in Boscoville, and that he will never be able to have the same confidence in them. Preoccupied with his departure in the near future, he pretends to attach no importance to this impression which visibly disturbs him and about which he avoids speaking in any more detail. Conscious of the radical change that has taken place within him, and convinced that we believe in this change as much as he does, he still wonders, as a result of recent experience, whether or not he is always going to come up against a similar skepticism from all those whose clearly manifested confidence would mean they recognize his rediscovered integrity, the sincerity of his intention, and the competence he has just acquired. Suddenly he perceives clearly that he will no longer be able to count on the understanding and discreet advice of an educator when he arrives at his parish or school, when applying for a job, or when returning to his family. In short, it is the thorny problem of a rehabilitation and effective reintegration into society that now fills his attention and tests the validity of the tremendous effort of his reeducation. To solve the problem, he feels completely alone, unable to prevent himself from asking the same question over and over again: will those he is about to meet be capable of enough human understanding to grant him the only favor he asks of them: to have faith in him—complete faith?

How the Delinquent Sees His Rehabilitation

Of those who are actually interested in the rehabilitation of the delinquent, very few suspect the intensity, significance, duration, and implications of the doubts I have just described, as they exist in his mind. Most rehabilitators feel that they have completed their task when their protégé manages to keep a modest job (often obtained out of pity) and lead a fairly quiet life that does not attract the attention of the police for one or two years. For this individual, on the contrary, one cannot speak of rehabilitation as long as he cannot live in the open, seek a job with a future, and accept important responsibilities without running the risk of being denounced and publicly humiliated. This means that rehabilitation in the true sense of the word has nothing to do with our present concern. One might wonder whether the criminal who avoids a form of treatment that will lead him into this impasse is not much more clearsighted and realistic than we are. May this logic of the absurd permit us finally to remove all the illogical aspects of an approach we have been obstinately pursuing for too long and encourage us to thoroughly reexamine a problem which is dear to our heart!

First of all it is a fact that society really does not take its responsibilities seriously with regard to its criminals. Society collaborates in the rehabilitation of criminals only to the extent that the criminals can be fed on the crumbs society drops from its table. As one climbs the social ladder, however, one immediately notices that society is very careful to defend itself against the criminal. With the help of constraints imposed from the outside by insurance companies, purely arbitrary internal regulations, and even outdated laws that people refuse to abolish, large companies and public services draw up barriers against ex-offenders which close the door to positions that their abilities could allow them to fill.

As an excuse, we concede that such an attitude, even if it is inhuman in certain cases, is reasonably justified by the facts. Experience proves only too often that the typical criminal seems as incapable of avoiding a relapse as if he were, to employ one of Freud's comparisons, a toy in the hand of a demon or an inexorable fate. Likewise, experience has long since taught us that punishment and incarceration are certainly not appropriate and effective ways of freeing a man from this compulsion to keep on repeating indefinitely the same criminal gestures. Moreover, such threatening expectation is no surprise to us, because similar compulsions, although less dangerous, may exist in each one of us. However, who would dare to affirm that prison is the best way of helping an alcoholic, a car driver who has many accidents, a competent worker who loses all his jobs, a lover whose every attempt at marriage is a failure, or a person who is always engaging in law suits that are lost in advance? Why should it be any different for the criminal who is always in the same mess?

Let us agree on this point. We are neither considering all criminals as sick people nor are we suggesting that our prisons should be turned into psychiatric hospitals. On the other hand, if the great majority of our criminals are not sick people, we can hardly conclude that they can exert effective control over certain of their impulses and return to normal behavior without any outside assistance. In certain circumstances, some people do not hesitate to speak of treatment. Since this expression seems to be a source of constant misunderstanding, however, we have preferred to use the term *reeducation* to refer to a highly specialized type of work using techniques that are rapidly approaching the point of reasonable efficacy. This leads us to understand why so few people are anxious to have confidence in the criminal who has just been set free. We know only too well that our prisons are not reeducation centers in which the prisoners may hope to receive the assistance absolutely vital to their ability to lead normal lives in society. In short, the most elementary logic suggests that our attempts at rehabilitation should take the form of a prolonged serious program of reeducation if we do not want these attempts to be in vain, as is too often the case. A similar approach would also permit us better to understand the profound expectation of the person who, at the end of a successful period of reeducation, shows himself willing to collaborate in his rehabilitation with the enthusiasm, provided one consents to guide him in this difficult enterprise as long as he feels a need for it. Without this he would, in effect, be strongly inclined to limit his meetings to some of his friends in misfortune who, like him, are too advanced in their reeducation to return to a life of crime while at the same time too insecure vis-à-vis society to think of becoming fully integrated once more into society.

It is therefore important to insist from the very beginning upon an essential fact that is not ordinarily taken into account. For the reeducated delinquent, rehabilitation means above all else the implicit recognition that a profound moral change has taken place that allows him as a person to rediscover his human dignity. Simultaneously, on the social level, the reeducated delinquent must sufficiently increase in esteem to be welcomed everywhere without the slightest reservation as an honest and responsible citizen. Only the assurance that can be given him by the experience of rehabilitation in this sense will allow the former delinquent to accept the idea of a reintegration into society, limited only by his abilities and competence, and having nothing in common with a superficial and precarious adaptation that will condemn him to live under the sign of pretense and shame.

As we can easily understand, a successful rehabilitation implies a delicate and difficult step during which the delinquent has to retrace the stages that led him toward social alienation. His reeducation has in itself made him aware of the extent to which his social alienation has occurred. Certainly he has long since become aware of the stupidity of the sweeping prejudices he has entertained with regard to all those claiming to contribute to the well-being of society and the self-excusing use he has often made of them. But he knows that others have not yet abandoned their prejudices toward him, even if these prejudices are more veiled and subtle. It is only too clear that they distrust him when they see him in his true light. In turn, he will have to explain himself and establish normal frank relations with people who live in his district, with a school principal, later on with an employer, with a young girl he dreams to marry, and finally with the members of his family, who will almost always be the last to believe that he has changed. In this way, we can see the close links between the rehabilitation process and the reeducation process. Likewise we realize that the suggestion and support of an expert adviser will prove indispensable throughout this new phase, which is as beset with difficulties as the first phase. We are especially conscious of the prodigious effort that will have to be expended with regard to all those most important to anyone trying to rediscover his place in society. Priests, teachers, employers, neighbors, or parents must possess an understanding that will make them capable of meeting the offender's expectations without his needing to disclose them. Soon, in fact, all those who are responsible for the quality of the welcome given the delinquent when he returns to his natural milieu will have to become aware that, all things being equal, the support he is expecting from them as he pursues his rehabilitation is very much like the support he received from his educators during his reeducation. In other words, for the purposes of his rehabilitation his natural milieu will have to offer a setting that is just as favorable as the one offered by the correction center for his reeducation.

Conclusion

In my previous works devoted to juvenile delinquency, my attention was almost entirely drawn to problems met in the study of the delinquent personality, or in the concrete work of reeducation. From a few observed facts, the implications of which I am only just beginning to glimpse, I thought I might take advantage of this opportunity to break new ground in the still sparsely explored field of rehabilitation. In fact, rehabilitation is an extremely important element of applied psychology in which, except for a little statistical research, the work is still at the elementary stage. By showing where its roots are, I have been able to clarify its significance and discern its principal stages. This has led to very suggestive hypotheses that I will soon try to put to the test. To this end, I have conceived the ambitious project of preparing a human community—I am speaking here of a Montreal parish—to take charge of the rehabilitation of its delinquents and criminals. Hoping in this way that a model approach can be established that would be used elsewhere, I hope at the same time to take advantage of the opportunity for a better understanding of the final stages of a delinquent's return to society.

Part IV
Trends in the Administration of Justice

13 Police Theory: New Perspectives

Bernard Cohen

Introduction

Theoretical concepts pertaining to the police are few, and theories of police organizations and performance, particularly from a sociological perspective, are even less numerous. For this reason this chapter attempts to develop certain theoretical concepts dealing with large police organizations which hopefully will provide a better understanding of the sociological mechanisms accounting for the genesis, persistence, and performance of these organizations. Throughout this discussion, the objective is to determine the effects that certain occupational experiences of police officers have on the structure of the police organization. I do not elaborate why police exhibit certain consistent patterns of behavior. For example, in the discussion of violent force utilized by police, I am interested more in "what effect violent force has on the police organization," than in the traditional question, "why do the police utilize violent force." Similarly, I consider determination of the effects of various forms of discretion on the police organization more significant than merely why police officers exercise discretion.

The chapter begins with a discussion of how bureaucratic and legal elements shape the police organization, producing structures which invariably conflict with the basic job demands of police officers serving in the field. Afterwards I discuss the police subculture, which is the structural response by police officers to this problem. Several factors, including the exclusive use of violent force by the police and the exercise of broad discretion, are analyzed in terms of their impact on the genesis and persistence of the police subculture.

The Police Bureaucracy

Most major urban police departments in the United States constitute huge bureaucracies. The largest police bureaucracy in this country is the New York City Police Department, with nearly 30,000 sworn personnel and approximately 5000 civilian employees. Its personnel are organized into well over a hundred police divisions or units, and each of these is broken down into numerous sections and subsections. Other large departments include Chicago, with nearly 13,000 sworn personnel, and Philadelphia and Los Angeles, each with approximately 7000 officers. At least 75 other departments in the United States range in size from 500 to 6000 police officers.

175

These departments exhibit the major characteristics of bureaucracy, which include division of labor, specialization, a hierarchy of authority, an administrative staff, compensation related to one's position, continuity of operation and employment, and use of contracts or agreements that specify in advance a person's obligations to the organization.

Several scholars argue that the central problem characterizing most large police agencies in the United States is related directly to the conflict between the rule of law, or the legal order, on the one hand and the bureaucratic structure on the other hand. Skolnick, for example, is a proponent of this point of view. He states,

The police in democratic society are required to maintain order and to do so under the rule of law. As functionaries charged with maintaining order, they are part of the bureaucracy. The ideology of democratic bureaucracy emphasizes initiative rather than disciplined adherence to rules and regulations. By contrast, the rule of law emphasizes the rights of individual citizens and constraints upon the initiative of legal officials. This tension between the operational consequences of ideas of order, efficiency, and initiative on the one hand, and legality, on the other, constitutes the principle problem of police as a democratic legal organization.[1]

Skolnick perceives the police bureaucracy as a dysfunctional force shaping the behavior of its officers because the impersonality, calculability, and emphasis on efficiency by a bureaucracy imposes pressures on the individual officer to sacrifice legality for the exigencies of law enforcement. Accordingly, an officer may violate the civil and legal rights of a suspect in order to effect an arrest that will in turn satisfy the demands of the organization. According to Skolnick, the bureaucratic pressures automatically lead the officer to behave in an unlawful manner. On the other hand, the legal system attempts to protect the rights of the suspect by controlling the authority of the police officer.

In this chapter I suggest an alternative to the point of view that the major police problem in a democratic society is a result of tension between the legal order and the police bureaucracy. Admittedly, it is the legal order which attempts to restrain illegal forms of behavior by police officers, but this objective usually is accomplished only within the context of the police bureaucracy. Accordingly the police bureaucracy, when *properly* structured and organized, can be the mechanism for channeling and implementing directives emanating from the legal order.

The police bureaucracy, then, rather than invariably conflicting with the legal order, can be the social structure through which its goals may be achieved. Ideally, all bureaucracies strive for efficient achievement of organizational objectives, and the police bureaucracy is no exception. However, bureaucracies must also operate within a specified and definable societal value system which serves as a mechanism of constraint and control in selecting means to carry out its operations and goals.

A major objective of a corporation is the maximization of profit, but it still must pursue this goal within the framework of the law. Although price fixing might be the best and most efficient means for earning profit, its illegality may restrain most corporations from its practice. Similarly, one of the major objectives of the police bureaucracy is to detect and then arrest individuals who violate the law. In order to accomplish these ends, however, the police must conform to a rigid set of rules and procedures. It may very well be that among the most efficient means to detect crime and effect an arrest are stopping, searching, and interrogating suspicious persons without probable cause or on false pretexts. But because these practices constitute blatant violations of the law, most police departments have established policies aimed at reducing these forms of misconduct. Instead, all arrests must be effected within the framework of legal prescriptions. The important point is that although a bureaucracy must strive toward maximizing efficiency, it must also provide the structural mechanism for limiting this objective whenever it comes into conflict with the rule of law. Similarly, the police bureaucracy must conform to the legal system and implement its policies within the framework of the law, particularly since it is society's most visible and pronounced representative of the law. On the action level, a well-established police bureaucracy will subordinate considerations of efficiency so that its higher objective of "upholding the law" will be achieved. Police efficiency therefore must bend to the higher principle of conformity within the framework of the legal system.

Max Weber was one of the earliest scholars to recognize these positive aspects of bureaucracy. According to Weber,

Fully developed bureaucracy operates in a special sense *sina ira ac studio* [without bias or favor]. Its peculiar character and with its appropriateness for capitalism is the more fully actualized the more bureaucracy "depersonalizes" itself, i.e., the more completely it succeeds in achieving that condition which is acclaimed as its peculiar virtue, namely the exclusion of love, hatred, and every purely personal, especially irrational, and incalculable feeling from the execution of official tasks. In the place of the old-type ruler who is moved by sympathy, favor, grace, and gratitude, modern culture requires for its sustaining external apparatus the emotionally detached, and hence rigorously professional expert. . . .[2]

Following Weber's lead, Blau and Meyer added, "This is another way of saying that bureaucratically organized enforcement agencies are necessary for all members of the society to be equal under the law."[3]

Bureaucratization of the police may tend, in several ways, to uphold the rule of law rather than undermine it. First, employment is based upon technical qualification and ability, rather than ascribed status. Efforts are made to minimize the effects of race, color, or creed in the selection of officers. Promotions and career advancement are based to a large extent upon civil service examinations rather than the number of arrests or other questionable measures of police performance. Also the uniform standards, rules, and procedures of the police organization help to prevent discrimination at the same time buttressing equal protection under the law. In this writer's opinion, the legal system, operating through rather than in opposition to the police bureaucracy, produces certain pressures that exert control over the police organization thus assuring the public that police officers will strive to carry out official duties within the context of the law. Of course, some police organizations have systematically violated the law, but this may be due to a malfunctioning bureaucratic structure or to external factors.

If the legal system exerts pressures on individual officers to conform to the law, what then accounts for widespread violations of the law by police officers and, sometimes, by entire police organizations? The answer to this question is complex, but it is partially related to the tension which exists between the legal system and the police bureaucracy, on the one hand, and the police subculture, on the other hand.

The Police Subculture

The police subculture is a product of certain conditions inherent in the nature of police work which frustrate the realization of bureaucratic goals. Police officers in the field usually work alone or with partners, under minimum supervision. They perform varied functions ranging from simple ones, such as assisting a child in crossing a busy intersection, to the most complex, such as intervening and providing guidance in a family dispute. It has been suggested that at various times, an officer must perform the functions of a social worker, a minister, a teacher, a physician, and an ombudsman; and in any one situation, he may serve as a mediator, enforcer, disciplinarian, and counselor. While providing services to the public, an officer is a generalist, while in performing the law enforcement function, he is a specialist whose training includes the use of lethal force.

The wide range of tasks required by police work, as well as its complexity, does not lend itself easily to bureaucratization. Efficiency as perceived by the organization is constantly undermined by the complexity of the officer's job. Moreover, broad discretion exercised by police officers run counter to efficiency and bureaucratization. The peculiar and difficult nature of police work and the powers which society invests in the police are especially conducive to the formation of the police subculture.

The police subculture exhibits certain characteristics, some or most of which are found in other organizations. These include regimentation, fear of danger, secrecy, isolation, authority, and discretion. What distinguishes the police subculture from other subcultures is that it alone possesses the exclusive and monopolistic authority to exercise legitimate physical and lethal force against a citizen population. It is significant that the police subculture exists within the framework of the police bureaucracy and yet is separate from it. The police subculture is an informal collectivity which surfaces in response to the complex occupational demands encountered by police officers in the field. It is not part of the formal organizational structure of the department. While the police bureaucracy includes all members and units of the force, the police subculture may only include those individuals whose work routinely brings them into situations where they may have to apply physical force.

In most large urban police departments, the majority of the patrol force, detectives, plainclothes officers, and many first-line supervisors belong to the police subculture. It is less likely, however, for commanding officers to be part of this fraternity, because they neither share the same experiences as low-ranking officers nor are they exposed to the myriad of specific pressures to which nonranking members are subjected. Not only is it unlikely for commanding officers to encounter situations in their daily work where application of physical force is required, but it is equally unlikely that they will be exposed to the same level of danger as patrol officers. Commanding officers often do not wear uniforms. They do not interact continuously with the public nor are they threatened by the legal system to the same extent as lower-ranking officers. Also, as we shall explain later, there is a distinction in the type of discretion utilized by commanding officers and members of the rank and file. Thus, the further up one is in the hierarchy of the police organization, the less likely he is to be a member of the police subculture. Because police commanders served as patrol officers at one time or another during their careers, it is probable that the majority once belonged to the police subculture. Whether or not most commanding officers of a particular force continue to maintain membership in this police fraternity depends upon certain conditions and processes, including higher education and the civil service system.

The police subculture differs from the police bureaucracy in several ways. The police bureaucracy stresses efficiency within the confines of the law, while the police subculture emphasizes improvisation and shortcuts. On the surface it appears that the aim of an individual officer is to satisfy the demand of the police bureaucracy, but in fact, in most police departments he is controlled by the police subculture. A natural tension exists between the police bureaucracy and the police subculture. The police bureaucracy provides an officer with formal rules and procedures to accomplish organizational aims, while the police subculture offers the officer informal but realistic means for attaining these same ends. The different situations encountered by the police officer are of such variety, uniqueness, and complexity that only the police subculture can provide him with the means to accomplish specific tasks. This situation creates a tension between bureaucratic means and the legal order, on the one hand, and realistic means provided by the police subculture, on the other. The police bureaucracy requires conformity and behavior within the structure of the law, while the police subculture demands that the officer perform his tasks in the simplest, safest, and most direct manner, while protecting himself from physical harm. In many instances, the tension between the bureaucracy and the police "entity" places the officer in a conflicting or compromising situation.

The Police Subculture and Violent Force

Several factors contribute to the formation of the unique structure we have referred to as the *police subculture*, but the authority to use violent force probably is the single most significant element. Perhaps the significance of this element in shaping the police organization is reflected by the fact that a police organization in this country is routinely referred to as a *police force* rather than a *police service*. While the legal order and the police bureaucracy attempt to provide definitions, rules, and regulations to guide and control individual officers in the use of violent force, the police subculture is the vehicle through which violent force usually is exercised. Participants in the police subculture, unlike police commanders, encounter situations where they must use violent force. While the nearly exclusive potential right of police to use violent force against the citizen population helps shape the police bureaucracy, it has an even greater impact on the police subculture. This is because participants of the police subculture are the implementors of violent force, while the police bureaucrats or commanders are charged with its control.

Types of Violent Force

There are three distinct forms of violent force. The first is *legal* or *necessary violent force*. This force is generally exercised during the commission of a felony in the officer's presence or when a suspect resists arrest for any crime.

Another form of violent force utilized by the police is *unnecessary violent force*. Unnecessary violent force is used in conjunction with necessary force. It emerges in situations where the officer is authorized by law to engage in necessary force but more force than is needed is applied to effect the arrest. Here unnecessary force is a direct extention of necessary force, because the initial motivation for the use of force was required by law, although its continuation and escalation is in violation of the law.

A third form of violent force may be termed *police brutality*. This generally emerges in situations in which the officer does not have the legitimate prescribed authority to use violent force. For example, if a crime is committed, a suspect may be placed under arrest. Although the suspect may be subdued and can no longer offer resistance, the officer, nevertheless, exercises violent force for personal reasons. This type of behavior is little different from the routine violent behavior of ordinary citizens.

Violent Force and Its Impact

In order to understand the police as an institution, and particularly the police subculture, which is the organizational entity through which violent force is implemented, we must understand more about the monopoly of the use of this force vested in the police by the state.

In this connection one traditional question is, "why do the police engage in various forms of force and violence?" It may very well be that this question does not address the critical issue of police behavior, and, therefore, its discussion will be deferred. A more immediate task is to determine, "what are the effects of the legitimate use of violent force on the police organization and on its individual officers?" This question is particularly significant because the police service is the single organization in our society which, under certain conditions, is authorized to use force against a civilian population that has not been labeled criminal through formal procedures.

Violent force, more than any other form of behavior, is what distinguishes deviance in police work from forms of deviance displayed by members of other professions. Few if any peacetime professions outside the police are invested by the state with the formal power to inflict violent force, albeit legitimate, on its citizens. The use of violent force, for example, by corrections personnel may be viewed as a police function. Nevertheless, it is imposed on a select population that has been formally identified and given a special legal status by society. A similar explanation may be offered for violent force exercised by custodial personnel in mental institutions. In this example, as well, violent force is inflicted on a limited population that has been defined as "different" or "unique" by certain formal legal procedures.

As stated previously, the critical question concerning police organizations is not, "why police engage in violent force," but rather "*what effects* does the use of violent force have on the police organization and the individual officer?" In what ways does exclusive and monopolistic use of violent force by a relatively small collectivity of individuals affect their behavior? The solution to these related questions is complex because the use of violent force apparently affects the social, cultural, and psychological structure of police. Yet, few scholars have approached the complex issues of police organization from this vantage point.

The use of violent force ultimately affects the character and composition of the police subculture. It is suggested that one reason why police are recruited primarily from the working class is because society requires persons for police work who will not hesitate to use violent force. Persons recruited from the middle class may not be able to serve as the implementors of violent force against a civilian population because of powerful internalized prohibitions against this form of behavior. On the other hand, the working class contains a subculture of violence where several forms of this behavior are acceptable. In addition, the police salary schedule and educational requirements may be determined partially by society's overriding concern to recruit police officers who will readily use violent force. The relatively low salary schedules and educational requirements of most large police organizations tend to attract individuals from lower rather than middle classes. The police subculture thus will be comprised of persons primarily of lower-class backgrounds. This does not contravene the argument that the police occupation also is a means of upward mobility for persons from the lower class. On the contrary, the potential for the use of violent force probably tends to attract persons from the lower class because police work offers a means by which individuals may express their need for violence through a more sophisticated structure and legitimate channel. Here lower-class violence is transformed into respectable middle-class force.

The use of violent force is not only significant in determining the character of the police subculture, it also adds to our knowledge concerning its persistence. The fact that only police officers and not others are permitted to use force against citizens creates and strengthens solidarity among group members. Socioculturally, the police are sacred and are set apart from and by the population at large as a result of their special powers to utilize violent force.

Group cohesion is further solidified by the potential ease with which legitimate violent force may be transformed into unnecessary violent force or police brutality. Force is a form of behavior which, once initiated, is difficult to control; and only a hair-splitting difference exists between legitimate force, unnecessary force, and police brutality. Indeed, the dividing line between these three forms of force is razor thin. Police officers, more than anyone else, are aware of this fact, and they realize that their actions are particularly susceptible to misinterpretation by others. A defensive reaction further reinforces the unique solidarity exhibited by the police subculture.

The personality of a police officer also undergoes change as a result of the unique authority to use violent force. Behavior once forbidden has now become legitimate when expressed in the role of police officer. An officer's personality is affected by this change in the sense that a form of behavior hitherto repressed is now being released. An officer must grow accustomed to the fact that situations will eventually arise where legitimate violent force must be exercised. And if he is to maintain membership in this subculture, he must abide by its rules.

The police subculture serves as the immediate social mechanism which triggers the release of whatever internalized constraints exist against the use of violence. The police bureaucracy neutralizes prohibitions against the use of legitimate violent force and by and large strives to control unnecessary use of force. The police subculture encourages legitimate violent force and even unnecessary use of force, but censures police brutality except in certain situations and under extreme conditions.

In sum, the exclusive use of violent force by police creates the social and psychological conditions that result in the establishment of strong bonds of solidarity among police officers, which in turn reinforces the cohesiveness of the police subculture.

Police Use of Violent Force

Several attempts have been made to explain the use of legitimate and illegitimate violent force by police organizations. Emile Durkheim was one of the earliest theorists to present a meaningful theoretical framework for those forms of behavior, utilizing the concepts of repressive laws. Although Durkheim concentrated on force used by organized society, his concept of repressive law also provides an explanation of violent force utilized by the police. Concerning a law that is violated, Durkheim stated,

Denied so categorically, it (i.e., a law) would necessarily lose its energy, if an emotional reaction to the community did not come to compensate its loss, and it would result in a breakdown of social solidarity. It is necessary, then, that it be affirmed forcibly at the very moment when it is contradicted, and the only means of affirming it is to express the unanimous aversion which the crime continues to inspire, by an authentic act which can consist only in suffering, inflicted on the agent.[4]

According to Durkheim, a cohesive group such as the police is likely to apply repressive law, which ultimately results in a form of punishment and vengeance. The application of violence serves several useful functions for the police. First, it provides summary punishment of the criminal, especially in situations when the courts may be excessively lenient. Second, it attempts to deter the criminal as well as others from committing the same or similar acts. Third, it serves to protect the police from injury and harm. Finally, it strengthens police solidarity and cohesion, while at the same time reaffirming who the real criminals are. For these reasons the police "entity" is a social structure particularly suitable for the use of violent force as an expression of repressive law.

A more recent explanation of violent behavior by police is offered by William Westley, who conducted a classic case study of a municipal police department.[5] He argued that the main reason police utilize illegal forms of violence is to defend and improve their social status. Accordingly, police may use illegitimate violence to coerce a suspect or to ensure an arrest. The illegitimate use of violence is directly related to a police officer's occupational experience, in that the police employ violence to persuade the public to respect their occupational status.

Another reason police use illegitimate force, according to Westley, is the belief by police that the courts will not adequately punish the offender. Consequently, the police utilize unnecessary force in obtaining informal control over certain forms of criminal behavior, especially those acts which are particularly offensive to the community (e.g., sex crimes).

Westley summarizes his thoughts on police violence in the following way:

These results suggest (1) that the police believe that these private or group ends constitute a moral legitimization for violence which is equal or superior to the legitimization derived from the law and (2) that the monopoly of violence delegated to the police, by the state to enforce the ends of the state has been appropriated by the police as a personal resource to be used for personal and group ends.[6]

Discretion, Bureaucracy, and the Police Subculture

Perhaps the second most significant factor in shaping the structure and character of police organizations is the element of discretion. *Discretion* is the act of making certain decisions based on one's judgment or pleasure in a particular set of circumstances. The decision is not controlled by fixed rules but rather involves free choice, individual judgment, and indiviudal expression.

I would like to conceptualize and distinguish between two types of discretion displayed in police organizations: *formal discretion* and *informal discretion*. *Formal discretion* is accorded to police organizations officially. At times it is dictated by law, and in most instances it is legitimized in order to increase the efficiency and effectiveness of a police organization. Formal discretion may be limited or revoked by the authority which bestows it. It is significant that formal discretion is one of the legitimized and officially recognized operational components of the police bureaucracy. When police commanders formulate policy concerning the allocation of resources for purposes of selective enforcement, they are carrying out their prerogative of formal discretion. Accordingly, one department may assign 20 percent of its personnel to plainclothes duty in order to enforce laws pertaining to victimless crime, while another department might allocate only 5 percent for this purpose. Decisions involving formal discretion usually are made by the highest echelon of police commanders rather than by the rank and file or the representatives of middle management. Also, formal discretion usually does not require instant decisions under great pressure and often is not applied by a single individual but rather is an expression of two or more persons in consultation.

Informal discretion is not consciously or formally delegated to police officers by the police organization, nor is it usually a result of a clearly defined bureaucratic policy. It exists because of areas of ambiguity in police work in which the police organization cannot easily issue guidelines about how to handle a particular situation. It also arises because it is very difficult to supervise and control the behavior of individual officers in the field. Unlike formal discretion, in which decisions are reached by police commanders, informal discretion is primarily promoted and exercised by members of the rank and file. In many instances informal discretion requires a split-second decision by officers acting in the field individually or in teams. Examples of informal discretion include situations where the officer must decide whether or not a crime has occurred; whether to stop, frisk, interrogate, or arrest a suspect; or whether necessary force is required. Informal discretion usually tends to increase with decreasing rank, while formal discretion increases with higher rank.

Bureaucracy is a form of organization which places emphasis on routine and conservative action. It operates through a narrow, rigid, and formal system which depends upon precedent. There is little or no room for initiative or resourcefulness. Bureaucracy entails efficiency in the sense of a capacity to produce desired results by specific, calculated means toward specific and definable ends. For these reasons, we would expect formal discretion to be exhibited by the police bureaucracy. However, the nature of police work, particularly at the operational level, is such that one cannot always specify beforehand the most efficient and rational means toward an end. Indeed, many situations require innovation, common sense, and on-the-spot judgment.

While bureaucratic efficiency requires "depersonalization," emotional detachment, rigorous, dispassionate application of the law, and professional expertness, individual officers must respond to situations of ambiguity where elements of subjectivity are necessarily introduced. Accordingly, members of the police rank and file will exercise informal discretion in these situations. Informal discretion leads to the introduction of emotional, incalculable, and often irrational behavior into police work, and it permits the purely personal to enter the situation so that feelings of love, hatred, sympathy, compassion, kindness, grace, and gratitude become important. It is for this reason that individual officers fear being blamed for miscalculation or for acting in specific ways that others term inappropriate. Thus, the element of discretion in police work creates and maintains an environment in which police officers, especially new recruits, must come to rely on their fellow officers for advice and assistance. As a result, informal discretion supports and reinforces the establishment and persistence of the police subculture.

George Kirkham, a professor of criminology who became a sworn and full-time uniformed member of the 800 man force of Jacksonville-Duval County, illustrated this point in recounting the following incident.

He and his partner had just gone off duty when they spotted two long-haired teenagers running from an area where the unmistakeable sound of breaking glass came from a church. Upon displaying his police identification, Officer Kirkham requested one of the boys for his identification. The youth sneered, cursed at him, and started to walk away. Thereupon, Officer Kirkham grabbed the youth by his shirt, spun him around, and shouted, "I'm talking to you, punk." At that moment his partner placed his arm on his shoulder and in a reassuring voice said, "Take it easy, Doc."[7]

Although at the time of the incident Officer Kirkham was the director of a human relations project designed to instruct police officers in emotional control and had frequently advised his students that a person who cannot control his emotions at all times has no business being a police officer, he nevertheless required guidance in the instant case from his more experienced partner, who helped calm him down.

As the scenario shows, the informal discretionary elements that continuously arise in police work are one reason officers tend to seek the guidance and advice of their fellow officers. This need for mutual assistance creates an extremely cohesive police group, or police entity, with exceptionally strong feelings of solidarity. Several additional factors related to the formation of the police subculture are discussed below.

Fear of Danger. Officers are repeatedly exposed to physical danger and threats of harm which require the assistance of fellow officers. This element of police work provides constant pressures for officers to interact with each other and to work together.

Uniform and Equipment. The uniform, shield, gun, and other visible police apparatus sets the officer apart from ordinary citizens and reinforces further group solidarity and cohesion.

Isolation. Police officers tend to be placed in a position where either they are pressured by their friends and family to reduce social contact when off duty or to withdraw altogether from this type of interaction. This isolation is promulgated not only by an officer's uniform and awkward working schedule but also results from the authoritarian image police officers project in society. For example, police officers tend to complain that when they socialize with nonpolice friends or attend parties, they are frequently forced into defensive or embarrassing positions as a result of personal incidents involving fellow officers. Officers discover that they are frequently identified with the behavior of their colleagues, which behavior they are called upon to apologize for, defend, or explain. The power underlying the role of "police officer" is so strong that it tends to surface even when the individual is not actively performing the role of "police officer." The status "police officer" accompanies the individual whether on or off duty.

Secrecy. Sources of pressure exist within and outside the police organization which create an atmosphere of secrecy. The police bureaucracy by its very nature must often be secretive if it is to realistically pursue and achieve organizational goals. Indeed, few criminals would be caught if the police divulged operational plans. As a result, society expects the police to be secretive, and to act otherwise would result in accusations of misfeasance. This could result in a general decrease in the level of respect on the part of the public for police authority. In addition, the complex nature of the police officer's task and the ambiguity underlying the situations encountered by the police result in many actions that automatically lead to violation of rules and procedures.

Constantly, incidents arise in which police officers are forced to compromise themselves. Every officer knows that sooner or later he will be placed in a situation where his acts will be termed inappropriate by his superiors or by the public. Secrecy is one of the mechanisms that provides some measure of protection from this understandable "occupational hazard."

The Legal System. Pressures exerted on a police officer by the legal system exceed similar pressures experienced by the ordinary citizen. Special laws have been enacted in an attempt to limit the police officer's discretion. Nearly every facet of an officer's everyday work, including stops, searches, interrogations, arrest, and detention, has been defined, circumscribed, or delimited by legislation. Eventually, officers begin to perceive that the rule of law has a differential effect on their behavior as compared with ordinary citizens, and this perception further increases the cohesion of this group.

Summary and Conclusions

In this chapter I have attempted to develop and apply several theoretical concepts which will provide a deeper understanding of large police organizations in the United States. I have shown how the police bureaucracy and the legal system can be mutually supportive and that the tension in large police organizations may result from a clash between these two institutions and the police subculture. This point of view takes issue with previously developed positions that organizational tension in police departments is due to the internal contradiction between the legal system, on the one hand, and the bureaucratic pressures interacting with the officers' occupational experience, on the other hand. It is suggested that the police bureaucracy is suitable for implementing the prescriptions required by the legal system, but both come into conflict with the police subculture.

I have developed the concept of the police subculture within the theoretical framework of the exclusive right of police officers to use violent force on a citizen population. This is the single factor which distinguishes the police subculture from other subcultures. Those aspects of the police work experience which have the most powerful impact on the genesis and persistence of the police subculture were identified. The most significant factor is the exclusive use by police of violent force. The key theoretical problem was to determine the effects of violent force on the police organization rather than to investigate the more popular issue of "why do the police use violent force." The second most significant theoretical problem in police organization involves police discretion. Two of its forms, formal discretion and informal discretion, were discussed in relationship to the police subculture and the police bureaucracy. Finally, several additional factors which contribute to the creation and persistence of the police subculture were discussed. These included the fear of danger, uniform and equipment, isolation, secrecy, and the legal system.

Large police organizations in the United States are increasingly becoming bureaucratized, despite strong cross pressures for decentralization. At the same time, police authority is being challenged with greater frequency, thereby expanding opportunities for increased police force and violence. The task now is to learn more about the character of legitimate violent force, particularly its institutionalization and control, in order that implementation of violent force is not perceived as the exclusive and personal right of its implementors but rather as a necessary, albeit undesirable, expression of a free society's obligation to maintain the rule of law.

Notes

1. Jerome H. Skolnick, *Justice Without Trial: Law Enforcement in Democratic Society* (New York: Wiley, 1966), p. 6.

2. Max Weber, in Max Rheinstein (ed.), *On Law and Economy and Society* (Cambridge, Mass.: Harvard Univ. Press, 1954), pp. 349-356.

3. Peter M. Blau and Marshall W. Meyer, *Bureaucracy in Modern Society*, 2d ed. (New York: Random House, 1971), p. 165.

4. Emile Durkheim, *The Division of Labor in Society* (Glencoe, Ill.: The Free Press, 1964), p. 68.

5. William A. Westley, "Violence and the Police," in Norman Johnston et al. (eds.), *The Sociology of Punishment and Correction* (New York: Wiley, 1962).

6. Ibid., p. 10.

7. George L. Kirkham, "From Professor to Patrolman: A Fresh Perspective on the Police," *Journal of Police Science and Administration* 2 (1974), 2:136.

14

Reflections on Israel's Legislation for Juvenile Offenders

David Reifen

Introduction

Israel is one of those states that has become independent since World War II. Following independence, laws and procedures dealing with juvenile offenders continued for the time being to be applied as before.

This chapter will in the first part be concerned with legislation until the first Israeli Youth Law of 1971[1] was enacted, and in the second part will deal with various aspects of that legislation, which regulates the adjudication of juvenile offenders. As we shall see, new and progressive procedures and methods of treatment were introduced. On certain issues, however, one can notice a rather conservative and even rigid approach by the Israeli legislators. This may indicate that ambivalent attitudes do exist which most probably have their roots in the subject matter as such, i.e., juvenile delinquency.

British Mandatory Legislation

The very first legislation concerning the adjudication of juvenile offenders was enacted in 1922.[2] This ordinance covered three areas, namely: punishment of young offenders, probation of young offenders, and miscellaneous. In this ordinance, the following points were noteworthy.[3] First, no punishment should be inflicted upon a person under nine years of age.[4] At a later date, when a Criminal Code Ordinance[5] was introduced—which replaced the Ottoman Criminal code—it was laid down that: "A person under the age of nine years is not criminally responsible for any act or omission."[6] The second part of the same section says that "a person under the age of twelve years is not criminally responsible for an act or omission, unless it is proved that at the time of doing the act or making the omission he had capacity to know that he ought not to do the act or make the omission." Whereas the first part of this section is a mandatory provision, the second part is liable to different interpretations.[7] The yardstick is not an objective, but rather a subjective, one.

It could have been expected that when the Israeli legislature introduced the Youth Law of 1971, the age of criminal responsibility would be raised so as to commence at twelve years. This seems to me imperative for the following reasons.

First, we are here concerned with age groups of at least nine and *under* twelve years. Official statistical data reveal that there in fact has been a decrease in offenders of these ages over the years 1960 to 1970.[8] Moreover, official statistical data which were published by the Juvenile Probation Department[9] for 1971 to 1973 reveal that a further decrease has taken place during these years. Apart from this, most offenses which were tried in Juvenile Courts were not of a serious nature. Yet, the number of recidivists reached about half the total rate each year. This fact points clearly to a failure of social services. It must be emphasized most strongly that prosecution in a criminal court can be no substitute for providing adequate and special educational facilities for this young age group.

Furthermore, for those instances in which the intervention of the Juvenile Court is required, the Youth (Treatment and Supervision) Law of 1960 should be applied.[10] In that law, the provision is made in section 2(3) that a minor may be regarded as being "in need" for the purposes of the law if "he has committed an act which is a criminal offence, but he has not been brought to trial for that act." Thus, the stigma of a criminal procedure would be avoided. Experience has shown that the civil procedure provided under this section is never applied in the Juvenile Courts in Israel.

The method of probation was then very seldom used, and no office for the administration of probation was established. Whenever a court convicted a juvenile offender under twenty years of age and decided that he should be placed on probation, a voluntary worker of one of the recognized religious communities was requested to supervise the probationer. Procedure was laid down for such events, as it was also in the case of discharge of the probation period.[11,12]

Many years had to pass before a Probation Service was established.[13] Probation officers were appointed on a full-time basis, but still at the service of Juvenile Courts alone. Functions and duties of probation officers were formulated anew, and a government department for the administration of that service was established.

With the enactment in 1944 of the Probation of Offenders Ordinance, the Probation Service was enlarged to include adult offenders as well.[14] That ordinance deals exclusively with matters of probation. It is still in force today, although revised by the Israeli legislature.

In Israel, probation has gained statutory recognition as a professional service.[15] According to certain laws, a court is obliged to receive from the Probation Service a written report before a final judgment can be pronounced. It is not my intention, however, to deal with matters of probation as such in the context of this chapter.[16]

The enactment of the Juvenile Offenders Ordinance of 1937 was a turning point for the trying of juvenile offenders in Juvenile Courts.[17] This was the first legislation in which provision was made for the establishment of such courts.

Judicial competence in relation to age and type of offenses was laid down, as were matters of arrests, release on bail, punishments, and other methods of dealing with juvenile offenders. Juvenile Court procedures pertaining to the evidence of witnesses and the role of the judge were defined, as was a procedure for acquisition of information on the personal backgrounds of each juvenile offender. "For the purpose of obtaining such information or for special medical examination or observation" court hearings could be adjourned from time to time, without necessarily remanding the juvenile offender to a place of detention.[18] It can be said that this legislation brought the procedures and functions of Juvenile Courts in line with developments in this field in England at the time.

Changes by the Israeli Legislature

Following the establishment of the State of Israel, previous legislation continued in effect. Yet, amendments and changes were introduced. Since 1950, Juvenile Courts have been in the charge of judges who have served exclusively in this field. Thus, the idea that adjudication in Juvenile Courts requires special knowledge and experience has been accepted and put into practice.

The Probation of Offenders Ordinance of 1944 was also amended in 1953.[19] Among the innovations that were thereby introduced was the provision that a probation order could henceforth be made only after a written report by a probation officer had been submitted to the Court.

In 1955, regulations were published, based on the Juvenile Offenders Ordinance of 1937, according to which a Youth Authority was established within the Ministry of Social Welfare.[20] Accordingly, it remains the duty of Juvenile Courts to fix the period of a placement order, but the place of residence is selected by the Youth Authority.[21]

Another amendment to the Juvenile Offenders Ordinance of 1937 was introduced which dealt, among other things, with matters of early release of juvenile offenders who were committed to an educational establishment by Court order.[22] A Release Board was constituted which consisted of five people, with a judge of the Juvenile Court as chairman. Since then, the Release Board has been meeting regularly once a month, at which time applications are scrutinized and all parties involved are given an opportunity to express their opinion on early release.

The Juvenile Offenders Ordinance of 1937 also contained a chapter that laid down the procedure for Juvenile Court trial of children who are in need of care and protection. The Israeli legislature decided to delete this chapter and to enact a new Law instead.[23] The opinion prevailed that jurisdiction in those matters should not be part of a criminal law and of criminal proceedings.

First Israeli Law

Competence

The first Israeli legislation regulating the competence of Juvenile Courts in trying juvenile offenders was enacted on August 23, 1971.[24] As of that day, the Juvenile Offenders Ordinance of 1937 was repealed. Now, in addition to the Juvenile Court at the Magistrate's Court level, there is also a Juvenile Court at the District Court level. The prevailing definitions are as follows:[25]

"Juvenile Court" means a Magistrate's Court or a District Court when a Juvenile Court Judge is sitting therein; "Juvenile Court Judge" means a Judge to whom the function of a Juvenile Court Judge has been assigned as provided in section 2; [it is further stated that] the trial of an offence with which a minor is charged, including the hearing of an appeal, shall be before a Juvenile Court.[26] [Yet,] the Minister of Justice may, by order, empower a Magistrate's Juvenile Court to try minors for felonies under the section specified in the order.[27]

Indeed, the Minister of Justice ordered by special proclamation that a large number of felonies should be tried by a Juvenile Court Judge of a Magistrates' Court.[28] The scope of that order was larger than that of an earlier one of the same type.[29] The reasons for such wide judicial competence can be summarized as follows.

1. Juvenile Court Judges attached to the Magistrates' Courts deal exclusively with minors. It can be assumed that these judges gain a great amount of experience while adjudicating juvenile offenders. Their alertness to the manifold and special problems of such offenders becomes an important asset for all concerned.

2. Although observance of law and procedure is a basic tenet of any Juvenile Court, one cannot forego an individualized and informal approach which can become part of the rehabilitation of juvenile offenders. On this score one has to be aware of many intangible factors that may be latent or may become manifest in this special setting.[30]

3. If an informal Juvenile Court (at the Magistrates' Court level) is a priori the appropriate place to adjudicate juvenile offenders who have committed minor offenses, it is even more the place to adjudicate juvenile offenders who have committed serious offenses. The latter may even be more in need of that individualized and expert approach which is accorded juvenile offenders in a Juvenile Court at this level.[31] For it is a fallacy to consider a Juvenile Court as a replica of a court for adults and to obliterate basic differences between them. Generally speaking, one can maintain that in a criminal court for adults the seriousness of an offense is a determining factor, whereas the commission of a felony by a juvenile (in Israel even by a child above nine years) has very often no other meaning than the commission of a minor offense.[32]

4. Last, but not least, the Juvenile Court at the Magistrates' Court level has at its disposal a very wide range of treatment measures. The fundamental element remains: the rehabilitation of juvenile offenders by means of educational methods. Failing this, that Court can make use of all the methods of punishments available to a Juvenile Court at the District Court level.

Another innovation was introduced by raising the age of competence for trying juvenile offenders in Juvenile Courts to "under eighteen years of age." In practice, it means the inclusion of male juvenile offenders aged between sixteen and eighteen who were hitherto excluded from the jurisdiction of Juvenile Courts. It was also stated, however, that, "in respect of male minors who have completed their sixteenth year" the law should come into force on April 1, 1975, or "any other day not more than two years thereafter."[33,34]

Such deferral seemed justified in order to reorganize or establish the educational facilities appropriate for the inclusion of the additional age groups. For the time being, matters developed differently, and as "the determining day" approached, the following order was issued:[35] (a) as from October 1, 1975, the age group of sixteen years and under seventeen was included into the jurisdiction of Juvenile Courts of first instance; (b) the age group of seventeen and under eighteen are going to be included as of April 1, 1977;[36] and (c) the competence of jurisdiction is limited to offenses for which the maximum penalty is under ten years imprisonment.[37] It remains to be seen which steps will be taken subsequently.*

Police Interrogation and Arrest

There are two new provisions, complementary to one another, which deal with police interrogation and arrest of minors. One cannot but be impressed with the importance the Israeli legislature has attached to these matters. There are two general laws which regulate matters of arrest, confessions, searches, and confiscations.[38,39] These laws apply to juvenile offenders as well. Yet, concerning matters of arrest, release, and detention, the Youth Law of 1971 introduced innovations and provisions more stringent than those which exist for adults.[40]

The Youth Law of 1971 states that a minor above the age of fourteen shall not be kept under arrest for more than 24 hours without a warrant from a judge.[41] A police officer who is in charge of a police station may, however, direct the continuance of such arrest for an additional 24 hours. The reason for the extension of the arrest shall be recorded and brought to the notice of the judge before whom the minor is brought.

If a minor under fourteen is involved, the law is still stricter.[42] The period of detention is curtailed to 12 hours only. Here, too, an extension for another

*Editors' note: As of April 1, 1977, the Law applied in its totality to all minors under the age of eighteen.

12 hours is permitted in special circumstances. In this instance a police officer in charge of a police station may only direct the continuation of such detention if one of the conditions specified by the law is fulfilled, such as the need to protect the safety of the public or of the minor himself.

Furthermore, a judge is also restricted in ordering a period of detention following arrest of a minor.[43] In instances in which a judge may order 15 days detention for an adult, such arrest cannot exceed 10 days if a minor is concerned; and if 30 days arrest can be ordered for an adult, it cannot exceed 20 days for a minor. In both instances, the arrest is for purposes of police interrogation or, when release from detention seems ill-advised, before Court hearings begin.

A police interrogator of a minor who denies having committed an offense of which he is a suspect generally regards the minor as a nuisance. The minor therefore usually encounters a rigid and harsh attitude. Sometimes, moreover, an order of arrest is made by way of intimidation, even prior to interrogation. The contact with the police at this stage is of major importance because any statement on the part of a suspect in which he admits having committed a particular offense can be held against him at the trial.[44] It may be sufficient evidence to prove the commission of the offense. The very fact of an early court hearing as to the alleged offense thus enables the minor to convey to the judge his version of events. Furthermore, parents or probation officers can also be alerted at this stage. Both have statutory status under the Youth Law of 1971.

As to the place of detention of an arrested minor, there is a provision in the new law which states that "A minor may only be held under arrest in a separate place of detention for minors."[45] The implementation of this provision was postponed to April 1, 1975. Yet, no adequate preparations were made for the establishment of separate places of detention. Consequently, an order was published postponing the implementation of this section until April 1, 1977.*[46] It proves again how inadequate social services are, and how little the underprivileged minor can rely on them. This is in gross contrast to his actual needs.

Status of Parents

The legal status of parents in Juvenile Courts, their legal responsibilities for the delinquent behavior of their children, and their emotional involvement are all

*Editors' note: On March 15, 1977, an amendment was passed to the Youth (Trial, Punishment and Modes of Treatment) Law of 1971, which both diluted the provision referred to here by Judge Reifen, and further postponed its implementation. Section 13 of the law now provides that minors may be detained *either* in a separate place of detention *or* in a separate wing of a general place of detention, while for the purposes of interrogation they may be detained in a police station; and section 49 postpones the implementation of the new section 13 until April 1980, with the possibility of postponement for a further two years. The absolute principle that a minor may not be detained in the same cell as an adult is, however, reaffirmed in the amendment.

matters with which a judge in a Juvenile Court is constantly confronted.[47] Some believe that parents should be held legally responsible if their child commits an offense. If that is the case, some sort of punishment could be levied on them. Such an argument is open to doubt because it would mean an oversimplification of a very intricate situation. Others place the emphasis on the consideration that punishment of a parent is not the major issue. Rather the question is to what extent can a Juvenile Court have an impact on parents so that they will become more concerned with their responsibilities towards their children. Some parents have made great efforts in raising their child in a proper way but have failed for reasons that are beyond their comprehension.[48] They may expect the judge to help them in their despair, because he embodies, in a way, the powerful authority of the state.

There are a great number of viewpoints involved in this issue; but whatever view one may adopt, it cannot be approached with fixed and preconceived ideas. For this issue is one example of many present-day problems. In a society like Israel, where changes in the functions of family members are constantly taking place, an authoritative setting, like a Juvenile Court, may become particularly important. It is especially in such a setting that great attention has to be paid to the bridging of disrupted parent-child relationships.[49]

The Youth Law of 1971 included several provisions concerning parents, a brief discussion of which will follow.

1. When a child is tried in the Juvenile Court, should attendance of parents be mandatory, or should it be left to their discretion? The Youth Law of 1971 allows for a variety of possibilities on this point. It is mandatory for the Juvenile Court to furnish a parent with information as to the summons and as to his right to be present at the hearing. For many parents this is merely information of no consequence at this stage. From my experience, I would make it mandatory for parents to be present at the hearing when the minor is under sixteen years. A hearing in the Juvenile Court can have far-reaching consequences for a minor and parent alike; and for this reason, attendance of a parent should not be left to the parent's own discretion. The second part of the same provision states, however, that for special reasons a Court may decide *not* to invite a parent to the hearing, or even to furnish him with copies of the summons and of the other relevant documents. What is meant by "special reasons," and who has to convey to the Court the existence of such "special reasons"? Is the Court informed of them in open court and under oath? Are the minor and the parent part of these proceedings, or has that parent been deprived of his right to be heard even on the issue of his subsequent participation?

At the same time, there is another provision which is, from the point of view of its content, at the extreme opposite point of view.[50] There, the law provides that a parent may file on behalf of the minor any application which the minor himself would be permitted to file. A parent may also examine witnesses and make statements, whether in lieu of the minor or together with him. This is an innovation in the procedure which is of limited practical importance, because parents are usually not proficient in matters of law and procedure. The innovation nevertheless has great psychological importance in the sphere of parent-child relationships. The minor becomes aware of the fact that his parent stands up for him in Court, even in instances where relations between them are strained. In fact, it may well be that in such cases, active interference by a parent is especially meaningful to a minor.

2. In another section, the 1971 law prescribes an innovative procedure, which contrasts with those previously mentioned.[51] This section states that if a minor is arrested by the police, the latter are obliged to inform one of his parents of the fact. If a police officer is of the opinion, however, that such information may prejudice the welfare of the minor, a probation officer may be informed instead. This is meant to safeguard the welfare of the minor, which might be endangered by a spontaneous reaction of a parent. In this connection a few points have to be mentioned. What is the yardstick for a police officer to believe that informing a parent of such an arrest may have detrimental results for a minor? On what ground is the police officer given authority to make such a decision? Is it based on assumption, information, the seriousness of offense, or just superficial impression? The position of a probation officer in this context also has to be examined; for example, does he have to be informed of all the details of the alleged offense? What message, if any, is he to convey to the parents? Does a possibility exist that his interference at this stage may enhance rather than diminish the parents' anxiety? Is the probation officer going to be involved in police interrogation? What can the probation officer do if the parents do not bail out the minor? Is there reason to believe, as I do, that in such circumstances the authority of the police carries more weight than that of a probation officer? Finally, for how long should a minor be kept under arrest in such cases?

3. In another context, there is a provision that bears a large degree of similarity to the concept underlying the previous statements.[52] Among the modes of treatment that are available to Juvenile Courts is "the committal of the minor to the care and supervision of a fit person." During the period of such a committal order, or during part of it, as decided on by the Court, a parent may be restricted in his rights over this child. This is a very serious matter, because it amounts to the deprivation of a parent of his natural rights even for a limited period. What are the conditions that permit a judge to make such an order? Is there a procedure to prove that such restriction is necessary for the welfare of the minor? What are the qualifications of a "fit person" in whom such powers may be invested by the Court? What possibilities are available to the Juvenile Court to supervise a fit person order? Under what conditions can such an order be altered or canceled?

The points raised here are not exhaustive. The intention is to convey the considerable amount of ambivalence in attitudes toward parents. Parental cooperation is of vital importance in a genuine effort to rehabilitate juvenile offenders. Here is a challenge for fresh thinking and for a dynamic approach, which in the end may be beneficial for all concerned.

Defense Counsel

A clumsy formulation in the Juvenile Offenders Ordinance of 1937 was interpreted in such a way that a judge in the Juvenile Court had to give his consent if a minor intended to be represented by legal counsel at his trial.[53] That interpretation was challenged,[54] and the Youth Law of 1971 regulated the matter of defense counsel. It is there laid down that the Juvenile Court may appoint a defense counsel if this is in the interest of the minor.[55] In such instances, fees and other expenses of the defense counsel and of witnesses are borne by the state. Furthermore, a defense counsel so appointed is not allowed to receive from the minor, or from any other person, any other renumeration, compensation, gift, or other benefit.[56] These provisions do not derogate the right of the minor to be represented by a defense counsel of his own choice and on his own account.[57]

The significance of this provision is apparent and should be made use of particularly in two instances, namely:

1. If a minor denies in Court having committed the alleged offense and
2. When two or more minors are accused of having committed an offense together, and one or more of them is represented by a defense counsel of his own choice, while the others are not, it should be mandatory that the Juvenile Court appoint a defense counsel for those unrepresented. This is in the interests of justice.

Although there is a provision to the effect that "the Court shall help him [the minor] to examine the witnesses," this cannot be a proper defense.[58] According to Anglo-Saxon legal tradition, which prevails to a large extent in Israel, a judge is not supposed to interfere in the trial except in unusual instances. The wording in that provision to the effect that the Court "shall help him to examine the witnesses" is far from being the equivalent of providing him with proper legal defense. This applies, incidentally, also to the status of a parent who is permitted to examine witnesses, whether instead of the minor or together with him.[59]

These two resources, the judge in the Juvenile Court and the parent of a minor, are limited in their ability to provide an appropriate defense in its true sense. By virtue of their status, the judge and the parent are able to examine only those matters and points which are brought to the notice of the Court at the trial itself. They have no opportunity to scrutinize the particular police file, nor are they in a position to interrogate police witnesses—in particular those who have not been called upon to testify in court. Safeguarding the legal rights of suspects begins with the inspection of the police file and any other material pertaining to a particular case. Such material would normally not come to the notice of the Court. Yet it may well determine the issue of the guilt or innocence of the suspect.

There is now general agreement that legal rights of minors who are suspects or juvenile offenders have to be taken more seriously than has previously been the case.[60] This is ultimately in the best interest of all concerned.

Methods of Disposal

As to the methods of disposal available to the Court, whether treatment measures or methods of punishment, the Youth Law of 1971 includes a number of innovations. Yet, here again, one encounters, on the one hand, a liberal attitude and, on the other, a punitive approach. It is particularly in these areas that comparisons may fruitfully be made with the law existing prior to the 1971 enactment.[61] It is also in these areas that the attitude of the judge in the Juvenile Court finds its individual expression.

1. Treatment Measures

The common denominator of *treatment* (as opposed to *punitive*) measures is the following:[62]

1. No conviction is attached to any of them.
2. One or more of them can be made simultaneously.[63]
3. As long as the order has not been fully implemented, it can be changed for another measure of treatment.[64]

Most of the treatment measures as such were available in the Juvenile Offenders Ordinance of 1937,[65] the main novelty of the new law being reflected in the three above-mentioned points. Among the measures now available to the Court are: a committal order to an open or a closed educational establishment; payment by the minor or his parent of a fine and compensation for sustained damage; and an order for an undertaking as to the minor's future behavior. It should also be noted that if the minor fails to comply with any of the provisions of a probation order, which is made without conviction, that order can be changed only by providing another treatment measure instead.[66]

One innovation is the subsection which provides for a Court order to the effect that the minor should stay at a "day center" instead of being sent to an open or closed educational establishment.[67] Such day centers do exist already, and cater to those who cannot keep up with the standards required at schools or at work. They are administered by a department of the Ministry of Social Welfare. So far, however, they have not been available for the admission of minors by Court order, and in this respect no progress has been made since the enactment of the Youth Law of 1971. This is astounding because a day center could enable a juvenile offender to be within a structured environment based on a definite educational and rehabilitational program. There the curricula for studies and trades are especially designed to strengthen potential abilities and create an atmosphere of acceptance and achievement. Moreover, minors who are sent there by Court order would remain within their own families, the possible emotional upheavals and other disadvantages of institutional life thus being avoided.

2. Punishments

Punishments, in contrast with treatment measures, can be ordered only after a conviction. Some of the treatment measures may also be ordered as punishment following a conviction, for example, a committal order to a closed institution, a probation order, or a fine. There are, on the other hand, methods of disposal, such as imprisonment and conditional imprisonment, that can only be ordered after a conviction.

The possibility of committing a minor to imprisonment has taken a new turn as a result of the Youth Law of 1971. Under this Law a minor who at the time of being sentenced has reached the age of fourteen years can be committed to imprisonment.[68] The wording of this section is plain, i.e., even if the offense of which the offender was convicted was committed at the age of thirteen, the minor may still be sentenced to imprisonment. This is a retrogressive step as compared with the previous law.[69] The earlier provision laid down that a person under sixteen should not be sentenced to imprisonment, "if he can be suitably dealt with in any other way, whether by probation, fine, corporal punishment, committal to a place of detention, reformatory school, or otherwise."[70]

It was only when all these measures were in vain that a person above the age of fourteen could be given a prison sentence. It is of interest to note that among the methods of disposal that were then listed in the main section of disposals, a prison sentence was mentioned only for those who were above the age of sixteen years.[71]

The attitude of the Israeli legislature on this point is most regrettable. The extent to which the belief apparently survives that a prison sentence for young people, especially those under sixteen, has a salutary effect on delinquent behavior is truly amazing. Experience the world over indicates the opposite.[72]

Conclusion

My brief remarks in this chapter deal with various legal aspects of the Juvenile Court in Israel. They provide the structure, as it were, within which the judge of a Juvenile Court adjudicates juvenile offenders. As we have seen, there are features of a legal nature that are particularly designed to fit this special setting. It should be emphasized that these legal aspects have to be adhered to very strictly, because they provide the safeguards for the protection of the basic legal rights of the parties concerned.

However, it is not sufficient in my view to conform to law and procedure alone, or to impress the offender by the solemnity of Court procedure. It is my contention that the judical setting of a Juvenile Court presents, by its very nature, a dynamic situation which entails inherently varying individual reactions, and in which intrafamily situations and conflicts express themselves. In fact, the salient feature of a Juvenile Court is that one is constantly confronted with crisis and stress situations, with failures of children and parents, and in many instances with inadequate community resources. It is self-evident that a judge of a Juvenile Court will have to deal with these issues in a competent manner. He need not, of course, be an expert on different treatment matters, but he has to have firsthand knowledge of their implications, the process of their implementation, and also their limitations. Otherwise it may happen that adequate diagnostic treatment and correctional resources will not be used in an appropriate way.

The Juvenile Court essentially has two functions. It adjudicates juvenile offenders within the judicial system, and it makes use of social services for the rehabilitation of juvenile offenders. A judge of a Juvenile Court should therefore possess the highest available qualifications in two disciplines: jurisdiction of juvenile offenders and the dynamics of human behavior.

Notes

1. Youth (Trial, Punishment, and Modes of Treatment) Law, 5731, 1971, in *Laws of the State of Israel*, vol. 25, p. 128.

2. Young Offenders Ordinance, no. 1, 1922, in *Palestine Gazette*, part II. chap. 156, p. 1556.

3. During the British Mandate statutory enactments were called "Ordinances." In February 1949 the first elected Knesset decided to use the word *law* for its statutes.

4. Young Offenders Ordinance, no. 1, sec. 2.

5. Criminal Code Ordinance, no. 74, 1936, enacted on January 1, 1937.

6. Ibid., sec. 9.

7. David Reifen, *The Juvenile Court in A Changing Society* (London: Weidenfeld and Nicolson, 1973), pp. 85-89.

8. Central Bureau of Statistics, Jerusalem, Special Series on *Juvenile Delinquency*, nos. 168; 24; 265; 301; 322; 370; and 408.

9. Ministry of Social Welfare, Jerusalem, *Minors under Care of the Juvenile Probation Department*, for 1971-1972, Tevet, 1973; for 1973, Shwat, 1975.

10. Youth (Treatment and Supervision) Law, 5720, 1960, in *Laws of the State of Israel*, vol. 14, p. 4.

11. Young Offenders Ordinance, no. 1, 1922, secs. 12-14.

12. Ibid., sec. 17.

13. Juvenile Offenders Ordinance, no. 2, 1937, sec. 9, in *Palestine Gazette*, no. 667, part I, p. 137, enacted 12/9/1938; and *Palestine Gazette*, no. 817, part II, p. 1240.

14. Probation of Offenders Ordinance, no. 42, 1944, in *Palestine Gazette*, no. 1380, p. 174, 28/12/1944 enacted 1/3/1945; *Palestine Gazette*, no. 1394, p. 161.

15. Probation of Offenders Ordinance (Amendment) Law, 5714, 1953, in *Laws of the State of Israel*, vol. 8, pp. 44-45; Penal Law Revision (Modes of Punishment) Law, 5714, 1954, in *Laws of the State of Israel*, vol. 8, p. 206; Penal Law Amendment (Modes of Punishment) Law, 5723, 1963, in *Laws of the State of Israel*, vol. 17, p. 102; Criminal Procedure Law, 5725, 1965, in *Laws of the State of Israel*, vol. 19, p. 158; Youth (Trial, Punishment and Modes of Treatment) Law, 5731, 1971, in *Laws of the State of Israel*, vol. 25, p. 128.

16. For further discussion of this topic, see David Reifen, "Some Observations on Treatment Aspects of Probation," in *Delinquency and Society*, vol. 3, no. 1, Israel Society of Criminology, July 1968 (Hebrew); David Reifen, "New Law for Juvenile Offenders," *Law Review, Tel-Aviv Univ.*, vol. 3, no. 1, May 1973 (Hebrew); David Reifen, "New Ventures of Law Enforcement in Israel," *The Journal of Crim. Law, Criminology and Police Science*, vol. 58, no. 1 (March 1967); David Reifen, *The Juvenile Court in a Changing Society* (Univ. of Pennsylvania Press, 1972), pp. 154-167; and David Reifen, *Das Jugendgericht in Israel* (Berlin: Walter de Gruyter Verlag, 1974), pp. 261-274.

17. Juvenile Offenders Ordinance, 1937.

18. Ibid., sec. 8(7), 8(8).

19. Probation of Offenders Ordinance (Amendment) Law, 5714, 1953, in *Laws of the State of Israel*, vol. 8, pp. 44-45.

20. Youth Authority Regulations, in *Kowetz Hatakanot*, no. 516, 1955, pp. 886-887 (Hebrew).

21. David Reifen, "The Israel Youth Authority," *The British Journal of Criminology*, vol. 9 (1969) no. 3.

22. Juvenile Offenders Ordinance (Amendment) Law, 5717-1957, in *Laws of the State of Israel*, vol. 11, pp. 49-50.

23. Youth (Care and Supervision) Law, 5720, 1960, in *Laws of the State of Israel*, vol. 14, p. 44.

24. Youth (Trial, Punishment, and Modes of Treatment) Law, 5731, 1971, in *Laws of the State of Israel*, vol. 25, p. 128.

25. Ibid., sec. 1.

26. Ibid., sec. 3(a).

27. Ibid., sec. 3(b).

28. *Kowetz Hatakanot*, No. 2741, 2/9/1971 (Hebrew).

29. *Kowetz Hatakanot*, No. 2542, 2/4/1970 (Hebrew).

30. David Reifen, *The Juvenile Court in A Changing Society*, pp. 85-128.

31. Israel S. Drapkin, "Criminological Aspects of Sentencing," in *Studies in Criminology*, vol. XXI (Jerusalem: Scripta Hierosolymitana, Magnus Press, 1969), pp. 40-52.

32. Children and Young Persons Act, 1969, chap. 54 (London: H.M.S.O., 1970). A person under seventeen who is now charged before a Magistrates' Court on an information shall be tried summarily, unless the offense is one of homicide (par. 6, enacted, 1/1/1971).

33. Youth Law, 1971, sec. 49(b).

34. Ibid., sec. 49(e).

35. *Kowetz Hatakanot*, no. 3315, 30/3/1975, sec. 1(a) (Hebrew).

36. Ibid., sec. 1(c).

37. Ibid., sec. 1(a).

38. Criminal Procedure Law, 5725, 1965, in *Laws of the State of Israel*, vol. 19, p. 158.

39. Criminal Procedure (Arrest and Searches) Ordinance (New Version), 5729, 1969, in *Dinei Medinat Yisrael*, no. 12, p. 284.

40. Youth (Trial, Punishment, and Modes of Treatment) Law, 5731, 1971, in *Laws of the State of Israel*, vol. 25, p. 128.

41. Ibid., sec. 10(1).

42. Ibid., sec. 10(2).

43. Ibid., sec. 10(4).

44. David Reifen, *Yeud Wematarah, Mifaley Tarbut Wechinuch, Tel-Aviv*, 2d ed., 1969, pp. 119-138 (Hebrew).

45. Youth Law, 1971, sec. 13(a).

46. *Kowetz Hatakanot*, no. 3315, 30/3/1975, sec. 1(d).

47. Youth Law, 1971, Definitions, par. 1: "parent" includes a step-parent, an adopter, and a guardian.

48. David Reifen, *The Juvenile Court in a Changing Society*, pp. 101-114.

49. Youth (Trial, Punishment, and Modes of Treatment) Law, 5731, 1971, sec. 19(a).

50. Ibid., sec. 19(c).

51. Ibid., sec. 11.

52. Ibid., sec. 26(1).

53. Juvenile Offenders Ordinance, No. 2, 1937, sec. 3(4).

54. David Reifen, "Legal Defence in the Juvenile Court," in: *Hapraklit*, vol. XXIII (Oct. 1967) no. 4 (Hebrew).

55. Youth (Trial, Punishment, and Modes of Treatment) Law, 5731, 1971, sec. 18(a).

56. Criminal Procedure Law, 5725, 1965, in *Laws of the State of Israel*, vol. 19, p. 158, secs. 14, 15, 17, 18, and 19.

57. Youth Law, 1971, sec. 18(d).

58. Youth Law, 1971, sec. 18(c).

59. Youth Law, 1971, sec. 19(c).

60. Sanford J. Fox, *The Law of Juvenile Courts in a Nutshell* (St. Paul, Minn.: West Publishing Co., 1971).

61. Juvenile Offenders Ordinance, no. 2, 1937.

62. Youth Law, 1971, sec. 26.

63. Ibid., sec. 24(2).

64. Ibid., sec. 30.

65. Juvenile Offenders Ordinance, no. 2, 1937, par. 11 *in toto*, sec. 18 *in toto*.

66. Youth Law, 1971, sec. 26(2).

67. Ibid., sec. 26(4).

68. Ibid., sec. 25(d).

69. Juvenile Offenders Ordinance, no. 2, 1937, sec. 12(1), (2).

70. See Punishment of Whipping (Abolition) Law, 5710, 1950, in *Laws of the State of Israel*, vol. 4, p. 140.

71. Juvenile Offenders Ordinance, no. 2 of 1937, sec. 18(j).

72. See, for example, the English Children and Young Persons Act 1969, Chapter 54, sec. 7(1). The minimum age for a conviction has been raised from fifteen to seventeen years, and no court can now impose a prison sentence on any person under seventeen years old.

15 The Future of Sentencing

J. E. Hall Williams

In 1968 Professor Drapkin contributed the Report of the International Society for Criminology to the Second International Colloquium held at Bellagio, Italy in May of that year. This paper on the subject of the sentencing process was subsequently revised and reappeared under the title "Criminological Aspects of Sentencing" in the volume *Studies in Criminology*, published in 1969 under Professor Drapkin's editorship to mark the tenth birthday of the Institute of Criminology of the Hebrew University of Jerusalem. Professor Drapkin's paper, written with his characteristic verve and style, passed under review a number of features of the sentencing process that have from time to time attracted the attention of criminologists. These were (1) the training of judges and lawyers involved in the criminal justice system; (2) the presentence report; and (3) the aims of sentencing.

This chapter reviews essentially the same general areas of the sentencing process, with the omission of the aims of the sentence. Instead, as my third topic I have written something on the structure of sentences, leading to some reflections on the current discussion of the whole question of power-sharing between the judge and the executive. My hope is that this may be seen as a worthy tribute to a scholar whose companionship I have been privileged to share on many occasions and whom I respect so much. In this chapter I draw extensively on the report hereinafter called the Strasbourg Report, of a subcommittee of the European Committee on Crime Problems on the subject of, and entitled, *Sentencing*, published in 1974, over which I was privileged to preside.

Training of Judges

The Strasbourg Report stated that "every effort should be made to promote the training of judges. In particular they should be provided with the available scientific and technical information."[1] The experts felt strongly that sentencing seminars and conferences should be organized in the member states of the Council for Europe at which prospective probation officers and social workers as well as criminologists should participate on an equal basis with judges. This had already been done in Sweden. In France the subcommittee was informed that a national school for the training of magistrates had been established and seminars were organized by judges. One might add that in England and Wales, for a

205

number of years, seminars and training exercises have been organized for High Court Judges, Judges of the Crown Court, and lay magistrates.

In the United Kingdom, Sir Kenneth Younger, chairman of the Home Office Advisory Council on the Penal System, speaking in a personal capacity to the Howard League for Penal Reform in 1973, called for judges to be required to have some training in penology. This demand has been echoed since in various quarters, and the Home Secretary announced in July 1975 the setting up of a working party under Mr. Justice Bridge (now Lord Justice Bridge) on judicial training and information. The terms of reference are: (1) to review the machinery for disseminating information about the penal system and matters related to the treatment of offenders and (2) to review the scope and content of training and the methods whereby it is provided. In his speech the Right Honorable Roy Jenkins MP said he hoped that the working party might in the long term lead to the setting up of more permanent machinery for judicial training and the flow of information to sentencers to help them in the proper understanding and use of the increasing range of alternatives to custody that were becoming available.

The question I must ask is how far the judges should be expected to become expert in the field of criminology and penology. How much detailed knowledge of the operation of the penal system and of the psychology and sociology of crime and criminal statistics is required for one to choose the right sentence? I suspect that the answer to these questions will vary in different jurisdictions in accordance with different systems of organization of the judiciary and different, traditions. Where one has a judicial service that one enters as a young man or woman soon after university, one can expect more thorough training to be provided in these areas than where the judge, as in the common law systems, tends to be appointed to the bench later in life after many years of legal practice at the bar. Where one has full-time criminal judges who have never tried civil cases, one can expect a higher degree of specialization than where one has judges who combine both civil and criminal jurisdiction. Where one has lay magistrates, one cannot expect so much in the way of sophisticated study, though one is bound to say that in England and Wales today the training arrangements for lay magistrates are in some respects superior to those of Crown Courts and High Court Judges. This is hardly surprising considering the very limited effort put into training the latter group.

As I remarked in reviewing Professor Drapkin's suggestions on the training of judges, my main concern with the demand that judges should become better acquainted with the social sciences is not that they may thereby become more competent, but they may become more vulnerable to criticism because they may be insufficiently competent in those social science aspects of the case to really do a professional social science job, and at the same time not realize their insufficiency. To know where you are in need of professional guidance and advice and to be willing to take it is a very different thing from believing you know all the answers because you have acquired a veneer of scientific training.[2]

Lord Devlin has recently expressed serious reservations about the extent to which judges should be required to become expert in penology and criminology.[3] He sees no more case for this than in regard to many other matters of scientific and professional knowledge, for example, medical science, which is very relevant to assessing the extent of personal injuries in civil litigation. The judge should not get too closely involved but should remain aloof, he seems to be saying, and let the experts advise him on these matters. He must bring to the decision of these questions the same kind of common sense and common experience which jurors and lay magistrates are expected to apply. While this philosophy will no doubt command a wide appeal, particularly among judges, whom it lets neatly off the hook, I submit that it is unrealistic and insufficient to respond to the needs of today. In order to make intelligent use of expert advice, and to then understand the guidance that is being offered, a modern judge needs to know a little more about the penal system, the probation and aftercare facilities, and the state of our knowledge about offenses and offenders than can be divined from "common sense," or assumed from past experience.

The question surely must be how much more he needs to know. Here different answers are possible. Some, like Professor Drapkin, would require a thorough knowledge, including the following: basic knowledge of criminalistics, forensic psychiatry, criminology, and penology, preferably gained in a certificate program. But even he warns of the danger of extreme specialization or exaggerated professionalism. Herein lies the problem, where to draw the line. Professor Drapkin recognizes that the degree to which specialized training should go will vary according to the operational requirements in different countries, and even within the same country, with respect to judges with different kinds of jurisdiction.

Presentence Reports

Professor Drapkin says there is a general consensus regarding the vital need for a presentence report in order to facilitate the task of the sentencing judge. Yet, as he observes, there are many different opinions about the details concerning the kinds of cases where such a report is required, when it should be produced, what kind of information it should contain, and the nature of the advice or opinions expressed, as well as about confidentiality of the contents.

In the United Kingdom, the Streatfield Report recommended for England and Wales that presentence reports should normally be available for a wide number of cases.[4] These recommendations were embodied in Home Office circulars to the courts, which have no binding effect but are merely advisory. The Criminal Justice Act of 1967 sec. 57 allows the Home Secretary to give directions to courts on this matter, but so far the "advisory" circular has been preferred as a means of persuading the courts when to require a presentence report. The way the higher courts were organized prior to the Courts Act of

1971 (which carried out an extensive reorganization), it was usually necessary for probation officers to carry out the investigation of the offender and prepare the report pretrial. It was made clear that in the event that the offender was pleading not guilty, he should have the option to refuse to cooperate in the preparation of the report pending the decision as to his guilt. But it should be explained to him that the consequence might be delay at the sentencing stage. Now the English probation service, through its representative association, is seeking a revision of the procedure, since many probation officers fear that prejudicial information about an offender may be contained in such a report and made known to courts before the finding of guilt.[5]

Another question concerns the confidentiality of the contents of the report. In England and Wales copies of the report must be served on the defendant or his legal representative, but there is no need to read out the whole of the report in court. Various devices are adopted to avoid embarrassing or harming the offender by the disclosure of certain kinds of information in open court, and sometimes by the way the report itself is phrased. In other jurisdictions the practice is different, and Professor Drapkin, after reviewing the arguments for and against confidentiality, concludes that the matter should be left to the discretion of the judge, who may himself decide whether the entire report or only parts of it should be known to the defendant or his representatives. Professor Drapkin's view that the matter can safely be placed in the judge's hands was queried in my review in 1972, and I think myself that the law must take a stand on this matter and make the position clear: though in practice one can avoid embarrasing the defendant in open court, he should have the right to receive a copy of any reports submitted to the court. Where a defendant is legally represented, it can be left to the representative to decide how much of the report his client needs to see. This appears to me to be a safer rule than reposing the whole discretion in the judge.[6]

The question that has been arousing considerable interest among researchers has been how far courts accept the recommendations contained in a presentence report, and how they use the information contained therein. There is some evidence to suggest that courts use this information selectively, picking out those bits of information which fit into their already established view of the case or coincide with their conclusion. John Hogarth showed this to be the case with Ontario magistrates,[7] and Wilkins and Chandler,[8] Carter and Wilkins,[9] and Hood and Taylor[10] have shown something similar to be true in the case of English magistrates. According to Trépanier, even probation officers tend to select the items of information they feel needed in order to arrive at their recommendation on a highly selective basis, and according to their personality and their own particular background and training.[11] Few items of information are required by probation officers to reach a decision, and the addition of further items makes very little difference to the choice. Moreover, courts rarely change their minds as a result of the additional information supplied in such reports, after having formed a provisional view about the case. All this is tending to cast doubt on the value of presentence reports.

The Strasbourg Report gives an account of some research carried out by two of the committee members in Scandinavia and the Netherlands about the degree of agreement between probation officers' recommendations in presentence reports and the actual decisions of the courts.[12] A large measure of agreement was found between such recommendations and court decisions. This can be interpreted in various ways, but the most likely explanation is that sentencers by and large shared the treatment orientation of the social workers. Differences in the legal provisions and procedures in the different countries made exact comparison difficult. There were also important differences in the nature of the reporting agencies. Naturally there were different levels of agreement between social workers' reports and court decisions. These reflected not only differences in the role and responsibility of the judge and the social worker but also differences in the frequency with which, and the purpose for which, presentence reports were made available.

The trend today, at least in the English courts, is toward limiting and reducing the use of presentence reports, partly to make better use of scarce resources, partly because experience shows that the cases where they are decisive are few in number.

This discussion will make little sense to those from jurisdictions following the inquisitorial method of trial, as distinct from the adversary system, where the practice is that an elaborate dossier is prepared containing a great deal of information about the personality and character of the accused person. There are some, even in those jurisdictions, who believe that justice would be better assured if the information was fed into a trial divided into two stages, and that division of the trial in this way (la césure) should be optional.[13] The result would be that highly prejudicial information (e.g., about previous convictions) would be screened from the trial court's view until after a finding of guilt. Recent developments concerning the role of the *juge d'instruction*, or investigating magistrate, in Germany have been attracting some interest in France, and it may well be that both jurisdictions will move further toward the adversary model. But in the meantime, the investigation of the personality of the accused *in extenso* has become the model for the practical operation of criminal trials in these jurisdictions, strongly supported by the writings of criminologists like di Tullio and Jean Pinatel.

The Structure of Sentences

A fresh debate is now opening up over the legal framework of the judge's decision concerning sentence. Whether the judge's decision should take place in the context of choices about definite sentences or indeterminate sentences is an old argument now being given fresh vitality by the criticisms of English and American scholars of the operation of indeterminate sentence laws and parole provisions. It is claimed that these confer too much power on the executive to decide about the date of the offender's release that such decisions involve injustice and arbitrariness, since research findings give little ground for confidence in the ability to distinguish good risks from bad; that operational considerations, such as rewarding conformist behavior in prison in order to preserve order and improve control in institutions, tend to be given undue prominence; and that discriminations are made against those very persons whose needs as ex-prisoners for support and supervision may be the greatest, such as the homeless and jobless.[14]

Without for the moment pursuing the argument into the area of parole and executive release, let us concentrate on sentence structure. Here, on the whole, one is bound to conclude that, with the important exception of cases exhibiting clear evidence of mental disorder, and possibly all murder cases, the definite sentence is to be preferred to the indeterminate sentence.[15] It has the advantage that it is pronounced in open court at the time of conviction for the offense, or soon thereafter. It can be the subject of review by appeal, where the principles on which it is based can be examined and any serious errors adjusted. This allows a jurisprudence of sentencing principles to develop, which as in the case of the decisions of the English appeal court can be made the subject of academic analysis and exposition, so that future courts can learn what principles there are and how to apply them. It is difficult to see how a jurisdiction conferring on the judge wide powers to choose an indeterminate sentence can develop such a jurisprudence of sentencing, or how, in such a jurisdiction, an appellant can meaningfully challenge a sentencer's choice. This creates pressure to review the choice elsewhere, transferring it to the agency of executive discretion over release, frequently the parole board.

The legislature must, however, provide the judge with a suitable framework within which to exercise his choice about sentence. While many new powers have been conferred on the judges in English law by the legislation passed in 1967 and 1972, these mainly concern alternatives to prison. On the custodial side, the judge is free to choose within the maximum laid down by the law, bound only by the constraint provided by the guidelines laid down by the court of appeal when deciding sentence appeals. It is only now that a step has been taken to review those maxims, by the decision of the Home Secretary (announced in July 1975) to ask the Advisory Council on the Penal System to undertake a major inquiry into the existing structure of maximum powers of sentence in English criminal law. Apparently, the object will be to consider whether the principles underlying the maximum statutory penalties are valid to support the present level of those penalties, in the light of current thinking about the objects of sentencing.[16]

The point here is that some concern has been expressed about the level of prison sentences imposed in England and Wales, as compared with that in other European countries. Scandinavia and, in particular, the Netherlands are held out as jurisdictions where a much more selective use of imprisonment is made, and the prison terms are ordered on a much milder scale.

The Strasbourg Report says that the experts found it difficult to carry out a scientific comparison of the level of sentencing between member states of the Council of Europe. This was because of the different laws and administrative practices and methods of record-keeping, which make comparison almost impossible.

Statistics on sentencing are dealing with the results of very complex processes in defining what behavior is illegal and in actually bringing a case to court. These processes occur before the judge can begin to exercise his judgment and select the most appropriate sentence to apply in the individual case. In order for the mass of statistical information available from member states to be useful for comparative purposes, it would be desirable to provide a set of definitions specifying the exact nature of the offences, the categories of offender to be included, and the precise nature of the sentence disposals themselves. Since the existing statistics do not meet these requirements and since it is virtually impossible to thread one's way through the data with any assurance of selecting any relevant figures, the experts were very sceptical of the value of publishing cross-national comparisons in statistical terms.[17]

The conclusion indicated here is that the league tables that have been widely used to indicate the standing of different countries with regard to sentencing, and particularly the use of imprisonment, are in fact rather unreliable since the basic data on which they rest are so much influenced by legal and administrative variations. Nevertheless, it can be taken as an observed fact that rates of imprisonment are lower in some countries than in others, and those who want to reduce the use of imprisonment and the length of prison terms are entitled to point to highly populated and heavily industrialized countries like the Netherlands and say, if they can get by with so few offenders in prison and for such short terms, why cannot we too move in that direction?

Lord Justice Scarman has suggested that Parliament should consider whether there is any justification for permitting a court to impose a sentence of more than five or seven years, save in exceptional circumstances that should be specified by statute.[18] Mr. Justice McKenna has argued against the practice of imposing long sentences for deterrent purposes and seeks to persuade sentencers to experiment with shorter sentences, for some at least of the more serious offenses.[19] Professor Sir Rupert Cross has argued in favor of the reduction of the length of sentences currently imposed for periods of three years or less,[20] and Dr. Roger Hood has expressed similar views.[21] Lord Justice James would like to see many of those now convicted for minor property crimes and who are socially inadequate persons treated more as social problems than as cases for punishment in the criminal courts.[22] Lord Justice Lawton has repeatedly expressed doubts about the value of imprisonment, especially for first offend-ers.[23] All this discussion takes place in the context of the situation where the English courts have inflated the length of prison sentences considerably in the last 20 years or so, ostensibly to cope with the crime wave. Already by 1958 one could see a vast increase in the average length of sentence compared with 1938,[24] but the process did not stop there, and the criminal statistics have revealed a steady inflation in sentence lengths as well as the proportion of persons imprisoned, expressed in relation to the population at risk. It is true that there is some evidence that fewer people now go to prison for a short period, but the proportion received into prison with sentences of more than five years is greater.[25] Statistical analyses published in July 1973 threw some new light on the situation. The conclusion suggested by the Home Office was that a smaller proportion of men over 21 convicted of indictable offenses were being imprisoned and that there had been no evidence in recent years of an upward movement in the index of average length of sentence. But the number of prisoners serving life sentences or very long terms of imprisonment is very disturbing.[26] Home Office spokesmen have more recently pointed to the fall in the proportion of offenders sent to prison, from 440 per 1000 convicted of indictable offenses in 1953 to 197 per 1000 in 1972.[27] The most recent figures tend to show, however, a rise in the English prison population of an unacceptably high level, which has led the Home Secretary to press for the greater use of bail and an extension of the granting of parole.[28]

Sharing Sentencing Responsibility with the Executive

The other strand in the current debate about sentencing is the argument about how far judges should remain wholly responsible for determining the length of sentence and to what extent this responsibility should be shared with the executive, acting administratively or with the advice of a semi-independent parole board. This argument became acute in England and Wales during 1974 following the publication of the Younger Report on young adult offenders, which recommended drastic changes in the legal and administrative arrangements concerning young adult offenders. On the whole the report has received a hostile response, stemming not only from those who, like Dr. Roger Hood,[29] see danger in conferring more power on the administration, but also from probation staff who fear the extra burden it is proposed to thrust upon them to supervise young adult offenders in the community without provision being made for adequate resources to be made available.[30] The more extreme case of the judge simply determining which offenders should be the subject of the community's interven-tion, leaving it to the authorities to decide what form that intervention should take, if it is to commence with a period of custody rather than supervision in the community, and how soon an offender shall be released—all this appears to be too far-reaching a change to be acceptable.[31] Indeed, in the light of what has transpired by way of public debate, one cannot be sure precisely in which direction changes will be made. All that one knows for certain is that the many years we have awaited decisions about the kind of regimes for these young adult offenders pending the recommendations of this report are now likely to be followed by still more years of delay until vital decisions are reached and implemented.

There is a strong lobby building up against the operation of parole, notwithstanding that since its introduction in Britain in early 1968 it has proved to be rather successful and commands considerable public and parliamentary support. The arguments against parole are basically these: (1) research shows that it makes very little difference to outcome, judged in terms of reconvictions; (2) it is essentially unfair in that it discriminates by making choices of the good risks against those with unfavorable records and backgrounds and poor prospects of satisfactory resettlement because of employment difficulties or domestic situation; (3) it takes away from public view the actual decision about restoring liberty to a prisoner; and (4) it deprives the prisoner of a right to be heard, to be represented, and to appeal, and since no reasons are given to prisoners for parole decisions, does not fulfill the requirements of natural justice. Elsewhere I have discussed the latter claim.[32] About the wisdom of evaluating parole on the basis of reconvictions, I have reservations, which apply to any such evaluation of custodial sentences, on the ground that they oversimplify what is basically an extremely complex question. The prisoner coming to prison brings with him not only his record of previous offenses and possibly many failures with regard to alternative measures like probation, fine, and suspended sentence, he also brings the total effect of his background and previous experience which has contributed so much to the making of his personality. On leaving the custodial institution and resuming his life in the free community, he experiences many of the disadvantages and deprivations which were familiar to him before he went in, to which are now added new disadvantages and experiences stemming from the fact that he is now an ex-prisoner. The black-box model of research, which gauges success of a treatment by measuring what comes out of a certain experience (in this case, custody) by comparing it with what goes in, is hardly appropriate, or if applied, would require a much more elaborate test than the simple fact of reconviction. One needs to ask, reconviction for what kind of offense? Was it the same or similar to those offenses he committed which led to the custodial sentence, or entirely different? If different, in what respects? Did it lead to recommital or was it not sufficiently serious to merit that course, so that some other measure was held to be adequate? How soon did the reconviction occur following release? How long had the offender "gone straight"? Is there any evidence to suggest that he had made a real effort and that this was an isolated lapse? Or, on the other hand, is the offense-free period one during which there is some suspicion that he was involved in criminal behavior but simply evaded detection. Along the lines of Glaser's concept of "marginal reformation," one has to depart from a simple arithmetical measure of reconviction.[33]

As regards the second charge made against the executive decision to release, that it is essentially discriminatory, one can answer on two levels. First, one can say, why should it not be? What is wrong with making choices of that kind, preferring good risks to bad, and those with better prospects of resettlement over those with poor prospects. In any case, the experience of the English Parole Board suggests that a great many cases are resolved in terms of the need for support and supervision precisely because to release later without such help is a recipe for disaster. But, it is objected, parole boards rely too heavily on prison response and good adjustment to the prison program.[34] This is to accuse parole boards of naiveté. Everyone knows that the prisoner who settles down to doing his sentence quietly and presents no problems in terms of prison behavior, which may be exemplary, is frequently a poor risk in practice on release. Prison staff learn to spot such cases and alert parole boards to them. If they fail in this, then they do not know their jobs. But, it is objected, the prisoner with a bad disciplinary record in prison does not stand a chance of getting parole—the staff will see to that. This again is a gross exaggeration. It all depends upon what the nature of the disciplinary offense was. If it appears to have little connection with the offender's crime and his prospects of succeeding on license, then it does not necessarily bar parole, though days of remission lost may lead to the postponement of the parole date—otherwise one would be nullifying the loss of remission.

Enough has been said to indicate the writer's belief in the parole system and its viability in any scheme for the reform of sentencing. Indeed, it seems now such an obvious improvement in the English system that one marvels that its introduction was so long delayed. Of course, there is room for improvement in the legal basis and in the administrative procedures. Lord Hunt has already said he would like to see the Parole Board concern itself less with the nature of the offense and the time served and be free to concentrate on the needs of the offender and the problems surrounding his release and resettlement.[35] This can hardly be a development likely to occur while the date of the earliest parole release is fixed by law, as it now is, at one-third of the sentence or 12 months, whichever is the longer. There might be something to be said for requiring the trial judge to fix the nonparole period, as is done in New South Wales, following certain well-settled principles.[36] The nonparole period would then be the subject of legal argument at the trial and could be the basis for an appeal, where its propriety could be reviewed. Provided that one avoided the situation that has occurred in some American jurisdictions, of the trial judges fixing the minimum sentence so close to the maximum as to preclude parole,[37] then I see no real objection to this system. It necessarily involves the right of the trial court to decline to fix a nonparole period and to preclude parole altogether, though the New South Wales statute says this must only be done on account of the nature of the offense or the antecedent character of the offender, and that again would be appealable. The court must give its reasons in writing for refraining from specifying a nonparole period. No doubt other amendments of the parole procedure and reforms of the administration could be introduced to give effect where practicable to some of the criticisms. But this is a very different matter from abolishing altogether the system of executive release on the recommendation of an independent board.

One argument advanced in favor of the trial court fixing the sentence is that all the essential information has already been assembled and is known to the trial judge or can be communicated to him so that he may decide not only how long an offender is liable to serve in prison but when, within those limits, the offender is to be released. This is simply not the case. Lord Justice James has described the disadvantages that a trial court suffers from this point of view, arising from the English practice of passing sentence immediately following, or shortly after, the finding of guilt.[38]

At that time the court will normally have a history of the offender in relation to education, employment, and previous convictions, prepared by the police. Usually it is the bare outline of those matters. There is insufficient time, and there are no facilities to investigate to the degree necessary to produce a full and detailed report; nor, until guilt is formally established, would it be right in many instances to investigate in depth. At the time of sentencing the court will normally have, in respect of those classes of offender in which social inquiries are likely to yield relevant information, a Social Enquiry Report. Uusually it is a pretrial report. Often it is prepared upon a basis of fact in respect of the offense reported by the accused to the Probation Officer, which is completely invalidated by the evidence given to the court. Normally the court will have at the time of passing sentence, in a case in which it has been recognized that medical evidence may be relevant, a medical report upon the offender's mental or physical health. But not always is the desirability of obtaining medical evidence recognized, and it is not unknown for accused persons deliberately to conceal facts as to personal or family medical history. When such social inquiry reports and medical reports are available, the risk of the court acting on incomplete information is minimized.

Clearly from this account it can be seen that the idea that a court necessarily has all the information which is desirable in order for it to make a satisfactory sentencing choice is disproved, though in practice, as Lord Justice James observes, this disadvantage is largely overcome, by, for example, remanding for further inquiries to be made.

Lord Hunt speaking in a House of Lords debate on parole in June 1975, made a slightly different point, when he said:

It is nonsense to claim, as some have done, that all the factors reviewed by the [Parole] Board and the local committees are already known to the courts at the time of the trial. It is tantamount to saying that time and circumstances have stood still over an appreciable period of time.[39]

It is sometimes suggested that instead of the judge fixing the length of sentencing, including the date of release, the executive should as a matter of administrative discretion decide within a short time of the prisoner's arriving in custody what the likely date of release should be and so inform the prisoner. Professor Norval Morris makes a strong case for determining the date of first parole release within the first few weeks of the commencement of the sentence.[40] The prisoner then has something in the way of a goal to aim for, and steps could be outlined for him to take on the way to ultimate release, involving "graduated testing of his ability to adapt to increasing increments of freedom."[41]

The Younger Committee has suggested something similar in its recommendation about "target-dating," under which an early initial review of each case would be undertaken, say, within a month of the offender's reception at a training establishment, and the needs and prospects of the offender would be reviewed by the staff in order to recommend a "target release date." This recommendation would be referred to the advisory committee in each establishment for their approval, and presumably, though this is not made explicit, if approved, the offender would be informed.[42] Already in the English borstal system an informal system of target-dating is operating, dependent on the particular institution to which the offender is allocated. If one is sent to a particular institute X, one knows that all being well one will be released in Y months' time. Of course, time can be lost for bad behavior, but very little time can be lost or gained one way or the other.

Whether one would be well advised to shift from the present basis of parole consideration, which commences at the earliest for some prisoners after a period of eight months or so in custody (which is the time when consideration of a parole application with a view to processing it for a local review committee should commence, in the English system, if one is to comply with the parole eligibility date of 12 months or one-third, whichever is the longer), toward a system based on automatic and almost immediate consideration of target dates for release is a difficult question to resolve. Clearly there would be some gains, but there would be losses too. The idea that parole must be applied for or sought and granted as a privilege would have to give way to the idea that it was automatically a feature of every sentence. The comprehensive investigation and documentation of the case in all its aspects, which presently occurs, would hardly be possible in the time available. The decision taken at the early stage would be more likely to be governed by administrative convenience (all chaps here go out normally in 10 months) than by the real needs of the case, the target release date being governed heavily by the initial allocation, which may itself be governed by operational considerations. The system of target-dating as at present operated in the borstal institutions is hardly defensible and is the result more of such administrative pressures than any conscious decision about the needs of the offender. It might be better to have the matter resolved by the trial court after an initial remand for a period of investigation than to perpetuate the present muddle and confusion of goals and practices. My conclusion is that early decisions concerning dates for release are inconsistent with the making of well-informed decisions about the needs of the inmate and the resources likely to be available to him on release and are not preferable to later decisions made nearer to the likely date of release on the basis of much fuller information.

Judges and the Penal Administration

The Strasbourg Report discusses the changing role of the judge in relation to the penal administration and reaches the conclusion that developments are likely to take place in the direction of giving the judge additional roles in the supervision of the sentence.[43] The possibility of the judge assuming a wider role than at present in the supervision of sentences was extensively discussed, and considerable interest was expressed in the institution of the judge charged with the duty of supervising the administration of the sentence, which exists in France and Italy. Belgium has not seen fit to introduce this institution, but it should be observed that in that country, as in Sweden and the United Kingdom, judges play an important role in the administration of probation and parole. The German model appears to be a compromise involving the creation of a special chamber of the criminal court charged with responsibility for matters concerning the execution of the sentence.

There was some hesitation about firmly recommending the extension of the judge's responsibilities in this direction, partly because it might involve the judge in difficult social and political issues, partly because it was felt that this would impose an extra burden on judges who are already under considerable pressure. Nevertheless, it was felt that these developments which had occurred in certain jurisdictions deserved to be more widely known.[44] The general conclusion reached was that

increasingly judges will be involved in making decisions about prisoners in contexts other than the choice of the actual sentence. It is in many ways desirable that this should be so, and much can be learned by the judges and by those with whom they work in the administration from this mutual contact.[45]

A Look Ahead

It seems likely that a new formula must be sought to define the role of the judge with regard to sentencing and express its relationship to the complementary roles of penal administrator, social worker, and persons charged with discretionary powers concerning the offender's conduct following conviction, such as parole board members and medical doctors. If it is accepted that the judge remains the sole repository of wisdom at the sentencing stage, it follows that he needs information and guidance relevant to the discharge of his sentencing function, if not training. It must also be true that the decision of the judge arrived at in court, whether immediately after the trial has resulted in the offender's conviction or later after information has been obtained and considered, cannot remain the last word about the matter. The sentence imposed at this time should not remain inviolable, it may be questioned on appeal, but should it not also be reviewable in some way other than by the operation of parole decisionmaking? Ideas about minimum sentences fixed by the trial judge, which would be reviewable on appeal, barely solve this problem.

In England and Wales, in connection with dangerous offenders, the Butler Committee has recently proposed a new kind of reviewable sentence, which would be available for a limited category of psychiatric cases, where the qualifying conditions were satisfied.[46] Such a sentence should be subject to a regular two-year review to be carried out by the Parole Board. Moreover, release would be on an unlimited license, as with the present life sentence, which would also be reviewed every two years by the Parole Board. This is to enable the license to be terminated when it is no longer necessary to maintain supervision.

Here we may have the seeds of an idea that could be generalized and applied not only to a limited group of psychiatrically disturbed offenders, but to a wider range of offenders, if not to all offenders, or at least all offenders receiving custodial sentences. At present under English law, if their sentence exceeds 18 months' imprisonment, it is one that makes the offender eligible for parole. This means he may apply to the Parole Board for early release on license. What is suggested here is not in derogation of parole but rather in extension of the power of the judge to fix the sentence at the trial. Why not make all sentences of two years or more reviewable sentences, in the sense that after 18 months the offender may apply to the court for the length of the sentence to be reviewed? Which court should be applied to, whether the court of trial, its equivalent, or the appeal court, might have to be considered carefully in terms of logistics and justice before authorizing such a scheme. But there is a lot to be said for not treating the trial court's decision on length of sentence as final. In this way adjustments could be made to allow for changing circumstances and conditions, related not necessarily to the offender, but rather to society's attitudes, needs, and values, e.g., on such a question as mugging offenses. It would give recognition to the fact that changes occur in these matters that cannot be reflected sufficiently or at all in any other discretionary release decision, such as a parole recommendation.

Notes

1. European Committee on Crime Problems, Council of Europe, Strasbourg, *Sentencing*, Report by the Subcommittee, 1974, p. 30.

2. Book review of *Studies in Criminology*, edited by Israel S. Drapkin, 1969, published in *Israel Law Review* 7, no. 3 (July 1972):455.

3. Lord Devlin's address to the annual meeting of the Howard League for Penal Reform, 30 September 1975, on "The Judicial Role in Sentencing."

4. *Report of the Interdepartmental Committee on the Business of the Criminal Courts* (February 1961), Cmnd. 1289.

5. *The Times*, 25 September 1975.

6. See J.E. Hall Williams, *The English Penal System in Transition* (London: Butterworth, 1970), pp. 34-35, for further discussion and references.

7. J. Hogarth, *Sentencing as a Human Process* (Toronto: Univ. of Toronto Press, 1970).

8. L.T. Wilkins and A. Chandler, "Confidence and Competence in Decision-making," *British Journal of Criminology* 5, (1965):22-235.

9. R.M. Carter and L.T. Wilkins, "Some Factors in Sentencing Policy," *Journal of Criminal Law, Criminology and Political Science* 58, (1967):503-511.

10. R. Hood and I. Taylor, "Second Report of the Study of the Effectiveness of Pre-sentence Investigations in Reducing Recidivism," *British Journal of Criminology* 8, (1968):431-434.

11. J. Trépanier, unpublished Ph.D. thesis, Univ. of London, 1976.

12. The Strasbourg Report, Appendix II, by N. Altahr-Cederberg and W.H. Hammond, pp. 49-60, and see also pp. 23-25 of the text of the main report.

13. The Strasbourg Report, pp. 26-27 under the heading "The investigation of the personality of the accused under the system of undivided trial."

14. See generally, Roger Hood, *Tolerance and the Tariff* (NACRO pamphlet, 1974).

15. See J.E. Hall Williams, "Alternatives to Definite Sentences," *The Law Quarterly Review* (January 1964).

16. Rt. Hon. Roy Jenkins, MP in a speech to the annual general meeting of NACRO, July 21, 1975.

17. The Strasbourg Report, p. 14.

18. Lord Justice Scarman's address to the annual general meeting of the Howard League for Penal Reform, 20 September 1974, on "Control of Sentencing: the balance between the judge and the executive," p. 10 of the published version.

19. Sir Brian McKenna, "General Deterrence," in *Progress in Penal Reform*, Louis Blom-Cooper (ed.) (London: Oxford Univ. Press, 1974), pp. 182-195, especially pp. 193-194.

20. Rupert Cross, *Punishment, Prison and the Public* (London, Stevens & Sons, 1971).

21. Hood, *Tolerance and the Tariff*.

22. Lord Justice James, "A new approach to the criminal process," The Riddell Lecture, 1974, *The Law Society's Gazette* 71, no. 22, (12 June 1974).

23. Lord Justice Lawton, Lecture at Police College, Bramshill, *Police Journal* (October 1971).

24. Cross, *Punishment, Prison and the Public*, pp. 98-99.

25. Home Office, *People in Prison* (pamphlet), Cmnd. 4214 (November 1969), pp. 14-16.

26. Home Office, *Report on the Work of the Prison Department*, 1972, Cmnd. 5375 (July 1973), pp. 2-6.

27. Sir Arthur Peterson, speech to the annual general meeting, ISTD, 4 December 1973; Dr. Shirley Summerskill, MP, at the NACRO annual conference, 23 March 1974.

28. See Rt. Hon. Roy Jenkins' speech of 21 July 1975.

29. Hood, *Tolerance and the Tariff*; also *British Journal of Criminology* (October 1974).

30. See *Report of Working Party of the London Branch of the National Association of Probation Officers* (January 1975).

31. As proposed by Louis Blom-Cooper. See his essay on the subject of "Sentencing structure—a paradigm for the future," in *Progress in Penal Reform*, Louis Blom-Cooper (ed.) (London: Oxford Univ. Press, 1974), pp. 174-181.

32. J.E. Hall Williams, "Natural Justice and Parole," *Criminal Law Review*, (February and April 1975), pp. 82 and 215.

33. Daniel Glaser, *The Effectiveness of a Prison and Parole System*, 2d ed. (Indianapolis: Bobbs-Merrill, 1969).

34. Professor Norval Morris, *The Future of Imprisonment* (Chicago: Univ. of Chicago Press, 1974).

35. Lord Hunt in the House of Lords, *House of Lords Debates* 361, col. 441 (11 June 1975).

36. John A. Morony, *A Handbook of Parole in New South Wales* (1975).

37. See the *A.L.I. Drafts of the Model Penal Code* for discussion of this point.

38. Sir Arthur (Lord Justice) James, "The sentencing process: present practice and future policy," in Louis Blom-Cooper (ed.), *Progress in Penal Reform* (London: Oxford Univ. Press, 1974), pp. 168-169.

39. Lord Hunt, *House of Lords Debates*, col. 440.

40. Morris, *The Future of Imprisonment*, pp. 39 and 49.

41. Ibid., p. 41.

42. Home Office, *Report on Young Adult Offenders* (1974) par. 218, p. 74.

43. The Strasbourg Report, p. 31, also Appendix III.

44. Ibid., p. 33.

45. Ibid., p. 35.

46. (U.K.) Home Office, Department of Health and Social Security, *Report of the Committee on Mentally Abnormal Offenders*, Cmnd. 624 (October 1975).

16 Clemency in Perspective

Leslie Sebba

Introduction

The pardon that was granted to ex-President Richard M. Nixon has drawn the attention of both the academic (see, for example, MacGill, 1974) and the general public to an institution the historic roots of which are almost as ancient as society itself but which has generally played a somewhat marginal and unseen role in the functioning of the legal order. The time is now ripe to examine this role in an historical perspective, with a view to determining how far there is a need for a clemency power in the fourth quarter of the twentieth century.

The reason for asking this question does not arise primarily because of the furor surrounding the Nixon pardon, which can to a considerable extent be attributed to the special circumstances of this pardon, from both the political point of view (President N appoints Vice-President F who becomes President F and pardons ex-President N) and from the legal point of view (a "blanket" pardon, granted prior to the filing of charges, in respect of acts which might have given rise to an impeachment which in itself cannot be pardoned). The grounds of attack on the clemency powers are much more substantial than this and may be considered under two headings—political theory and penal policy. From the point of view of political theory, what place is there for an institution rooted in the concept of an omnipotent sovereign tempering justice with mercy as he is swayed in the mood of the moment in a twentieth century constitutional democracy? In such a democracy the application of principles of justice is the prerogative of the judiciary, the principles themselves having been determined by the legislature which in turn is answerable to the people.[1] Why should the sacred principle of the autonomy of the judiciary permit of derogation in the form of outside interference by the executive arm of government, be it even a titular head of state, a source of interference considered anathema to the makers of the Glorious Revolution in seventeenth century England and to the legal and political reformers of the eighteenth century throughout Europe and America, whose ideas constitute the foundation and inspiration to contemporary democracies?

Second, from the point of view of penal policy, it is evident that there was a need for a clemency power in an earlier age, when justice was either arbitrary or, worse still, resulted in harsh and oppressive punishments being automatically inflicted without regard to the circumstances of the offense or to the personality of the offender. However, in the professionalized twentieth century scheme of

221

criminal justice, the public prosecution is expected to instigate proceedings according to certain criteria determined by the law and public policy. The courts are expected, following a verdict of guilty at a fair trial and having considered all available information respecting the personality of the offender and the circumstances of his offense, to determine a sentence based upon a delicate balance of the need to protect society on the one hand and the need to rehabilitate the offender on the other. Even developments subsequent to the sentence, whether related to the personality of the offender or otherwise, may be taken into account by a qualified body specially established for this purpose, namely, the parole board. What is the need under such a penal system, which reflects in such manifold aspects the results of positivist thinking and, in particular, the need for the individualization of justice, to bestow upon the head of state, a political or symbolic figure remote from the issues described above, the power to upset the fruits of this delicate and complex chain of decisions? In sum, the pardoning power appears on the face of it to be an anachronism from all points of view—political, legal, and penological.

How is it, then, that a clemency power has existed in some form under almost all recorded legal systems since time immemorial and that, even today, no constitution is known to the present writer which does not provide for such a power?* Is the time now ripe to do away with an archaic institution? Or is it possible that the above rhetoric does not do justice to the pardoning power and that the sentence of banishment indicated above should be commuted? We shall endeavor to answer these questions in the remainder of this chapter.

Scope of the Topic

Considerable confusion surrounds the terminology applied to the institution or institutions under discussion here. Terms such as *clemency, pardon, amnesty,* and *reprieve* have been subject to varying interpretations according to the particular geographical or temporal context. The French, with commendable Latin clarity, developed clear distinctions between *la grâce* (of which *le pardon* was a historic form), denoting the discretionary individualized prerogative of mercy on the part of the executive head, *l'amnistie*, representing a reorientation on the part of the legislature in respect of a particular type of offense or offender, and *la réhabilitation*, signifying the judiciary's powers to expunge the criminal record of the ex-offender—all of which derived historically from the same roots. A degree of cloudiness was produced, however, when they evolved a composite form, *la grâce amnistielle*, an individualized form of the amnesty (there is also a somewhat different version, common in other Latin countries,

*Editor's note: An apparent exception has now emerged in the new constitution (1975) of the People's Republic of China; see L. Sebba, "The Pardoning Power—A World Survey," *Journal of Criminal Law & Criminology* (forthcoming).

the *indulto*). The pragmatic English, on the other hand, developed their own hybrid, the Act of Grace, which combined royal discretion with parliamentary sanction (Attorney General's Survey, 1939)–but subsequently allowed this institution to fall into desuetude. American jurists have differed not only over the question of the demarcation of powers between executive and legislature in this sphere–with special reference to the question of whether or not executive heads can grant general pardons or amnesties (L.C.K., 1869) and whether legislatures can grant individual pardons (Weihofen, 1939a; Radin, 1939); they are not even in agreement as to whether American law recognizes a concept of amnesty as distinct from pardons. Finally, the endeavors of the Israeli lawmakers to draw inspiration selectively from all the above systems (as well as from Biblical sources) has, needless to say, resulted in a degree of confusion that has been compounded by both the linguistic and the juridical problems of translation (Sebba, 1975).

There is no place in this essay to explore the above complexities. Suffice it to say that I am primarily concerned here with the so-called prerogative power, generally invested in the head of state, to interfere with determinations of the courts (or sometimes even to preempt their decisions) as to the guilt or the punishment of the accused. This power, selectively applied to individuals, is generally known as the clemency or pardoning power.[2]

A Historical Review

Although the requirements of justice in ancient and primitive societies–namely, appeasement of the gods on the one hand and of the victim and his clan on the other–allowed for little flexibility in the implementations of sanctions, nevertheless early manifestations of the exercise of clemency have been discovered among the laws and lore of such societies (Attorney General's Survey, 1939; Gvaryahu, 1968; NCCD, 1973). The Almighty Himself apparently relented of his condemnation of the fratricide Cain to be "a fugitive and a vagabond," by permitting him to "dwell in the land of Nod";[3] and while there is some doubt as to whether God's human agents were authorized to modify the execution of His laws in this way (Mendelsohn, 1890/1968), the Kings of Israel had few inhibitions about exercising such powers, as reflected in David's relenting the banishment imposed on Absalom for the murder of his brother,[4] and Solomon's commutation of the death penalty which awaited Aviatar the priest for his conspiracy.[5]

Section 129 of the Code of Hammurabi provided specifically for the pardon of the adulterer under certain circumstances (Driver and Miles, 1952). The Greek Thrasybulus is accredited with having granted the first amnesty (although ironically the Greek term employed was not *amnesty* but *adeia*), while Demosthenes and Thucydides are also known to have been pardoned. Not surprisingly, however, it was the Romans who developed the most sophisticated legal institutions in this as in many other spheres, differentiating as they did (although the precise significance of the different concepts is not entirely clear today) between *venia, indulgentia, abolitio privata*, and *abolitio publica*, of which the *leges oblivionis* (passed on the coronation of an emperor and some other holidays) appear to be an example.

It naturally followed that similar types of distinction were made in the subsequent legal development of continental Europe. In medieval France pardons were frequently granted by the King (as well as by the Church) on joyous occasions, such as the birth of an heir or on a military victory (or, in the case of the Church, a religious festival). By the sixteenth century French Law distinguished *abolition, rémission*, and *pardon*, on the one hand, all of which resulted in the equivalent of an acquittal, where the crime was committed under special circumstances, such as for self-defense or on provocation; and *commutation* and *rappel* (the recall of the offender from banishment or the galleys), on the other hand, which resulted in mitigation of the sentence—the predecessors of the modern concept of *grâce*. These developments were followed by the recognition of *réhabilitation*, entailing the subsequent removal of the adverse consequences of a conviction, as a separate institution. Finally, when political, military, or religious considerations rendered a general amnesty appropriate, it became the practice to use a legislative form—*ordonnances* or *édits* (Foviaux, 1970).

In England, as in France, the pardon served in early times to compensate for the strictness of the criminal law. Pardons were granted to persons who were lacking in criminal capacity owing to their mental unbalance or their tender years, or where the circumstances of the offense were such as to negate an evil intent. In some of these instances the custom even acquired Parliamentary sanction. The Statute of Gloucester, 1278, decreed that "... if it be found by the country that he did it in self-defence or by misadventure then, on the record of the justices, the King shall pardon him if he will."[6] Similarly, in certain cases a reprieve of the death penalty came to be granted *ex necessitate legis*[7] (Blackstone, 1765/1962).

Second, the pardoning power was also used to develop new forms of punishment—notably transportation. Prior to 1717, when legislation empowered the courts to impose this penalty directly, the same objective was achieved by granting a conditional pardon to a felon who had been sentenced to death, the condition being that he agreed to be transported to the colonies and work the plantations.[8] Mention may also be made of the use of the conditional pardon as a means of recruitment to the navy—much to the chagrin of its commanders (Craies, 1890). This type of pardon also became a recognized means of avoiding capital punishment.

Pardons were also used to enable an offender to be rid of the stain of his conviction. The pardon, in the words of Hawkins (1771), made its recipient "a new man." It opened the way for his reappointment to various offices from which he was disqualified and made him eligible to give testimony in court and to bestow an inheritance.[9]

Finally, the promise of a pardon became the established method of inducing an accomplice or a coprincipal to testify against the principal offender. By ancient practice, an "approver" could instigate an "appeal of felony" against his codefendants. If he succeeded in securing their conviction, he might be pardoned; but if he failed to do so, or if his courtroom testimony deviated one iota from his original statement to the coroner (e.g., as to the color of the horse or the hour of the day[10]), he would be executed. While this procedure fell into disuse, the practice of granting pardons to suspects who turned "King's evidence" became increasingly common and appeared to be the mainstay of the administration of criminal justice in the late eighteenth and early nineteenth centuries. Statutes were passed incorporating such promises of pardon. Moreover, victims were encouraged to offer financial rewards to such public-spirited felons (Radzinowicz, 1957), who would then have the most persuasive grounds for manifesting the contrition appropriate to a repentant criminal seeking the forgiveness of his sovereign—which had in actual fact been guaranteed in advance.

Clemency under Fire

The Age of Enlightenment is renowned for the forcefulness of the attacks directed at the established political and legal institutions of the day, and the clemency power did not emerge unscathed from the barbs of the critics.

Cesare Beccaria (1764/1963) is well known for his view that pardons derogate from the deterrent power of the law. (The reformist magistrate and novelist Henry Fielding (1751) went so far as to claim that the pardoning power led more people to execution than it saved from this fate.) Beccaria took the view—often echoed since—that deterrence could better be achieved by certain execution of the law than by its severity. ". . . Clemency is a virtue of the *legislators* and not of the *executors* of the laws. . . . Let the laws, therefore, be inexorable, and inexorable their executors in particular cases, but let the legislator be tender, intelligent and humane." In principle he was thus in favor of the abolition of the clemency power. "As punishments become more mild, clemency and pardon become less necessary. Happy the nation in which they might some day be considered pernicious!" However, for his own day they remained an unfortunate necessity "to compensate for the absurdity of the laws and the severity of the sentences."

Mention may also be made here of a writer belonging to a very different school, but also a believer in the merits of the certain execution of punishment, albeit for entirely different reasons, the German philosopher Immanuel Kant.

For him the inevitable juxtaposition of crime and punishment was a sacred principle. "The penal law is a *categorical imperative*; and he is to be pitied, who slinks through the tortuous maze of Utilitarianism, in search of some (opposing) good which may absolve him from punishment (or even, from the due measure of punishment) where Justice requires him to be punished" (Kant, 1796).

Further, it was held that the existence of a power to pardon was an implied criticism of the prevailing criminal code. This was commented both by Beccaria and by his fellow countryman Filangieri, who observed that "If the pardon is just then the law is wrong, while if the law is a good one, the pardon constitutes its breach" (Monteil, 1959).

The pardoning power was also seen to be a threat to the role of the judge. Thus, Lord Mansfield was reputed on one occasion to have labeled such a proposed interference with the sentence "a most dangerous precedent" (Radzinowicz, 1948). More generally, and as we indicated earlier, the clemency power may be regarded as an infringement of the principle of the then emerging concept of the separation of powers. However, opposition to clemency was not usually voiced specifically in this context. Indeed, Montesquieu himself, to whom the main credit is given for the theory of the separation of powers, did not object to the use of pardons. On the contrary, in his view: *"Ce pouvoir que le prince a de pardonner, exécuté avec sagesse, peut avoir d'admirables effets"* (Montesquieu, 1748/1944).

A group of English critics directed their objections not against the institution of pardon as such but against the abuses in its practice which were then rampant. Fielding, William Eden (1771), and Patrick Colquhoun (1797) criticized the excessive use of pardons, the pressures and interventions, the failure to enforce the conditions attached, and, above all, the indiscriminate practice of granting pardons to accomplices who turned state's evidence. Similar criticisms were also voiced in France (Monteil, 1959).

The pardon was not, however, without its supporters. Both Montesquieu and the famous legal commentator Blackstone took the view that the pardon provided a system under which punishments could be individualized; to cite Montesquieu's example—differentiation could thereby be made between murderer and thief. Blackstone was aware of the possibility that such a power of differentiation could instead be placed in the hands of the courts, but he rejected this suggestion out of hand: ". . . the exclusion of pardons must necessarily introduce a very dangerous power in the judge or jury, that of construing the criminal law by the spirit instead of the letter" (Blackstone, 1765/1962). Both Montesquieu and Blackstone, however, were of the belief that the pardoning power could exist only under a monarchy, and was inconsistent with democracy.

Finally, one must add the not inconsiderable weight of the name of Jeremy Bentham to the supporters of the institution of pardon. For Bentham, one of the eleven essential properties of punishment was that of "remissibility"

(Bentham, 1789/1948), which he proposed to apply as a reward for good conduct. However, with an argument reminiscent of Beccaria's, he advocated this use of the pardon only so long as the severity of punishment was excessive. With the introduction of true proportionality in sentencing, this use of the pardon would disappear. The institution of clemency would still be required, however, to remedy miscarriages of justice.

All in all, it seems fair to say that the Age of Enlightenment was characterized rather by the critics of the clemency powers than by their supporters. Did this not inconsiderable body of criticism in any way affect the subsequent development of these powers?

The pragmatic critics of the pardoning policy as exercised at the time in England may be said to have achieved a measure of success which was gradual, but ultimately almost complete. For during the course of the nineteenth century, the main abuse against which they railed, the practice of pardoning informers and accomplices, virtually disappeared. This was probably facilitated by the establishment of the Metropolitan Police in 1829 by Sir Robert Peel, which rendered police investigation more professional and reduced the reliance upon informers. Apart from this, it became the practice of the prosecution to induce accomplices to cooperate and to testify simply by means of an undertaking to refrain from prosecuting them, without the need for recourse to a pardon.

The ideological opponents of the pardoning power won an earlier and more dramatic victory in Continental Europe where they themselves were the most vocal. The French Revolution of 1789 brought about a *"bouleversement des instituts de clémence"* (Foviaux, 1970). By way of reaction to the repressive measures of the *ancien regime* and to demonstrate the supremacy of the legislature in a revolutionary democracy, the institutions of executive clemency were thrown out lock, stock, and barrel. To cite the Penal Code of 1791: *"L'usage de toutes les lettres tendant a empêcher ou à suspendre l'exercice de la justice criminelle, l'usage des lettres de grâce, de rémission, d'abolition, de pardon, de commutation des peines, est aboli pour tout délit qui aura été jugé par voie de jury"*[11] (*Ire partie, titre* VII, art. 13). The legitimate requirements of the penal system were catered to, it was thought, by the recognition of the Penal Code of certain defenses to a criminal charge, such as self-defense, and by legislation providing for the legal rehabilitation of the ex-criminal.

This victory, albeit dramatic, proved to be ephemeral. First, the abolition of the clemency powers may be regarded as having been at least a partial failure, in that instances inevitably occurred in which the established judicial machinery was inadequate to the particular case, and the absence of a clemency power resulted in a resort to alternative methods for obtaining a similar result, viz., legislative *sursis, arrêt de cassation*, and amnesty laws (Foviaux, 1970). Second, while various proposals for restoring the clemency power in the immediate subsequent constitutions were not adopted, with the establishment of the

Consulate in the year X (1802), the pardoning power was revived and placed in the hands of the First Consul. "Abolition" had lasted little more than a decade.

The establishment of the Consulate of course signified a substantial transfer of power from the legislative to the executive branch, and the resurrection of the clemency power—traditionally associated with the executive—may partly be seen as an aspect of this transfer. In this respect, the constitutional history of France since the Revolution has resembled the action of a pendulum, swinging from executive to legislative dominance, and vice versa. However, this phenomenon does not wholly explain the revival; for while the precise mechanics of the clemency power and the identity of its wielder varied from time to time, since 1802 no regime or constitution (and there have been seven since the defeat of Napoleon) has been without such a power. Thus the experiment of abolition was not only short-lived, but also unique, never to have been repeated.

Clemency in the Contemporary World

Having briefly surveyed the role of the clemency power in the past, and having considered the objections launched against it, we are now in a position to take a look at the role of this institution in the contemporary world.

In the context of an examination of the institutions of clemency, there arise a multitude of constitutional and procedural problems—some of which were implicit in the observations of the eighteenth century critics and in our opening remarks. Such questions as whether it be appropriate that in the second half of the twentieth century the clemency powers be vested in the head of state, rather than in some alternative body (as is sometimes the case); the degree to which the legislative and judicial branches should be entitled to comment upon or review clemency decisions; the degree of publicity which should be involved; the extent to which formal procedural requirements should be laid down in respect to petitions for clemency—all these are matters worthy of reappraisal.

Regrettably, considerations of space do not permit us here to enter into such questions. Apart from the intrinsic complexity of these problems, the answers will vary from jurisdiction to jurisdiction, according to the political and legal scheme of things prevailing under the particular system. Such questions are, moreover, secondary to the more fundamental one: Given the present stage of development of the penal system, is there a need for clemency powers today? Until this issue of substance is resolved, it is superfluous to enter into questions of a procedural or mechanistic nature. I shall thus confine myself here to a discussion of the objectives of the clemency powers today. In each case, I shall consider how far clemency appears in fact to be the appropriate method for achieving the stated objective.

It is in fact hard to enumerate an exhaustive list of the uses of clemency today, even in respect to one particular jurisdiction. The reason for this is twofold: first, the relevant information is generally regarded as confidential and not open to public scrutiny;[12] second, clemency tends to be reserved for special cases, for which adequate solution has not been found under the prevailing system, and such cases may be difficult to classify. This problem is compounded inasmuch as I am not confining my argument here to any particular country. Nevertheless I shall endeavor to specify the main objectives of the pardoning power as indicated by my historical survey, as mentioned in the literature (see, for example, Cornil, 1949; Foote, 1959; and Rubin-Weihofen, 1963) or as declared by the official state representatives (Shapira, 1968).

One traditional function of the pardoning power referred to above was the creation of *new defenses in the criminal law*, the pardoning power serving as a means to avoid the criminal sanction where the defendant was insane, acted in self-defense, etc. Today such defenses constitute an integral part of the penal code and this use of the pardon is largely obsolete.

Another almost obsolete use of the pardon relates to *accomplices who turn state's evidence*. The search for alternative modes to the notorious English practice of inducing accomplices to testify with the promise of a pardon was described above. In the United States the authorities were faced with the additional obstacle that the privilege against self-incrimination under the Fifth Amendment inhibited such testimony, but this was overcome by the introduction and application of special Immunity Statutes (see Note, 1963).

A more commonly accepted use of clemency is for cases of *miscarriage of justice*, where the guilt of the convicted defendant was subsequently doubted. This seems to be one of the main recognized purposes of the pardon in England, as evidenced by the publication of the organization Justice (1968), which examines the exercise of the royal prerogative in reviewing such cases.

The need to pardon a wrongly convicted defendant was diminished from the day that judicial systems introduced the concept of appeal. *Cassation* in France has a long history, but the Court of Criminal Appeal in England exists only since 1907. Such courts provide for a reassessment of certain aspects of the case. In the United States there are, in addition, wider possibilities of "collateral attack" (Donnelly, 1952). What if serious doubts about the justice of the conviction arise only after the appeal has been heard, or when the time for lodging an appeal has passed? For this purpose French law developed a special institution, termed *révision*, which enabled the case to be reopened (for specified grounds) at any subsequent date. A similar institution was adopted in Israel in 1957.[13]

In other words, the function of investigating the propriety of the original conviction is increasingly seen as the function of the courts themselves, and not of the executive. This view is reinforced by provisions of the English[14] and Israeli laws[15] which enable the pardoning authority itself to refer a case back to the courts for reconsideration.

Finally, mention should be made of an ideological objection to the use of clemency for the purpose of remedying miscarriages of justice. "To pardon a man on the ground of his innocence is in itself, to say the least, an exceedingly clumsy mode of procedure" (Stephen, 1883). If the defendant has been found in retrospect to have been innocent all along, why should he have to fall upon the tender mercies of the head of state? In the words of a young recipient of one such act of mercy, "How can you be forgiven for something you didn't do?" (cited in Ducann, 1960).

Individualization of Sentences

Pardons were often used in the past to overcome the harshness of the sentence laid down by the law. However, the rise of positivism led to the development of a number of forms of punishment/treatment, such as probation and the suspended sentence, designed for first offenders and others for whom the full rigor of the law was inappropriate (see Saleilles, 1911/1968). At the same time, courts were invested with wide powers of discretion, enabling them to determine the sentence appropriate to the particular case. Thus in a regular case, individualization of sentence did not require resort to the clemency powers. The most notable exception related to the application of capital punishment. It is fair to say that over the last hundred years the commutation of sentences of death has been the focal point for discussion of the prerogative power, as has been well documented in the literature, both official and professional (Royal Commission, 1953; Abramovitz and Paget, 1964; and Bresler, 1965). This interest in the application of the pardoning power in capital cases derives from three causes: first, the dramatic nature of the decision, upon which a human life depends; second, the practice common to many jurisdictions whereby the courts have no discretion as to whether or not to impose capital sentences in cases (notably murder) where the law provides this penalty, thus leaving the executive as sole arbiter; and third, the controversy as to the morality, justice, and effectiveness of capital punishment, which has resulted in a close examination of every aspect of the implementation of this supreme penalty.

The importance of the clemency powers in this area, however, has undergone a spectacular decline in the last decade. The death penalty for murder was abolished in Great Britain in 1965. In the 1972 case of *Furman* v. *Georgia*[16] capital punishment as then practiced in the United States was held by the Supreme Court to be unconstitutional. In Israel capital punishment is not available for murder, while even for offenses such as genocide it is no longer mandatory.[17] The use of executive clemency to commute death penalty cases has thus fallen into disuse at present in these countries.

Under the heading of individualization of sentence, one may also mention the not infrequent cases where a prisoner who has served a part of his sentence has it reduced by the pardoning authority owing to a change in his circumstances or evidence of his good conduct. Here the individualization is based not on facts available at the trial stage, but on subsequent developments. This is the main function of *grâce* under the French system and indeed accounts for most of the cases in which the clemency power is exercised in Israel (Sebba, 1975) and by the state governors in the United States (Goldfarb and Singer, 1973).

However, the positivist and rehabilitationist philosophy which has dominated correctional thinking in recent times does not regard the sanction as something which should almost always be finally determined at the trial, only to be modified in exceptional circumstances. The punishment should fit the offender—taking into account subsequent developments in personality and circumstances—in *all* cases and in a systematic and institutionalized fashion. Thus systems of remission and parole were developed enabling a prisoner to be released prior to completion of his sentence or even after serving only a small portion of the term imposed. The institution of parole boards, pioneered in the United States, has expanded lately: England introduced this system in 1967, and in Israel it is now under consideration. Parole boards are supposedly expert bodies equipped with the knowledge and techniques required for penal decision-making; and much of the activity of pardoning authorities frequently derives, if not from the absence of such a board, from the restrictions imposed upon its powers (NCCD, 1973). Where, however, the powers of the parole board are sufficiently comprehensive to take into account all possible developments subsequent to the imposition of sentence,[18] the pardoning power would appear to become superfluous at this stage, except perhaps in those rare cases in which executive intervention is based on purely political considerations.[19]

Expunging the Record

An ex-offender who has reformed frequently encounters problems in reestablishing himself in society owing to his police record, which may be held against him when seeking employment—in particular an office of a public or professional nature (Gough, 1966). Other forms of civil disqualification may also ensue from criminal conviction. In the United States and in Israel, as well as in a number of other countries (see Damaska, 1968), it is not uncommon for pardons to be sought for the purpose of restoration of rights or "expungement of the record"—in spite of the doubts pertaining to their judicial effectiveness in this respect (Williston, 1915; Weihofen, 1939b).

Here, again, however, the problem is a general one, needful of a systematic and comprehensive solution (Feller, 1969). All offenders who have made a genuine attempt at rehabilitation should be entitled to shake themselves free of their past stigma. French law has recognized this since the Revolutionary era and even earlier. The British Parliament has now passed the Rehabilitation of Offenders Act, 1974, while Israel is in the process of introducing a Criminal Registration Law. These laws provide that after a predetermined number of crime-free years, varying according to the nature of the offense or the sanction imposed, the offender will be free of any handicap incurred by reason of his erstwhile sins.[20] Whatever the merits and demerits of these particular laws, it is clear that the universality of this problem requires a standardized social—and legislative—response and should not be dependent on the highly discretionary power to intervene in special cases which the clemency power represents.

It is also still the practice in some countries to use the power of executive clemency to exonerate or release whole categories of offenders. Two types of situation are involved. The first is where some public event giving rise to national jubilation leads the authorities (often in these cases a monarch) to echo the traditions of bygone days and remit the punishments currently being served by certain categories of offenders; examples of this were the general pardons issued in Belgium to celebrate the coronation of King Baudouin in 1951, and his marriage in 1960. The second type of situation occurs when certain political, social, economic, or military changes result in a transformation of the public or official attitude toward particular types of offenses or offender. An example of this is the President's Clemency Program recently established in the United States for the benefit of "Vietnam Era Draft Evaders and Military Deserters."[21]*

While these two cases are distinct, they have two factors in common; first clemency is applied on these occasions to groups rather than to individuals; and second, the rationale is based on national events or policies, rather than the individual characteristics of the particular case. For these reasons, it would be more fitting to rely upon the legislative arm in these cases; the commutation of sentence or exoneration could be achieved by statute, instead of by executive clemency. Moreover, a degree of selectivity of application—the Vietnam draft evaders who applied for clemency were considered by a board on an individual basis—is not precluded by such a solution, since such a board could equally have been established by means of legislation.

What seems to emerge from the above analysis is that whatever function of the clemency power is considered—whether the creation of new defenses in the criminal law, securing the testimony of accessories to the crime, the rectification of miscarriages of justice, the individualization of the sentence, the expungement of the record, or the implementation of national policy—the institution of clemency seems in no case to constitute the optimal means for fulfilling this function. In some cases, it has already been superseded by another institution, while in others some alternative institution could be adopted or expanded for this purpose; and the superseding or alternative institution appears to be more appropriate for securing the desired objective than the continued use of clemency. There thus seems to be at least a *prima facie* case for abolishing the clemency power altogether.

---

*Editor's note: The reference is to the clemency program of President Ford, and not to the even more recent measures announced by President Carter on taking office.

Moreover, this case has been presented without reference to the ideological objections to clemency mentioned earlier, and without entering into the problems of the appropriate machinery for implementing the sovereign's historical prerogative power in the twentieth century. Nor have I been concerned here with the legal effects of the pardon, and whether they enable the desired objectives to be achieved. I have been concerned here solely with the need for the clemency power as such, from the point of view of the legal or penological functions it fulfills; and the foregoing analysis has suggested that Beccaria's utopian age, when the clemency power will finally wither away, may be around the corner.

Let us now attempt to take a glimpse around that corner, in order to determine whether this utopia is indeed at hand. Lacking a crystal ball, our glimpse will necessarily have to be based on a closer scrutiny of some aspects of the penal system considered above, as well as an attempt to interpret current trends in criminal justice policy, on the one hand, and in criminological thinking, on the other.

The Future of Clemency

I will now admit to a degree of deception in the foregoing analysis of the contemporary scene. It is true that in all the situations described I genuinely believe an alternative solution to be both available and preferable to reliance on the clemency power. However, it is also true that in the majority of cases the solution adopted may not be exhaustively comprehensive, and special cases may still continue to require a special solution.

Let us briefly reconsider the most important contemporary uses of the clemency power—remedying miscarriages of justice, individualization of sentence, and expungement of the record. Whatever judicial machinery might be established for dealing with suspected miscarriages of justice, it will of necessity specify certain criteria, possibly even strict and narrow criteria, for reconsideration of the case—the objects of such strictness being both to guard against a flood of petitions for rehearings and to derogate as slightly as possible from the principle of the finality of judgments with which such retrials are thought to be inconsistent. Thus, for example, the relevant French and Israeli provisions stipulate such conditions as the discovery that the "murdered victim" is still alive, or the conviction of another defendant for the same crime, while even the more liberal proviso as to the emergence of new evidence which could not have been secured at the time of the trial may not always be easy to substantiate. Hard cases may therefore occur, deserving of consideration, which do not qualify for a judicial hearing. Clemency will remain the only alternative.

As to the mandatory death sentence, this may not be a problem today—at least in the countries considered here.[22] Yet, other forms of mandatory or minimum sentences may be provided by law, including sentences of considerable severity, which cannot be modified, however compelling the circumstances, except by means of the clemency power. In Israel, for example, murder is punishable by mandatory life imprisonment, while mandatory or minimum sentences of imprisonment have been introduced for certain other offenses (see Sebba, 1971). In the United States, habitual offender laws, providing for minimum terms of imprisonment without parole eligibility, still obtain under many state laws (Goldfarb and Singer, 1973). Thus the court may be prevented from taking into consideration even the most extreme of mitigating circumstances, or the trivial and technical nature of the infraction, while the parole board may similarly be unable to take cognizance of subsequent developments. The only available solution will thus be executive clemency.

As to expungement of the record, here also the alternative solutions adopted in various countries often involve relatively long "waiting" periods— often 10 years or more after the last offense was committed or the sentence served—as proof of reformation of character; and the most serious offenses may be excluded altogether from its benefits.[23] Here, again, clemency may occasionally be appropriate in special cases, where both the offender and society would benefit from the restoration of his rights and status where this has been precluded, or from an earlier restoration than provided for by the law.[24]

Even the archaic use of clemency to provide a defense to a charge where the criminal law is inadequate may need to be resurrected from time to time; for occasionally a lacuna emerges even in contemporary penal codes, and the courts are not always willing to fill such lacunae by means of judicial lawmaking. Thus, for example, the Israeli Supreme Court once held that a mental defective was obliged to stand trial for the offense imputed to him (and could subsequently be convicted of this offense), since the prevailing laws granted exemption on the grounds of insanity, but not on the grounds of defectiveness. The court added that judicial interpretation could not be employed to overcome legislative deficiencies.[25] The consequences of conviction in such a case could thus be alleviated only by an act of clemency.

The above analysis suggests that the abolition of clemency may be a utopian aim—constantly to be pursued but never to be attained. Beccaria was undoubtedly correct in his view that a clemency power would be unnecessary when laws were perfected; but even the enlightened thinking of the eighteenth century philosophers could not produce perfect laws. On the other hand, it is less unrealistic to suppose that the pursuit of an ideal, albeit unattainable, may at least result in its greater proximity. In terms of the clemency power, the effect of this should be the ever-narrowing scope of its ambit, as problems of substance in the penal system are solved by alternate means, and the laws, if not perfected, are at least improved. Moreover, our survey of the present-day functions of the pardon in the preceding section indicates considerable progress in this respect.

At present, however, it is by no means clear that in the immediate future we shall continue to progress in this direction. There are, on the contrary, indications that in certain areas at least the need for the clemency power may actually increase.

It will be recalled that one of the main functions of clemency was traditionally to obtain the individualization of sentence, but that this function has been rendered increasingly superfluous by positivistic thinking in corrections, which has laid emphasis on individualization in both the judicial and the executive branches in the penal system. However, the present mood, at least on the American scene, appears to be to move *away* from individualization of sentence, and the implications of this must be considered.

The trend away from individualization in fact stems from two different forms of pressure. On the one hand, the reported increased rates of violent crime have given rise to public pressure in favor of harsher laws, often of a mandatory character; and such provisions will no longer be restricted to habitual offenders. In Israel this legislative hammer has been used for such diverse offenses as pimping, "hit-and-run" driving, and the sale of narcotics to a minor. Similarly, under the United States federal narcotics statutes (as well as those of certain states), minimum terms are provided for without parole eligibility. More significantly, public demand—as perceived by the legislators—has resulted in the reenactment of death penalty laws in some 35 states, in spite of the Supreme Court's designation of the earlier laws as "cruel and unusual."[26] Such laws have laid down very specifically which categories of offender are to be executed, since it was the arbitrary nature of the implementation of the earlier laws that resulted in their nullification by the Supreme Court; the new laws are thus deliberately aiming to achieve inflexibility. However, those who drafted the laws did not, it seems, go so far as to exclude the possibility of executive clemency; indeed, this would in most cases have derogated from the constitutional powers of the governors of the states. Thus the only hope of the guilty defendant under these laws—in the absence of a new judicial holding as to their invalidity*—will be recourse to executive clemency.[27]

The other motivation for the trend away from individualization is the current disillusion with the concept of rehabilitation (Riedel and Thornberry, 1976), coupled with the belief that the criminal justice system is operating arbitrarily and unfairly. Both sentencing and parole practices which purport to adapt the sentence to the individual needs of the offender have been criticized. It has been suggested that it would be fairer to sentence the offender on the basis of the severity of the offense alone—or rather the severity of the offender's accumulated offenses (Wolfgang, 1975; Twentieth Century Fund, 1976). It has further been suggested that the parole system operates so unfairly that it should be abolished altogether (Vogel, 1975; Conrad, 1975).[28] Moreover, some profes-

---

*Editor's note: In a series of Supreme Court decisions handed down on July 2, 1976, three of the new laws were upheld, while two others (apparently the most inflexible) were invalidated; see, for example, *Criminal Law Bulletin* vol. 13, Jan.-Feb. 1977, pp. 51-60.

sional legal opinion, including the drafters of the model Penal Code, has been registered in favor of restricting both judicial and parole discretion.

Needless to say, I do not propose to discuss here the respective merits of these suggestions. It should be observed, however, that these proposals amount to a drastic reversal of positivistic trends in criminology and penology, and a revival of the approach of the classical school. The object of attack is no longer the cruelty of barbaric laws and the arbitrariness of despotic rulers, but the cruelty of pseudo-rehabilitative institutions and the arbitrariness of decisions made with a rehabilitative aim. The remedy, however, is essentially the same remedy: that the punishment should be proportionate to the crime. Further, the mechanistic application of this principle is thought by some to be enhanced by reviving the solution beloved of the architects of the French Revolution, namely, a legislative tariff of penalties. The reintroduction of classical proportionality (and the move toward mandatory punishments is of the same conceptual ilk) entails, of course, the decline, if not the total disappearance, of the positivistic principle of individualization in the sentencing process. The social reality which gave rise to the principles of individualization will not, however, disappear. A return to classicism cannot obliterate the infinite variety of human situations and the occurrence of "hard cases" to which the predetermined penalty will be manifestly inapplicable. Means will have to be found to take cognizance of such cases—either by reliance on such illicit forms of redress as plea bargaining and "jury equity" (Kalven and Zeisel, 1966), or by resorting to the sole remaining legitimate remedy—the clemency power. Ironically, the return to classicism will thus have ensured the survival of an institution it disliked. As far as his hopes for the disappearance of clemency are concerned, Beccaria will have dealt himself a death blow.

Notes

1. This point has more force when applied to democracies on the British model than to systems such as the United States or France, where the chief executive is also answerable to the people by elections.

2. The term *pardon* is sometimes used in a narrower sense, referring to a particular species of the executive power, as distinct from reprieves (see Blackstone's *Commentaries*, or Art. II, sec. 2, of the United States Constitution) or even from commutations and mitigations of sentence (see Israel's Basic Law: The President). On the other hand, the term *clemency* may also relate to institutions no longer involving the executive, such as legislative amnesties and judicial rehabilitation (see, for example, Garraud, 1898).

3. Genesis 4, v. 12, 16.

4. 2 Samuel 14, v. 26.

5. 1 Kings 2, v. 26-27.

6. According to Coke, the words *if he will* were added out of respect for the sovereign but were not intended to convey a discretionary power; the pardon was automatic.

7. Thus Hale distinguished "Pardons of Course and Right" and "Pardons of Grace."

8. It is interesting to note that the same technique was occasionally employed after the formal *abolition* of transportation as a recognized punishment, when the above-mentioned legislation was repealed in the mid-nineteenth century; a conditional pardon again became the only means of inflicting this sentence.

9. Where, however, the conviction was accompanied by attainder, it seems that only an Act of Parliament could remove the "corruption of blood" which this involved (L.C.K., 1869).

10. See *R.* v. *Rudd* (1775), 1 Leach 115, 120.

11. The jury was adopted comprehensively at this time; see J. Graven (1967).

12. The main exceptions to this are found in some states in the United States, where clemency decisions and recommendations are entrusted to a Board of Pardons. Thus Article IV, Section 9, of the Constitution of Pennsylvania provides for hearings by such a board in open session, and that "the board shall keep records of its actions, which shall at all times be open for public inspection." Even here, however, the board is not obligated to give reasons for its decisions (NCCD, 1973).

13. Section 9, Courts Laws, 1957.

14. Section 17, Criminal Appeal Act, 1968.

15. Section 10, Courts Law, 1957.

16. 92 S. Ct. 2726 (1972).

17. *Attorney General* v. *Eichmann*, 45 P.M.3.

18. Subsequent reconsideration of the sentence or treatment decision by the court is also not unknown; see Section 30 of Israel's Youth Law of 1971.

19. For example, cases involving the release of a foreign national. Such cases may be considered beyond the province of the parole board. On the other hand, they are not really in keeping with the traditional concept of clemency. Alternative methods of dealing with these cases are discussed elsewhere (Sebba, 1975).

20. Under some systems, including the French, the offender has in many cases to convince a judge of the genuineness of his reformation.

21. See Presidential Proclamation 4313, 16 September 1974.

22. This problem has now reemerged in the United States with the recent Supreme Court decision, handed down after this chapter was completed, endorsing at least some forms of quasi-mandatory capital punishment.

23. See Sections 14 of the two Israeli Bills of 1970 and 1975, respectively. See also Section 5, English Rehabilitation of Offenders Act, 1974.

24. Under Section 789 of the French Penal Code, the conditions of rehabilitation may be waived only in respect to a defendant who has rendered distinguished service to his country *"au péril de sa vie."*

25. Cr. App. 388/62, *Attorney General* v. *Cohen*, 16 P.D. 2710. The law in this respect has since been amended and the position of mental defectives has been substantially assimilated with that of the mentally ill.

26. See, however, note 22.

27. In France also the importance of the clemency power in this area appears to be increasing, but for a different reason. Since 1972 the few capital sentences imposed have been routinely commuted, but there is currently a demand that this power be exercised selectively.

28. Conrad emphasizes that the "service" arm of the parole system would be preserved. Early release, however, would be based essentially on a nondiscretionary system of remission—in effect a return to the "Good Time" laws.

References

Abramovitz, E., and D. Paget. "Executive Clemency in Capital Cases." 39 *N.Y.U.L. Rev.*, p. 136, 1964.

Attorney General's Survey of Release Procedures, Vol. III: Pardon. Washington: Department of Justice, 1939.

Beccaria, C. *On Crimes and Punishments* (trans. by H. Paolucci). Indianapolis: Bobbs-Merrill, 1764/1963.

Bentham, J. *The Principles of Morals and Legislation*. New York: Hafner, 1789/1948.

Blackstone, W. *Commentaries on the Laws of England*. Boston: Beacon Press, 1765/1962.

Bresler, F. *Reprieve*. London: Harrap, 1965.

Colquhoun, P. *A Treatise on the Police of the Metropolis*, 4th ed., 1797. Extracts in Heath, J., *Eighteenth Century Penal Theory*. Oxford Univ. Press, 1963.

Conrad, J.P. *Who Needs a Bell-Pusher?* Paper presented at the Annual Meeting of the American Society of Criminology, Toronto, 1975.

Cornil, L. *"Le Droit de Grâce dans le Cadre de la Constitution Beige."* 35 *Bull. de la Classe des Lettres et des Sciences Morales et Politiques*, 5e serie, p. 594, 1949.

Craies, Wm. F. "The Compulsion of Subjects to Leave the Realm." 6 *L.Q.R.*, p. 388, 1890.

Damaska, M. "Adverse Legal Consequences of Conviction and Their Removal." 59 *J. Crim. L. Crimin. & P. Sci.*, p. 347, 1968.

Donnelly, R.C. "Unconvicting the Innocent." 6 *Vand. L. Rev.*, p. 20, 1952.

Driver, R., and J. Miles. *The Babylonian Laws*. Oxford: Clarendon Press, 1952.

Ducann, C.G.L. *Miscarriages of Justice.* London: Muller, 1960.

Eden, W. *Principles of Penal Law*, 2d ed., 1771. Extracts in Heath, J. *Eighteenth Century Penal Theory*, 1963.

Feller, S.Z. "Rehabilitation—A Special Legal Institution Required by Reality." 1 *Mishpatim*, p. 497 (in Hebrew), 1969.

Fielding, H. *Enquiry into the Cause of the Increase of Robbers*, 1751. In Heath, J. *Eighteenth Century Penal Theory*, 1963.

Foote, C. "Pardon Policy in a Modern State." 39 *Prison Journal*, no. 1, p. 3, 1959.

Foviaux, J. *La Rémission des Peines et des Condemnations.* Paris: Presses Universitaires de France, 1970.

Garraud, R. *Droit Pénal Français*, 2ème ed., 11. Paris: Larose, 1898.

Goldfarb, R., and L. Singer. *After Conviction.* New York: Simon & Schuster, 1973.

Gough, A.R. "The Expungement of Adjudication Records of Juvenile and Adult Offenders: A Problem of Status." *Wash. U.L.Q.*, p. 147, 1966.

Graven, J. *"Evolution, Déclin et Transformation du Jury."* In *Le Jury Face au Droit Pénal Moderne.* Brussels: Bruylant, p. 79, 1967.

Gvaryahu, H.M.I. "Roots of Amnesty in Biblical Cultures." In Drapkin, I. (ed.), *Amnesty in Israel.* Jerusalem: Institute of Criminology, p. 21 (in Hebrew), 1968.

Hawkins, W. *A Treatise of the Pleas of the Crown*, 5th ed., 11. London: Sweet, 1771.

Justice, *Home Office Reviews of Criminal Convictions.* London: Stevens, 1968.

Kalven, H., and H. Zeisel. *The American Jury.* Boston: Little, Brown, 1966.

L.C.K., "The Power of the President to Grant a General Pardon or Amnesty for Offenses against the United States." 8 *Amer. L. Reg.* (n.s.), p. 513, 1869.

MacGill, H.C. "Nixon Pardon: Limits on the Benign Prerogative." 7 *Conn. L. Rev.*, p. 56, 1974.

Mendelsohn, S. *The Criminal Jurisprudence of the Ancient Hebrews*, 2d ed. New York: Hermon Press, 1890/1968.

Monteil, J. *La Grâce en Droit Français Moderne.* Paris: Librairies Techniques, 1959.

Montesquieu. *de l'Esprit des Lois* (ed. G. Truc). Paris: Lib. Garnier Frères, 1748/1944.

NCCD. *Clemency in Pennsylvania.* Austin, Texas: National Council on Crime and Delinquency, 1973.

Note. "The Federal Witness Immunity Acts in Theory and Practice: Treading the Constitutional Tightrope." 72 *Yale L.J.*, p. 1568, 1963.

Radin, M. "Legislative Pardons: Another View." 27 *Calif. L. Rev.*, p. 388, 1939.

Radzinowicz, L. *A History of the Criminal Law*, I. London: Stevens, 1948.

Radzinowicz, L. *A History of the Criminal Law*, II. London: Stevens, 1957.

Riedel, M., and T. Thornberry. "The Effectiveness of Correctional Programs: An Assessment of the Field." (Forthcoming).

Royal Commission on Capital Punishment. London: Cmd. 8932, H.M.S.O., 1953.

Rubin-Weihofen. "Pardon and Other Forms of Clemency." In *The Law of Criminal Correction.* St. Paul, Minnesota: West, p. 569, 1963.

Saleilles, R. *The Individualization of Punishment.* Montclair: Patterson Smith, 1911/1968.

Sebba, L. "Minimum Sentences: Courts v. Knesset." 6 *Isr. L. Rev.*, p. 227, 1971.

Sebba, L. *Pardon and Amnesty—Juridical and Penological Aspects.* Unpublished doctoral thesis, Jerusalem, Hebrew Univ., 1975.

Shapira, Y.S. Parliamentary debate reported in 53 *Divrei Haknesset*, p. 346, 1968.

Stephen, J.F.S. *Hisotory of the Criminal Law of England,* I. London: Macmillan, 1883.

Twentieth Century Fund Task Force on Criminal Sentencing, *Fair and Certain Punishment.* New York: McGraw-Hill, 1976.

Vogel, D. *"We Are the Living Proof": The Justice Model for Corrections.* Cincinnati: Anderson, 1975.

Weihofen, H. "Legislative Pardons." 27 *Calif. L. Rev.*, p. 376, 1939*a*.

Weihofen, H. "The Effect of Pardon." 88 *Univ. Penna. L. Rev.*, p. 177, 1939*b*.

Williston, S. "Does a Pardon Blot out Guilt?" 28 *Harv. L. Rev.*, p. 647, 1915.

Wolfgang, M.E. "Seriousness of Crime and a Policy of Judicial Sentencing." In Short, J. (ed.), *Crime, Justice and Society.* Chicago: Univ. of Chicago Press, 1975.

List of Contributors

Bernard Cohen, Department of Sociology, Queen's College, City University of New York

Haim Cohn, Supreme Court Justice; President of the Israel Society of Criminology

Simon Dinitz, Department of Sociology, Ohio State University; Academy of Contemporary Problems

Franco Ferracuti, Institute of Psychology, Faculty of Medicine, University of Rome

J.E. Hall Williams, Faculty of Law, London School of Economics; Secretary-General, International Society of Criminology

Nicholas N. Kittrie, Dean of the Law School, and Director, Institute for Studies in Justice and Social Behavior, American University

Simha F. Landau, Assistant Director, Institute of Criminology, Faculty of Law, Hebrew University of Jerusalem

Noël Mailloux, Institut de Psychologie, University of Montreal (Emeritus)

Sigmund H. Manne, Chief Psychologist, Patuxent Institution, Maryland

Graeme R. Newman, School of Criminal Justice, State University of New York at Albany

Jean Pinatel, President of the International Society of Criminology

Walter C. Reckless, Department of Sociology, Ohio State University (Emeritus)

David Reifen, Chief Judge, Israel Juvenile Court (retired)

*Stephen Schafer, College of Criminal Justice, Northeastern University

Leslie Sebba, Institute of Criminology, Faculty of Law, Hebrew University of Jerusalem; Secretary, Israel Society of Criminology

Thorsten Sellin, Department of Sociology, University of Pennsylvania (Emeritus)

Rita J. Simon, Director, Program in Law and Society, University of Illinois

Marvin E. Wolfgang, Director, Center for Studies in Criminology and Criminal Law, University of Pennsylvania; President, American Academy of Political and Social Science

---

*Deceased

About the Editors

Simha F. Landau is Assistant Director of the Institute of Criminology of the Hebrew University. A graduate of the Hebrew University, he was a Senior Fulbright Fellow at the Center for Studies in Criminology and Criminal Law of the University of Pennsylvania, and has taught at the University of Alberta. Dr. Landau is presently involved in an international project on comparative juvenile justice systems. He is a member of the Israeli Psychological Association and has contributed to various psychological and criminological journals.

Leslie Sebba is on the faculty of the Institute of Criminology of the Hebrew University. Educated in England, he holds degrees in law from the Universities of Oxford and London. He received his Doctor Juris at the Hebrew University and is a member of the Chamber of Advocates in Israel as well as of the English Bar. Dr. Sebba has worked as a research officer with the Home Office Research Unit in London and was Visiting Fellow at the Center for Studies in Criminology and Criminal Law at the University of Pennsylvania. He has published in various legal and criminological journals.